Beneath This Crown of Thorns

adventures of a mentally ill messiah

Jeffrey Wayne Wood

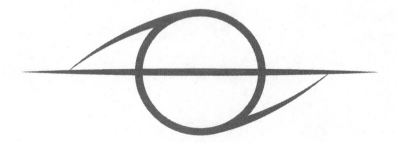

ISBN 978-1-945283-00-0

Krido Ishii Publishing
6455 Longwood Lane
Clinton Washington 98236
www.KridoIshii.com
Email: info@KridoIshii.com

Audio and e-book versions also available.

Ordering Information:

For U.S. trade bookstores and wholesalers special discounts are available. They are also available for quantity purchases by corporations, associations, and others. For details, contact the publisher at the address above or email Krido Ishii Publishing.

Cover art by Jimmy Nijs.

Printed in the United States of America

Contents

Preface

"Our deepest fear is not that we are inadequate. Our deepest fear is that we are powerful beyond measure. It is our light, not our darkness that most frightens us. We ask ourselves, Who am I to be brilliant, gorgeous, talented, fabulous? Actually, who are you not to be? You are a child of God. Your playing small does not serve the world. There is nothing enlightened about shrinking so that other people won't feel insecure around you. We are all meant to shine, as children do. We were born to make manifest the glory of God that is within us. It's not just in some of us; it's in everyone. And as we let our own light shine, we unconsciously give other people permission to do the same. As we are liberated from our own fear, our presence automatically liberates others."

-Marianne Williamson

As I search for the reasoning behind my decision to tell my story, this quote stands out, like a lamp post on a darkened street. I have spent most of my life hiding; laying low and allowing the confused community around me to dictate my sense of self-worth and value. I have been guilty of playing small and complying with the norms that are foundational to a highly dysfunctional society. The skewed perspectives that create and maintain such a system have provided me with an excuse for staying out of harm's way. "The highest nail is the first to get slammed... and the tallest tree, the first to be cut down." Most of my life has been a struggle to survive. My fear of handling the challenges that emerge when a person speaks out, have kept me quiet.

My choice to tell a story that few would share is based primarily in my ability to do so. What I mean by that, is that after decades of doubting, and finally embracing this option, it is a gift that only a fool would throw away. My entire adult life has been spent in the balance of whether or not I could ever overcome this affliction that haunted my every waking hour.

For decades I have pondered the notion of writing this book. I never felt quite mentally or emotionally stable enough to do so. To find myself in this position, knowing beyond a doubt that I have accomplished my highest visions of health and happiness against all odds, leaves me with a certain sense of responsibility. As unique as my story may be, the suffering I've experienced along this rugged road is not the least bit original. The path that I've carved through this jungle of madness, has the potential to serve others in a profound manner; a roadmap I would have found priceless thirty years ago.

How many people do you know who have suffered in one form or another with mental health issues; whether it be anxiety, depression, ADHD, Bipolar disorder, Schizophrenia or any of the other countless labels associated with mental/emotional health? Mental health is a prominent issue that eats at the very core of our social structure. If I believed that ignoring these issues would be of value, I would never have written my story. I absolutely do not! Shoving those of us who do not fit the mold, into the back corner of society's mind, is an enormous part of the problem. The time has come for us to be seen… and heard.

At a personal level it's been a lot like "coming out of the closet." Much like our gay community and more recently the transgender population, I have been taught to be ashamed of myself for being a round peg that wouldn't fit into a square hole. I have grown up in a social setting that forced me into a corner, with drugs and isolation as the only treatments available. My claim to fame is that I have not only survived, but also escaped the grip of the medical/judicial system that guaranteed my disability and drug dependency. In the process of breaking free, I have also unraveled a mystery that keeps millions of people enslaved. My goal in writing this book is to share with others my path and process of recovery; to make obvious Western Civilizations' systemic illness, and set free those capable of finding this path of light that shines through the darkest night.

Although the writing of this book has been spread out over the last decade, the story has taken a lifetime to form. I am forever grateful to the many who have encouraged me to write and particularly thankful for my spiritual partner and companion Christi, who has held my hand and steadied the light for this final approach to our landing. The divine certainly does work in mysterious ways...

Acknowledgements

As I look within for the list of people who have influenced my life and played a supportive role in one way or another, I am overwhelmed. The names and stories could easily fill several more volumes. I cannot begin to put that list on paper. I do, however, feel drawn to make clear that certain individuals have been core elements in my becoming the man I am today. My life story has been centered on what was perceived as my failings in life, and as such, often points to the characters who contributed to that misery. In reviewing the life of the Titanic, it is rare to hear of her magnificence and glorious attributes. The designers are not easily praised. So it is with my tale.

As for acknowledgements, it is important to state clearly that my father has been, by far, the most powerful influence in my life. As such, the finger gets pointed his way a great deal as I search for understanding the follies of my life's path. In truth, his influence has been far more beneficial and strengthening than it has been a detriment. Even as I highlight his shortcomings in great detail, I know in the deepest part of me how fortunate I am to have been fathered by a man like this. A hundred million young boys would give their left leg to have a father of this nature. Of all the acknowledgments that are due, this one is at the top of the list, beyond any shadow of a doubt.

Secondly, my mother has consistently modeled compassion and wisdom. When no one else could be there… she was. I am grateful for her unwavering support and also thankful to have inherited my mother's heart.

Along the same line, my brother too has played a significant role. I have often blamed him for not being all that I needed and generally slow to acknowledge his incredible contributions. He taught me how to play music, write poetically, and think creatively. He also led me to see the value in non-conformity, as he modeled the courage it takes to accept feeling unaccepted. To my brother I am forever grateful.

My surviving sister has also been an enormous influence in an equal, yet opposing manner. She showed me that you can shine just as brightly while conforming to proper rules of conduct.

I discovered by watching her, that rebellion is not a requirement for creating a life of honesty and happiness. She has been by my side in the heat of the battle and close enough to feel the burn from the pepper spray that drenched my face, on her own cheek. That tells it all. My gratitude for my sister runs deep.

As odd as it may be, I cannot proceed without mentioning my ex-wife, the mother of my children as one of the most powerful contributors to my emotionally healthy life. Although we divorced over twenty years ago, she has remained loyal and faithful to my role as their father. God only knows what she went through in my darkest hours. I am forever grateful for her strength and steadfast love.

My children are my heroes. They have been angels of light through the seemingly endless nights of confusion and suffering.

To all of the dear friends and family members who have been there for me through thick and thin... I hold you deep in my heart.

To my Warrior brothers and Yaga sisters... Aho!

To Christi, my sweetheart, spiritual partner and companion ... I will spend the rest of my life thanking you.

In sincere gratitude to all of you....

I bestow my deepest blessings.

This book is dedicated to and in memory of my little sister Cathy Jo Wood ~1962 - 2001~ Forever in my heart!

Part 1

Stumbling Upon the Heart of God

"See, this is my opinion: we all start out knowing magic. We are born with whirlwinds, forest fires, and comets inside us. We are born able to sing to birds and read the clouds and see our destiny in grains of sand. But then we get the magic educated right out of our souls. We get it churched out, spanked out, washed out, and combed out. We get put on the straight and narrow and told to be responsible. Told to act our age. Told to grow up, for God's sake. And you know why we were told that? Because the people doing the telling were afraid of our wildness and youth, and because the magic we knew made them ashamed and sad of what they'd allowed to wither in themselves."

— Robert McCammon, Boy's Life

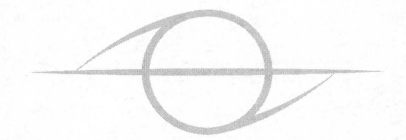

Chapter 1

❧ the early daze ❧

The journey of a thousand miles begins with one step.
—Lao Tzu

My story begins in 1957, on a blazing hot August morning, under the desert sun in Moses Lake, Washington. No twinkling star appeared in the heavens for this momentous occasion. No wise men gathered for the glorious celebration. My humble beginnings were not among livestock or doting onlookers. I was just another name on an insignificant list of births at the local Saint Joseph's Hospital.

I would love to share the memories of my early childhood but they are so few and far between. From what I've heard, I was a fat and happy baby. The pictures I've seen show a plump belly and a smiling face. I was the second son and eventually one of four children, as my two sisters came later. I was destined to grow up in a typical American family which, like so many, was highly dysfunctional.

As for nationality, I have always considered myself a Heinz 57. I generally check the box labeled *mixed* when forced to make a stand. I'm sure that outside eyes would see me as Caucasian but with the white man's reputation in this world, I have never appreciated the association. I would much rather be listed among the native tribes that were reportedly slaughtered by my forefathers. It seems like a better position when it comes to guilt and karma.

My father would tend to hold up the Italian ancestry as more important than the others for some odd reason; perhaps it was something he felt he could hold onto that gave him a sense of value. Maybe it relates to finding one's roots, which has become such a popular movement in this modern day. For me, it would mean holding my Scottish, Danish, Austrian, and the many other ancestors, as somehow inferior, including those unknown. I was never willing to make that move.

My personal search for my roots has pulled me into realms that are far beyond this world. I have found deep soul connections through visions of ancient indigenous peoples who held no label. My inner journeys have revealed more of a mystery than a sense of being rooted in any particular family tree. I trust that my story will reveal the motivation that has called me to look so much deeper than blood.

In my eyes, my father was a rather violent and aggressive young man. Regardless of his ancestry, he carried a substantial chip on his shoulder. He generally exhibited a mean-spirited nature that seemed central to his attitude toward life. As a child, to know him was to fear him. Kindness and affection were foreign concepts when it came to his fatherly influence. Apparently, this was an intergenerational attribute according to his own story, which includes a childhood filled with the physical and emotional abuse that he would so generously pass along.

My mother, on the other hand, was a passive, kind, and caring soul from an undefined European descent. Her grandmother on her father's side had raised her, while her biological mother separately cared for the four siblings that were to follow. My mother's early life has remained shrouded in secrecy; particularly in regard to her father, who was not in the picture as far as the stories go. Being one of five children from three different fathers, my grandmother's history was carefully kept in the closet as well. Like so many women of the day, my mother stayed home with the four of us, while our highly driven father was a busy and devoted workaholic. This set up was quite standard for that generation.

As a family, our situation was just as customary as the Cleavers in *Leave it to Beaver*, but perhaps a bit more realistic. Add a little mental, emotional, physical, and sexual abuse, throw in a few twisted perspectives on the meaning of life - and voila! Like I said... a typical American family.

Now just to set the record straight, the sexual abuse came by way of a third party. In other words, the abuser was not in my bloodline, although his intimate relationship with the family would put him in the same category. Even though he was considered a "friend" of the family, from a psychoanalytical standpoint, the child sexual abuse was ultimately considered incestuous. He had nestled into the heart of the family circle before I was born, and was there to welcome me when I arrived.

In the early years, it was confusing to have such an abusive father battering us boys while our softhearted, compassionate mother could only cry and retreat. The physical pain was actually only a small part of the suffering. Being treated in such a malicious manner by my father is where the real damage occurred. A young child can easily be at a loss in processing the emotional aspect of such trauma. It was challenging to do so without creating a generous portion of resentment, balanced with a comparable dose of self-blame. When my mother was sobbing and screaming in terror, *"Stop! ... Please stop,"* it became obvious that I was not alone in recognizing this repetitive violence as overkill.

For many years, I held bitterness toward her for not standing up to protect us; me as well as my older brother. It hurt on a deeper level to realize that she knew better, and still did nothing to prevent it. The early days of abuse seemed to twist these individual strands of hurt into an angry knotted braid of

5

yarn. My life mission would become learning how to unwind and disentangle this emotional spool that carried the memories and deeply ingrained patterns of such confusion and pain.

I have since come to recognize my mother's way as one of patience and compassion. Whether it came by way of her insecurities, or her religious discipline, the outcome was the same. While she has always called herself a Christian, I recognize her mindset as more fitting with the Buddhist path. She has certainly modeled tolerance, and through the many years of travail I have come to appreciate her gentle influence in my life.

Although the true culprit is ignorance, I do give my parents a great deal of credit for presenting the dynamics that would ultimately infuse me with perfectly oppositional postures and perspectives, instrumental in my breaking in two. Perhaps this was a necessary process on this path, to separate the wheat from the chaff.

I grew up with two very divided and distinct value systems that would lead me to sorting from the inside out, which aspects should be honored or rejected. I graciously received the impact of each of them equally, allowing two diametrically opposed forces to share the cramped quarters of a single mind. Having two polar opposite mindsets modeled so consistently is a powerful set up for a schizophrenic or bipolar point of view.

The mind, like a computer, can easily become compartmentalized and fragmented. Schizophrenia, bipolar disorder, and multiple personality disorder are all indicative of a seriously fragmented psyche. I had these two oppositional extremes displayed consistently in my life from day one. I can now see clearly how and why it played out the way it did. My life path and purpose became a quest to understand and resolve this deeply confused state that brought such intense suffering.

Oh, I know it sounds like a bum deal, and it certainly came with a high price, but in the long run... eventually... the blessing is revealed. So there you have it, a very brief synopsis of the beginning of this lifetime.

The pivotal event that is so central to my life story came 20 years later. This is where the Christ Complex enters the script. By the way, in case you didn't know, the word *Christ* means "anointed." This title is most often associated with Jesus. He was anointed in the *Holy Spirit*, and is considered by many of his followers to not only be "a Christ"... but to be "thee Christ." This is where it gets a bit sketchy.

An anointing in the Holy Spirit, the Light of God, is like the christening of a ship. Yet we commonly speak as though only one person has ever received this anointing. What a peculiar notion! According to the doctors who diagnosed this personal event, it is a classic syndrome, *The Messianic Syndrome*. When it occurs in Jerusalem, which apparently it does quite often, it's called *The Jerusalem Syndrome*. This bizarre archetypal psychological phenomenon occurs often enough to be deemed worthy of a classification as a full on syndrome. That's an impressive volume! This was a real eye opener for me, since I'd never heard of such a thing. It was like being accepted into a club that you didn't know existed. Welcome to the party!

Now let me tell you the story of this particular anointing. It doesn't come in the way you might expect. There is no baptismal font involved. I would not recommend this approach to anyone longing to be touched by God. In fact, it could easily fit on the complete opposite end of the spectrum.

In pursuit of God's grace, you would be more readily guided to fast and pray; purify your thoughts and strive for a compassionate and caring heart. Cultivate a true nature of kindness, forgiveness, and let go of all selfish desires. When you attain a level of purity worthy of God's grace, you will be allowed to enter the Gates to the Kingdom. These are the type of requirements I expected a genuine seeker would be held to, and I can only say, *"I was dead wrong."*

In this story, the aspirant fails miserably to reach even the lowest rung on the ladder, at least in the eyes of man. Nevertheless the anointing occurs. By the grace of God, it is given.

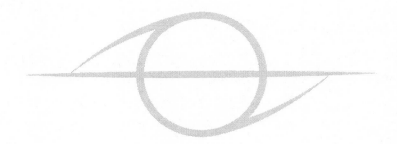

Chapter 2

❧ the american dream ☙

The individual has always had to struggle to keep from being overwhelmed by the tribe. If you try it, you will be lonely often, and sometimes frightened. But no price is too high to pay for the privilege of owning yourself.
—Friedrich Nietzsche

Growing up in a family that held such standard American values instilled a very materialistic perspective deep within my mind. As the son of an aggressive businessman who bought hook, line, and sinker the American dream of buying your way to happiness, I was vigorously molded.

Not only was the material realm highlighted; more specifically the dollar bill was established as the means to coercing that material world to conform to one's desires. It was simple and straightforward. Yes, money was the answer to all of life's needs, and of course it would ultimately bring the true happiness we all longed for. The family motto was, *"Never mind how you get it… just get it."* This was one of my father's most potent contributions to our misguided upbringing. Interestingly enough, it turns out that his take on life, this adopted value system, would be foundational to the situation that ultimately set in motion my *awakening*.

By the time I was expected to pave my own path, I knew full well that it was all about money. It was clear that if you made enough money, you could buy whatever you needed to make yourself happy, and that was all that mattered. It was all very simple. My child-like mind had soaked up "The American Dream" like an empty sponge. With such a materialistic mindset, I enthusiastically dove head first into the mess that it was bound to create.

When I was 19 years old, I dropped out of college after my first year. I was supposedly on my way to becoming a dentist when I realized that I was living a lie. This false sense of direction had begun when I was about five years old. I was given this little book called *School Days*, as a way of keeping photos and memories of each school year. It asked questions like, *"Who were your best friends?"... "What do you enjoy the most in school?"... "What do you want to be when you grow up?"* Well... that last one was the kicker. Who could imagine that this trivial act would play out with such an enormous impact?

I was very fond of a particular movie back in my early childhood that left a lasting impression upon my innocent mind. It was *Rudolph the Red Nosed Reindeer*, and we watched it every year during the Christmas season. Rudolph's best friend was one of Santa's elves and a misfit because he didn't want to make toys like all the other elves. Rebellious fella I guess you might say. He had a strange obsession with dentistry, and despite the opposing voices of authority, desperately wanted to become a dentist. This was very frowned upon by his mentors and peers, and yet he was a sweet and genuine little guy with a good heart.

He was a wonderful role model, and a bit of a hero in my youthful eyes. So I decided I would write his profession down in my little book. It certainly seemed like the best answer I could come up with as a kindergartener. *"When I grow up... I want to be a dentist."* My declaration was received in an overwhelmingly positive manner. My parents were so pleased that I continued to fill in the blank with the same answer year after year. It was definitely a winner. After a decade or so, I guess I actually came to believe it myself. It had become a given, *"I was going to be a Dentist."*

Well, as I said, I had done one full year of college and decided, *"That's enough!"* A year earlier, in 1975, when I graduated from high school, my course had been set. My academic records were not such that it would be an easy path by any stretch. Although I may have been accepted into a four year college, it was much more realistic in my mind to attend a local community college. I figured it would buy me time to get up to speed and transfer to a university before enrolling in a school for dentistry.

The truth is, I hadn't given it much thought. My high school grades were not that great to begin with, and I figured it was most likely due to smoking too much weed. I told myself I was far too wild and carefree to step into the highly disciplined world of a university.

My life thus far had been one of going to school, playing some sports and goofing off in between. Oh, I did Boy Scouts, had a paper route, and took piano lessons for a while, but the point is, there was a lot of *in between*. I had no idea what it would take to accomplish this incomprehensible goal of becoming a dentist.

I did my first year of college, and took on a fairly heavy load, including courses such as pre-calculus, biology, chemistry, economics, and sociology. I fulfilled many of the requirements that would allow me to enter the university, and I also came to realize, within my own mind, that this wasn't something I really wanted to do. I was burned out and ready to walk away after the first semester. How could I possibly keep up this pace for the years to come? I knew deep down I couldn't. One day while I was working with a friend, I inadvertently discovered my hidden destiny.

We were doing some landscaping, moving rocks, digging in the dirt, and sweating in the hot sun. We got to talking and sharing tales of our hardship. As college students, we were each struggling in our own way.

I told my buddy, *"There must be an easier way. I don't want to spend my life moving rocks and studying books about stuff I couldn't care less about."* He seemed to share the same youthful feelings of uncertainty. Our mutual complaining took us into the visions of the grass that was so much greener elsewhere.

He cautiously spoke of a fantasy he was secretly entertaining. That was the day he undeniably opened my eyes to an entirely new direction. He told me a story about the male hairdresser who had just cut his hair. He spoke of the girls that swarmed around him, the rock and roll music that played all day, and the cold beer that filled the fridge. *"Wow! Now that's the life for me!"* I thought out loud. This vision was fabulous! What more could a wide-eyed anxious teenager want? Maybe a joint… right?

My mind was made up. I would break the news to my parents and soon be set free. Who was I fooling anyway? I didn't want to become a dentist any more than I wanted to become a nuclear physicist. I couldn't quite imagine sitting in a sterile little office working on the teeth of people who despised the very idea of seeing me. Even if I could stand the many years of college, which I was sure I couldn't, I wouldn't like the outcome anyway. *"No… a hairdresser! That's the life for me!"*

I had seen the movie *Shampoo* with Warren Beatty, and that was a good sell as well. I could see myself relaxed and enjoying every moment of every day, and that's about how quickly my life changed. I quit school and told my parents the horrible news. By the expression on my Dad's face, you would have thought I had just announced that I was gay. The funny thing is, I hadn't even heard of this connection between hairdressing and homosexuality. Somehow I had missed that stereotype. In time, it would become quite obvious that I was one of the few who didn't carry this correlative. Believe me, this abrupt change of course would turn out to be vastly insignificant in comparison to the stunning calamity that was soon to follow.

That summer I began my cosmetology training, which sounds a little more sophisticated than beauty school. However, beauty school was a dream come true. The total enrollment included about eighty-five, mostly good looking young women, a few straight guys, and a handful of gay men. As for the dating pool, the odds were fabulous. This was a very attractive adventure I was about to embark upon. I could feel it in my bones.

I was about to discover a hidden talent that would carry me far into my future. It turned out that I actually enjoyed the trade, and had a definite aptitude and affinity for the art of hairdressing. I particularly enjoyed cutting and developed a genuine passion for this new form of *live medium* sculpture. It was downright exhilarating!

My parents seemed to be less attached to my choice of direction than I had imagined. They were actually supportive as they witnessed my sense of accomplishment and success in a field that still somehow rated on a much lower level than dentistry. Even so, it was all going very well as I stayed the course and finished my 2000 hours in one year to the day. I loved it!

I was now a fully licensed cosmetologist with big dreams. I went to work in a small local salon, which was owned by one of our visiting teachers. She was highly skilled and had a good reputation in the business. I was honored to be accepted into her company, but it wasn't long before I took interest in a gal who was selling hair coloring products to the salon.

I was very curious about her position as a distributor for a particular product line out of Los Angeles. The business aspect of selling products on a larger scale intrigued me, and my interest grew as I looked deeper. I quickly realized that a distributor took a much bigger cut of the profit than an employee ever would. Although she had secured the rights to the state of Washington, I was certain there would be opportunities available elsewhere. Looking back I see clearly how my father's overwhelming influence was suddenly at the forefront of my decision making. It was all about making money.

He was raised in a family that teetered on the brink of poverty throughout his early life. His parents raised him through the Great Depression, and at an early age his fears and values became centered on finances, and more specifically, on avoiding poverty. Money became the most important thing in his life and the social values of that entire generation seemed to support this shared perspective. My youthful mind had no idea how shortsighted or deep this programming was. Through my indoctrinated eyes, it appeared as though this was simply how the world worked. With good intentions, my father drove his shallow thinking into my mind like a high speed freight train through a darkened tunnel. An obsession with the pursuit of riches was pouring through my bloodstream in those early years.

I remember, I got my hands on a copy of *Think and Grow Rich* by Napoleon Hill shortly after finishing my schooling. After reading the book, I knew without a doubt that I could accomplish anything I could ever conceive of. If I could conceive and believe, I could achieve. It was like learning the art of magic; I had a sense of certainty inside that I had never known before. My father's money-driven blood was coursing through my veins, and I was too naïve to have any room for doubt.

I became decidedly determined to get a distributorship and a territory of my own. I made a few calls and soon had an appointment to discuss this possibility with the owner of the product line. I was anxious and enthusiastically running in high gear. I drove my sister's car from Seattle to L.A. and back in three days. Talk about a whirlwind!

The car was a rather beat up old Toyota Corolla, and I remember being sure to park it where it wouldn't be seen. I had put on a funny little three-piece suit to present myself as business capable. As silly as it seems now, somehow it all fell into place. The man whose name was on the label spoke directly with me, and he agreed to give me the distributorship for an entire state. I think he was impressed with my enthusiasm and willingness to make the effort to see him in person. That's exactly what I was hoping for. I was offered a choice between Oregon and Hawaii.

C'mon folks... Oregon isn't all that much different than Washington. It is beautiful for sure, but held up against white sand beaches, palm trees, surf boards, bikinis and coconuts...

it wasn't much of a choice. It was a no-brainer decision for a teen-ager. I took Hawaii in a heartbeat. So I was off and running just like Napoleon had suggested. I'd conceived, believed, and achieved my goal, like clockwork.

Looking back, I was obviously on the manic side of my mental energy, although I had no point of reference for such a notion in those days. I was very anxious, excited, and believed that if I could just stay in a positive frame of mind I could make all my dreams come true very quickly. Quickly was definitely the key to the plan. I didn't want to spend a lot of time making the money. I had more important things to do. I needed to make a lot of money rapidly so I could get on with the good part of life, which certainly wasn't *working*. I had no understanding of work as a form of enjoyment. Neither had I been introduced to the idea of work relating to fulfilling a personal purpose in life.

In my childhood training, work was a penalty and if you were lucky, money was the reward for the hardship. I realized much later in life that I had been unintentionally trained to hate work. It had been used as a form of punishment in my childhood. When we deserved chastisement, which was apparently quite often, we were put to work right after the "spankings."

My dad's favorite form of teaching us a lesson for bad behavior was to make us rake rocks; we were also blessed with a back yard that grew them. It was truly a never-ending job.

Apparently, our property had been used by the local housing development as a dumping ground before our home was built. You could rake all day, every day, and they just kept coming up. So somehow "work" in general became another four-letter word that seemed pointless. That's what you do when you are a bad boy. Boy Scouts, on the other hand, was instrumental in my cultivating good intentions for my purpose in this world. Although I was unaware of the value of work, I was certain that *being a good guy* was central to my path. At the ripe age of 19, I still held a very shallow view as to what it was all about.

I came home from the L.A. trip and told my folks about gaining the exclusive rights to a distributorship for the State of Hawaii. They seemed semi-impressed and openly supportive. However, what I needed now was more than moral support. I needed the financing to get this ball rolling. I mean, c'mon, the taste of success is dripping from my lips! For God's sake, don't forget that *"it takes money to make money. Let's get this party started!"* My father was very resistant at first, but soon gave in to my demands as I threw a tizzy fit over his denying me the chance to grab hold of this incredible opportunity. After all, it was the grand opening for me to step into the financial success that he so strongly believed in. He finally agreed to loan me a chunk of change to get me started, at least it seemed like a chunk back then. Looking back, it was just enough to ensure failure.

At the time, I was more than overjoyed and began my planning immediately. The Master Plan was about to unfold, and I knew for sure I didn't want to go it alone. I was certain that I needed some help because I didn't have a clue about running a business. I had the confidence to deal with the product end of things, including teaching and selling, but what about accounting and business in general? I was anxious to find a partner. My girlfriend had a buddy who had recently completed a two-year college program in business. *"Wow, what a break... and such a coincidence."* I gave him the low down on my business plan and offered to bring him on board which included taking him to Hawaii.

Now the truth is, I did't know this guy from Adam. I just knew I didn't want to go it alone. He quickly accepted and we just as quickly joined forces in putting our travel plans together. It seemed that in an instant we'd packed our bags and jumped on a plane headed for the middle of the Pacific Ocean, the island of Oahu to be exact. A short time later we found ourselves in a small apartment on Ala Moana Boulevard, centered deeply in the middle of the madness of Waikiki. We spent several months attempting to get the operation off the ground, all the while burning through my insignificant stash. I was busy talking to salons, ordering our first shipment of product and bringing a couple of sales people on board. It was an extremely disorganized and unstructured attempt. Probably exactly what you would expect from a couple of punk kids who had no clue about what it takes to set up a business, or the experience that would produce any kind of positive work ethic.

It soon became obvious that there was very little compatibility between us. He didn't seem too thrilled to be a part of the business, the confusion, or my personal trip. He just wasn't the kind of guy that would pass up a free handout that came in the form of an all-expense paid trip to Hawaii. Can you blame him?

About six months into the venture, I decided that I was due for a trip home. I really wanted to see my girlfriend and touch base with my family. I left the "partner" with access to the bank account as we were expecting another shipment of product. Looking back, I realize that I was either extremely naïve, ignorant, or unconsciously setting myself up for the fall that would forever change my life. Perhaps it was all of the above but for now let's just call it pure innocence. That feels much better.

You can probably see it coming. I returned from my visit to the mainland... and it was ALL gone. I don't recall there being a note and don't remember exactly how I came to realize what had transpired. What I did discover was that my partner was nowhere to be found. The sales staff had been brusquely informed that we were no longer in business and promptly let go. Last but certainly not least; the bank account had been drained. The several thousand dollars in the account had become his play money, and I soon discovered that he had flown a buddy over to join his party. What a shock! What a disaster! I didn't bother to hunt him down as I had problems that far exceeded my concerns with him. I never did see the guy again.

Now, this is where the critical point of my story comes in, the turning point that thrusts me into another dimension of life. My reaction to the situation was one of deep trauma. I was dumbfounded, flabbergasted, and extremely angry. After all, anger was one of the few male skills I had been trained in. It was also one of the only acceptable forms of emotional expression I was allowed. Big boys don't cry, but they sure do get pissed off!

Raging would be a definite understatement. I was livid beyond my ability to express it; hurt, sad, and scared to the core, not to mention confused. Did I mention confused? The emotional response was extreme and out of control. I was too upset and embarrassed to tell anyone, especially my parents. I had nowhere to go and no one to turn to. In spite of the severe upset, I was determined to find a solution on my own.

Beneath the rage, the fear, and the pain, the wheels were turning. I have Napoleon in one ear and the devil in the other. *"Quitters never win …and Winners never quit. I'm gonna kill that son of a bitch!"* I knew one thing for sure. I was not going to give up. I was devoted to navigating my way through this mess, one way or another. I would not accept defeat or failure. It wasn't even an option. So I was pacing around in circles, scrambling through my deepest reservoir of rationality, which wasn't very deep.

"Okay... what is the problem here? Money. That's right. That's all it is... Just money. This is not really a problem. You just need more money. So where can you get more money? More Money... aha... the bank! The banks have all kinds of money. Just go to the bank and get some more. You can always pay it back after you get this business up and running. Think Jeffrey... think.

But c'mon now, they aren't gonna give some punk with a funky little three-piece suit a loan! Get real man," I argued with myself, *"Well... then steal it! You can always make it up later. It's not like you're a criminal. You know yourself better than that. Just this once you can do what it takes to keep going forward... launch your business and never do it again. Just this once. You've got to remember, winners never quit! This one bad move doesn't make you a bad person. God knows your heart. Just imagine all the good you will do once you have achieved financial success! Yeah. Just once. I mean... what else can I do?"* That was it. I had the answer. I knew what to do. Quitters never win and winners never quit, and I choose to win. So there it is... the emerging of a brilliant plan for my salvation.

Chapter 3

♀ a plan for salvation ♂

There is no easy walk to freedom anywhere, and many of us will have to pass through the valley of the shadow of death again and again before we reach the mountaintop of our desires.

— Nelson Mandela

So, now I've got one quick little painless bank robbery to pull off, and then back to plan A. I began to investigate the situation, still out of my mind with emotional upset. I believe I was actually foaming at the mouth as I made my way through the streets of Waikiki to the local bank. I needed to check out the accessibility, as well as the security guards who were sure to be watching over the place. Upon my initial inspection, it didn't look too threatening or difficult.

There were two entrances and a guard stationed just inside each one. If I could enter the side door and disarm the first man from behind, I could easily hold him at gunpoint while I forced the other guard to drop his weapon. The customers will, of course, readily comply and lay on the floor as I have the tellers hand over the loot. *"This is certainly doable,"* I thought to myself. I had the solution to all of my problems at the tips of my fingers.

Now, it was a matter of working out the details. First of all, I needed a gun. I had no money, no idea of how to get a gun even if I did have the money, and quite honestly, I wasn't really comfortable with the notion of actually having one. I quickly decided that my best bet was to use what I had on hand to create something that *looked* like a gun. After all, I wasn't going to actually shoot anyone; I just needed to fake them out long enough to accomplish my goal. Besides, these guys are going to be so caught off guard that they won't be looking at whether or not I'm carrying a real gun. I'll blind side 'em and shake 'em up too much for anyone to be thinking about a fake gun. This gun-less situation could actually end up being twice as good, since nobody was likely to get hurt. Good thinking... right?

So I started digging around the apartment and noticed that the vacuum cleaner had a metal tube that could make a damn good alternative for a gun barrel. Perhaps it was a bit large, but on second thought, it was close enough. It could work. I also discovered that I had a wooden coat hanger in the closet that could be jammed into the chrome tube to resemble the butt of the gun. I found some medical gauze and wrapped it around the fake rifle from top to bottom. You could see the open barrel sticking out of one end and the wooden handle hanging out of the other. It looked real enough to me. Thank God for these items being so readily available. *"How divinely convenient!"*

I was looking it over. The length looked good. It could easily pass for a sawed-off shotgun. All the pieces were in place now. I had the plan, the weapon, and well... the moment of reckoning had come. It took three days to get myself prepared as the clock was ticking violently in the corner of an all but empty apartment. Meanwhile my heart was jamming to the same beat.

The big day had finally arrived. The preparations were complete with no more excuses for delaying. *"It's now or never pal - Time to do it!"* I threw on my clothes without any thought as to how I looked, and grabbed the gun. *"C'mon man, let's go!"* I snarled. *"What are you waiting for?"* I mustered up everything I had, but couldn't quite get myself to budge.

I was sitting there frozen in fear with my heart pounding like the bass drum at a heavy metal concert. I finally forced myself to stand up and began to move toward the door. I was shaky and sweating bullets. Every ounce of anxiety within me came to a head like a volcanic eruption. Suddenly there was a crescendo of emotion as I stumbled and dropped the gun. I turned around, staggered toward the bed, and like a dead man, fell face down as I cried out..."*Please help me GOD!*"

Chapter 4

℘ into the light ℘

Opportunity often comes disguised in the form of misfortune, or temporary defeat.

—Napoleon Hill

Now, looking back, those weren't just words. It was a cry from the depths of my shattered soul. My heart, mind, and spirit were unified in that heated moment, and the whole ball of wax cracked open like a broken egg. I never experienced landing on the bed. I didn't physically feel a thing. What I did experience was falling into a field of light that I would never be able to fully grasp or describe.

This light was glorious beyond comprehension. I was warm and floating in a timeless sea of pure Love. It was as if I wasn't there, as if I had been swallowed up into the vastness of space. The feeling was one of being held in the arms of an enormous Angel, Light Being, or Holy Spirit. I was enveloped in a divine light of consciousness that was inseparable from any sense of self. I was seeing from this awareness, and yet witnessing the entire experience simultaneously.

I also remember having the intense awareness of receiving data, like an immense download of information was flowing in. The influx seemed endless, and I was oblivious to the nature of the incoming content. Where it was coming from, I couldn't say, but the download was enormous. I could feel the clicking bars and the turning wheel as the gigabytes of information were being received.

The Divine Being, which I perceived to be Christ, just held me in a state of love, grace, and forgiveness. I felt as though

I was in the womb of an Angel of the highest order, and yet we were one and the same. All that is was in total unity and perfect harmony. To this day, I struggle to comprehend the experience. There was no division, pieces, or parts. Just one... and that one was wholly divine. This realm was beyond the reaches of space and time, and there was somehow a sense of timelessness within the presence of eternity. Certainly this was a heavenly realm. The experience never diminished or faded away. This divine light would ultimately serve to carry me through the many years of hellish episodes of madness soon to follow.

I slowly came back into conscious awareness to find myself lying motionless on the bed. I had no idea how much time had passed. It could have been three minutes or three days. I had no frame of reference and was never able to answer that question. I was contentedly in my own world.

When I came to, all of my troubles had been lifted and burned in a fire of divine ecstasy. I awakened from my deep sleep with an overwhelming sense of joy. I was floating in a state of euphoria. I remember feeling warm inside and overflowing with a deep-seated sense of inner peace and happiness. I couldn't even imagine what could possibly upset a person. None of the hurt made sense any more. It all seemed absurd from this new state of awareness. I didn't have a care in the world as I was saturated in a sense of being blissfully free.

I still carry a recollection of the descent as I reentered the stratosphere. As I was descending from this heavenly realm of consciousness back into my body, and just before awakening, a voice cried out. *"You are the Messiah of the Coming Age!"* Oh my God! In that instant I knew without a doubt that I was the Christ and the Messiah of the dawning age. I had no idea in my wildest imaginings the many years of pain and confusion that would accompany this realization. Floating in the joy and bliss of my newfound awareness, I drifted through the coming weeks in a mesmerized and mystical daze. I don't recall a great deal of what took place in the physical world during that time period. I do remember writing a letter to my girlfriend back home; letting her know who I was. Imagine that; finding out that your boyfriend is the new Christ. What a trip, huh? Now keep in mind she's a teenager as you try to imagine her position, as well as her response. Uh... not so good.

My family also became aware of the transformation and soon, my 18 year old sister and my aunt, who had just turned 21, came to help. Although my mind was slow to record or hold fast to the events of the day, I do know that I was consciously attuned to what was unfolding within my spiritual awareness.

I knew with deep certainty, the shift that was soon to come. I could feel it through every pore in my skin, every fiber of my being. My body was moving toward a state of dematerialization whereby I would soon become pure spirit. It was inevitable, and I was at peace with what was happening.

I was quite certain that it would be just as pleasurable as my most recent "spiritual" experience. This was God's plan and obviously orchestrated with only divine intentions for the highest good. Perfectly beautiful visions of my own dematerialization filled my mind like old movies playing on a dusty sheet. It was clear that my destiny was not of this world. That much was for sure.

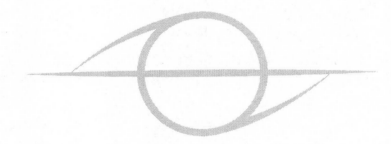

Chapter 5

❦ the path to paradise ❧

I took a walk around the world to ease my troubled mind
I left my body lying somewhere in the sands of time...
I watched the world float to the dark side of the moon
I feel there is nothing I can do...

—3 doors down, Kryptonite

As I recall the feelings and thoughts of those days leading up to my scheduled departure, it was as if a part of me had been obliterated by that Holy revelation of light. My personal ego had been burned in a fire of sweet ecstasy. It felt good and yet empty at an individual level of awareness. I had no need to live this earthly life any longer. It wasn't like I wanted to die or that I hated living. I just knew that it was my time to go and had a deep sense of peace about it.

I remember having twenty bucks to my name. I decided that I could best dissolve into the cosmos from a peaceful and serene setting in the jungles of a nearby garden of tranquility... Kauai. Although I'd never been, I had a strong knowing that this was the perfect place for lift off. I bought my ticket for nineteen dollars and kept a single dollar in my otherwise empty pockets. I had only a small backpack of clothing and a sleeping bag; I foresaw that I would have no use for money on this one-way trip I was about to embark upon.

As the plane came in for the landing at Lihue Airport and the doors gently opened, a sweet fragrance permeated the cramped quarters of the last flying machine I would ever need. I was stunned by the unexpected and exhilarating olfactory experience; the memory of which would stay with me the rest of my life. The plane's interior had been flooded with a heavenly fragrance of exotic flowers, wild grasses, and fresh air that was absolutely intoxicating. As I disembarked, I was filled with the scent of what may as well have been *The Garden of Eden*. I knew I was home and that my astral launching was being divinely guided. It was in the air. I could taste it.

I was totally blissed out as I wandered through the quaint little terminal and out into the Hawaiian sunshine. I meandered across the airport parking lot and found my way to the main road. I didn't know where it led, but it seemed to be pointed in a good direction. I stuck my thumb out as I approached the highway and was pleased to be picked up by the first passing car. To my surprise it was a young woman. This was a strange and rare occurrence back home. Women didn't often take that kind of risk in the big city. *"Where ya goin?"* she asked, with a reassuring smile. She didn't seem fazed in the least when I told her I didn't know. She spoke reverently of a trail that would lead me deep into the Kalalau Valley, as she drove down a country road to the Na Pali Coast and into the heart of paradise. She gracefully directed me toward a tranquil and beautiful white sand beach about eleven miles in. Her friendly, caring manner was almost enough to make me stay, but I knew better. Somehow, there was something more important than my personal pleasures of living another life.

In spirit form I could be much more effective in bringing the peace and love that was so needed on this earthly plane. I had full faith that God would not lead me down a dead end street. No way. The ascension was purposeful and necessary. This life, that wouldn't have amounted to a hill of beans, was being taken to a higher level of functioning. I would soon saturate the consciousness of mankind in a powerful way that held great value. That was fine with me. I wanted to be of value. The sacrifice was well worth the anticipated outcome. This transformational event was a generous gift from God; not just for me, but for the entirety of Mankind. Thank God for this peace and this purpose.

I soon found myself at the end of the road, the entry to the trailhead and the beginning of an adventure into the Kalalau Valley. As I mentioned earlier, I had Boy Scout experience, and hiking down a trail in the wilderness was not a scary thing for me. I was comfortable with making my way through a forested terrain; however, the climate, flora, and fauna of this landscape were very different from what I'd been exposed to in my Pacific Northwest adventures. I had no idea what might be considered edible, nor what was better left untouched.

About a half mile in, I came across a large avocado lying in the middle of the trail. Next to it was a note, finger scribbled in the dirt. *"This is for you!"* I couldn't believe it! How generous and what a sweet find! I tore the skin off and enjoyed every bite of the feast immensely as I continued hiking. Amazing! I was being supported along my one-way journey, and could easily see that I had nothing to worry about. Even my food was being laid at my feet. I hiked through a lush, beautiful jungle, and took a turn that led me onto an overgrown path that I can only imagine had been forged by pigs. The further I went, the skimpier it became until I was breaking my own trail. I could hear the rushing water of a nearby waterfall and stayed the course until I reached it. I sat, pondering the significance of the magnificent flowing waters and the sound of such beauty and power. Mesmerized by the tranquility, the aroma of heaven, and the overwhelming full sensory experience, I sat and gazed, open eyed... open hearted... and empty. It was surreal and this vision, like the initial blast of fragrance, has remained locked in my memory ever since.

In my ponderings, I've often wondered if my mind was in some sort of ultra-open state that allowed these experiences to be planted at the core of my consciousness as they are still so vivid nearly forty years later. The dreamlike exhibition was absolutely astonishing and breathtaking. Here I was, lost in this lush and dense jungle with a magnificent waterfall playing an angelic song, just for me. The entire experience was truly and utterly stunning.

It's hard to say what shifted me from that peace. Maybe it was hunger, or an inner sense of urgency to make camp. I looked around to quickly realize the undergrowth was far too thick to lie down in. The rock on which I was perched was the only clearing within sight and it certainly wasn't big enough to curl up on. I felt a twinge of fear as I began to trace my steps back along the faded separation in the bushes leading me to my original pathway. This was not a good place to get lost. I gained energy as I scurried toward the safety of the main trail. There was a definite sense of relief when my feet found this well-traveled path to security. As I ventured along that worn and welcomed dirt I was at ease, knowing that I was not alone.

The total distance to the end of the trail was eleven miles. It took me two days to reach my destination. The memory that stands out, beyond the heavenly gift of an avocado, was when two beautiful girls came around the corner bare breasted. I remember squinting and rubbing my eyes to be sure that it wasn't a hallucination. It wasn't and I was happily surprised to see their nakedness. We spent the night in the same camp and didn't find any reason to interact much. There was no sense in my pursuing any human relations at this point. I was about to exit this realm and felt no need to explain that to my traveling friends. I just drifted off to sleep in the gentle caress of the angels that were guiding my every step. The next day, I hiked through the winding path that seemed to take me in and out of a lush and aromatic primeval forest. It followed the grade of the landscape and wound back and forth along the deep valleys and peaks that hovered above the blue-green sea below. As I came around a turn in the path, and peered out of the dense tropical foliage, I was awestruck by the vision that awaited me. I gazed out at a sunset that revealed rich colors and textures of softness that seemed to envelope the curvature of the earth. As far as I could see... there was ocean. It was magnificent and spectacular beyond understanding.

I instinctively turned my head to share the moment, and realized there was nobody with me. I even began to speak, *"Wow... can you believe... ?"* as I swiftly searched for my non-existent companion. The strange incident left me dazed. The sadness that followed this realization haunted me for many years to come. Perhaps this was the undoing of what would have been a clean ascension. Maybe I had unknowingly latched onto the wanting, the deep desire for others that keeps us in this vicious cycle of life, death, and rebirth. At the time, my emptiness was filled with sorrow.

I continued my journey; eventually basking in the sun on a white sand beach that still ebbs and flows through the far reaches of my mind. It was an exquisite excursion, more than a person could wish for. The people here didn't wear clothing, and I soon found myself feeling rather odd to be dressed. It didn't take me long to join the ranks and quickly embrace this new sense of freedom. I swam in the ocean and found myself drifting among naked bodies, casually roaming a scene that was surely fitting for a heavenly fantasy. I soon discovered the wild tomatoes growing along the edges of the tropical forest, as well as fresh water flowing in a nearby creek. I could easily survive until I naturally dissipated into the formlessness I was so readily anticipating. No problem.

The beach was tucked in alongside the Na Pali Coast and looking up at the cliffs was as magnificent as the view across the ocean. I was trying to mind my own business, and yet the longing for company left me open to the interactions that came. A few idle conversations kept me feeling connected and at ease. About seven days into the journey, there was a rumor of a nearby tragedy. Apparently a poacher who was hunting mountain goats had fallen to his death on the slippery wet cliffs. It didn't look like a very safe place to be; the rugged terrain was extremely steep and downright slimy. I remember the guy who was telling me the story saying, *"Wow… talk about instant karma!"*

I didn't think about it at the time, but later on I wondered if the poacher had been taken in my place. I was scheduled for departure and yet it never came. I felt abandoned in some way, like a lost child waiting for an invisible bus. *"Alright already… when do I dissolve into the cosmos?"* I mumbled to myself. I'd been there two weeks and nothing had happened. I didn't get it. *"Now what?"* I remember thinking, *"What am I supposed to do with this body?"* I couldn't wait any longer, something had gone awry. I didn't know what to think, but I knew the ascension wasn't going down as planned. My divine exit would not be forth coming at this time and I was back on the game board, whether I liked it or not. *"Damn it! This really sucks! What on earth shall I do now?"* I gathered my belongings and hiked back out the same way I'd come in. No divine avocado gift on this leg of the trip. The deeply permeating beauty and fragrance of this heavenly realm were already starting to fade as I began to feel overshadowed by one minor, yet very disturbing detail. Me.

Part 2
Scorned

*"One day you finally knew what you had to do,
and began, though the voices around you kept
shouting their bad advice...
though the whole house began to tremble and
you felt the old tug at your ankles.
'Mend my life!' each voice cried. But you didn't
stop. You knew what you had to do, though
the wind pried with its stiff fingers at the very
foundations...
though their melancholy was terrible.
It was already late enough, and a wild night,
and the road full of fallen branches and stones.
But little by little, as you left their voices
behind, the stars began to burn through the
sheets of clouds, and there was a new voice,
which you slowly recognized as your own, that
kept you company as you strode deeper and
deeper into the world, determined to do the only
thing you could do... determined to save the only
life you could save."*

— Mary Oliver, The Journey

Chapter 6

❧ the road home ❧

Let us not pray to be sheltered from dangers but to be fearless when facing them.

—*Rabindranath Tagore*

I still recall deep feelings of sorrow as I look back at this stretch of my journey. It felt like a return to hell. Not because life had been such a terrible experience thus far, but in relation to my visions of turning into pure spirit, the direction I was headed in didn't appear quite so pleasant. I was climbing out of the frying pan and right back into the fire.

I reluctantly found my way out to the country road. It was mid-day and I was confident that I could catch a ride into town. The next step would certainly reveal itself from there. I was picked up while hitchhiking, by an older gentleman who was on vacation. He was a medical doctor that lived and practiced in Australia. He was friendly enough and seemed to take a genuine interest in my predicament. I didn't go into the inside story of what I was experiencing, I just told him that I was trying to get home and didn't have any money. I had an uncle who lived on Maui, and I knew that he'd be happy to see me if I could only find him. From there I was certain that I could eventually find my way back to the mainland.

My newfound friend took pity on me and generously paid the fourteen dollar airfare. I was grateful for the gift from above and one more caring soul in the world. I flew to Maui and was able to connect with my uncle. I knew the general vicinity of where he lived and asked around town until I found somebody that knew how to reach him. It was a small community back then. When we met he seemed genuinely pleased to see me. It was also obvious that he was well aware of my being a bit off course, not that he was in a position to be of much help.

This uncle was my mother's youngest half brother. He was ten years older than me, and a Vietnam Vet. He'd made the unfortunate choice, at an early age, to follow in his father's footsteps to becoming a tried and true war hero. His father had come back from the Korean War with medals of honor that left a real impression on my uncle's young mind. When the Vietnam War came along, it kicked the door wide open for him to step into the same path of finding that sense of self-worth and pride that he'd so unknowingly projected upon his father.

At age 19, he joined the Marine Corps Infantry and was sent straight to the frontlines. It didn't ultimately go down as planned and the war hero idea never really came to fruition. Actually, it fell through quite miserably. He shared very few stories of the nightmare he lived through during those frightful years. Although he did survive physically, he never really came home mentally or emotionally. Like so many Vietnam vets, his life had been swallowed up and lost in the violence and trauma. He was engulfed by the mental suffering of what he'd witnessed and willingly been a part of. I loved him dearly, and had deep compassion for his dreadful situation.

It was good to see him and I felt at home with my uncle. I don't recall how long I was with him or much of what I was doing beyond hanging out. I do recall his seriously entrenched habits of drinking alcohol and smoking pakalolo were more than I could bear to witness. It was painful to watch, and I remember drifting around the island until I found myself in the sweet embrace of a little town called Hana. It was lush and fragrant, just like Kauai. The memories for that leg of the journey lay hidden beneath a heavy cloud cover. I can only imagine that at some point my parents were notified, because I did eventually make it back home.

So I'm at a crossroads here. I wanted to speak of my return home, but as I reach inward for the memories to support this segment of my story, I realize that, like my uncle, I never fully returned. I spent the next twenty years in and out of mental institutions, trying to recover in spite of the oppositional force of the AMA and the American Mental Health system. The "I" that I thought I was before the transformation became a faded memory. That "I"… never returned.

I believe the next year was spent mostly ranting and raving about the end of days. My mind was busily occupied, scattered, and confused to say the least. Like so many bewildered folks, I had poked my nose into the book of Revelations just far enough to stir up the hornets' nest. I spoke incessantly of the many ways we needed to change, and the unbearable consequences that were sure to come if we didn't. I remember my parents bringing a couple of counselors over to talk with me one day. It was more than they could handle. Nothing came of it.

The memories are faded, but I clearly recall this phase as disturbing for everyone in my life. I had immersed myself into the many religious perspectives that were so readily available at the various local churches, as a way of coping with my disturbed state of mind. It was such a troubled time in my life, and I wanted everyone that I knew to listen to my deeply rooted words of guidance. It was apparent to me that I held considerable knowledge about life now and it was top priority that I be heard. I mean, after all, I was the Messiah of the coming age. This was important stuff! So I did a lot of reading and talking and …well… about a year after I had come home, I was officially declared a certified wacko. The official label went something like this; Schizophrenic with delusions of grandeur and a Messianic Syndrome. *(Try to say that in one breath!)*

Now… I saw that Mel Gibson movie *The Passion*. I have an idea of the horrendous and brutal thrashing that Jesus faced on his way to the cross. Being nailed to a wooden stake and hung up to die a slow, painful death isn't something I can ever imagine signing up for. However, the agony that I would endure in the coming years would leave me wondering if that painfully ugly crucifixion wouldn't have been an easier way to go.

During the decades of being "treated" for my disorder, I would never once have a health professional approach the subject of the *Christ Complex*. Through the years of ongoing "medical treatment" it was not once mentioned, let alone discussed. Apparently, it was forbidden territory for the medical professionals.

It certainly was not a subject to create a social conversation around, as it was smothered with shame and avoided like the plague. My so-called "alternative" studies were my only opportunity to gain any understanding or insight as to how I might proceed with such a dilemma. Beyond comedy routines and an occasional Charles Manson reference, it was basically a taboo subject in my world. My research would remain private and undercover. The battle I faced was in my own mind and so was my only source of hope.

There was nothing offered through traditional medicine beyond drugs. The prescribed drugs typically brought on more severe difficulties than what I was already facing without them. As you may already know, with many of the psychotropic drugs, the side effects and long-term repercussions can be debilitating, if not deadly. I have lost friends and family along the way and consider myself extremely fortunate to have survived such an extensive ordeal. It has been a rough road and it is with deep gratitude and by the grace of God that I carry on.

Long before my grand awakening, I had established certain behavior patterns, certain habits you might say that were standard for the kids in my neck of the woods. I was growing up in the seventies and smoking pot was like riding a bike. It was just another normal thing to do. Drinking and partying was one of my favorite past times, alongside the many peers I considered friends. Dropping a hit of acid wasn't quite as popular, and now, looking back, I wish I hadn't been so courageous or haphazard but the truth is… I was. I did take a few acid trips. LSD, they called it. *"Lucy in the Sky with Diamonds."* It was well known to produce flashbacks.

It's tough to be afraid of something you don't understand. I get it now. Through my rebellious teen years I had pretty much sampled everything that was put in front of me. Uppers… downers… hash… coke. Heck… I remember thinking it was cool to take a pill and not even ask what it was. God, that sounds crazy, knowing what I know now.

Only by the grace of God did I not fall into the death trap that I saw dear friends devoured by. Cocaine took a lot of people down in those days, and it didn't seem to be related to a person's strength or goodness of heart. It was just some kind of chemical reaction that caused one guy to crave and need something so badly that he would die for it. I was fortunate to have missed that boat. The only drug addiction I had at that age was pot. I smoked a lot of weed.

As I would discover later on, although it wasn't cocaine or heroin, it would prove to be something to contend with. The year preceding my diagnosis I was still smoking heavily. Drinking and partying with my friends was an outlet for the madness that resulted from my altered sense of being in this world. At least it provided a temporary escape from the confusion and painful loneliness of feeling like such an oddball. All of my friends knew that I was loopy, but they couldn't understand it. One saving correlation was when another one of our buddies had a very similar experience.

As strange as it still is to me, he too, went to Hawaii and came back believing he was the Messiah. I never did hear the details of his story or how it all went down, but I'm sure his situation was unique and quite different from my own. We were clearly separate strains of people. As for being a savior, he was a much nicer guy than I was. If it came down to it, I would have voted for him. All I'd ever heard about his vision was that he believed he had to write a particular set of songs and that when he'd completed his mission there would be great peace upon the land. I could only guess that he never did finish his assignment.

The saving grace for me was that I knew I wasn't alone in my madness. Unfortunately, however, my mission was not so concrete or measurable. I wasn't exactly clear on what I was supposed to do. I just knew what I knew. It was like having a string in your hand that leads to an enormous angelic kite in the sky. The kite was God and the catch is… I was the only one who could see it.

So here I am. I'm in my early twenties, my mind is fried and I am trying to get by. Meanwhile the wheels never stop turning. I am unable to halt the incessant churning and grasping for more; more knowledge, more understanding, and ultimately more peace of mind.

I have got to figure this thing out. By this thing, I mean life. I am drawn into deep places of thought, and even deeper places of pain. My mind hurts. It's like a wounded animal that is vicious and threatening. It bares its teeth and ravages all that enter its circle of need.

The drugs don't help, at least not in the long run. Now if a guy is running around barefoot in the snow, waiting for a spaceship to land and take him onboard, well, I guess the fact that drugs can debilitate him makes them of great value. It's a tough point to argue when that targeted individual is behaving in a highly self-destructive manner. So let me restate that. Drugs were not the cure for the state of mind I found myself in, but they may very well be one of the biggest reasons I have lived to tell about it.

On many occasions I was drugged and confined as a way of keeping me safe from myself. God that is hard to admit. How pathetic. How sad. I was my own worst enemy, and I was so angry and hurt that nobody could help me. Strange things can happen from a place like that.

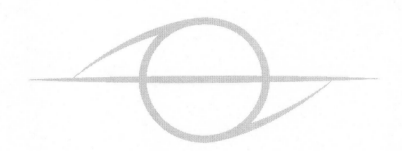

Chapter 7

❦ appointment with destiny ❧

In the quiet afternoon you left and went down into town, and I just watched the empty road behind you. Where the fog lies kissing the mountainside, you want to be sleeping, deep inside, believing that the hungry world won't find you.

—Heart, How Deep It Goes

One day I was on the move. I was bouncing off the walls at the peak of a manic high. Nobody was home and it was a bright and beautiful summer day. I had decided that I was going to visit my father at his business. He owned an auto body repair shop in Seattle, and my older brother worked for him as a painter. I could see them both in one shot, if only I could find my way there.

I was living in Lake Forest Park, which sits a few miles north of the city limits. They were in the Queen Anne area of downtown Seattle. I would guess that this trek is over twenty miles, through a spread out metropolis. There was no straight path through the many miles of highways, city streets, and densely populated neighborhoods that lay before me. So I hoofed it for miles and miles, and I'm not sure how I made it on foot, but I did. The energy that comes through the manic state of mind is tremendous. Absolutely amazing.

When I showed up in the office, my dad was a bit shocked to see me and I'm sure he could tell right off the bat that I was really flying high. He quickly put me to work. *"Go help your brother,"* he snarled. I went out into the shop and my brother assigned me a cleanup job. He gave me an air hose and told me to blow the dust off a car. By the time I finished, there was

45

an unacceptable amount of dust in the air. I had gotten a bit carried away, and was really over doing it. The other workers were upset with the disruption and my brother pulled me away as soon as he realized what was happening. He then put me to work sanding a car. The result was similar in that I was pushing far too hard. I was sanding too deep, and ultimately doing more harm than good. A few of the guys stopped working as they curiously watched from the sidelines.

In frustration, my brother went to my dad, who abruptly told him to take me to the doctor. I don't know who called who or what kind of arrangement was made, but we definitely had a destination. I was more than happy to hang out with my brother and take a ride in his car. I hadn't spent any time with him in a quite a spell.

He took me to a clinic called Mental Health North. I'd never been there before and he came into the building with me. We sat quietly in the small waiting room looking at magazines. I was utterly content to be in my brother's company. After a short wait, a voice came blaring from the adjoining office as a cranky old lady called out my name.

I remember feeling like a dog being called into the house. *"Next!!! Number fifty three!"* You know the feeling? Remember that Bob Seger song, *"Feel like a number"*? Yeah… like that. Her tone indicated neither respect nor compassion. Disregarding my gut instinct, I got up and went into the office as my brother quietly exited the building.

As I entered, I noticed a woman with short gray hair sitting at her desk with a less than friendly expression on her face. I casually walked into her office, and immediately noticed an ornate bookshelf with many interesting books arranged very neatly upon it. Without a second thought, I began checking out the books. I reached up, took a book down and opened it. The woman immediately yelled, *"Those are my books! Don't touch them!"*

Wow... I felt like a child being scolded. She was extremely rude, and it became quite obvious that I was in the wrong company. I approached her desk as she continued her grumbling and said, *"You know what Lady...You have way too many problems of your own to be dealing with mine."* I turned around and walked out. To this day I believe it was an accurate assessment and a wise choice. She was yelling threats as I casually departed. *"I'm going to report you to such and such!"* *"Yeah... whatever,"* I mumbled to myself on the way out.

It was a ridiculous display from someone who was supposed to be a point of support. I'm still amazed by the overbearing negative attitudes of these so-called educated people who work in the mental health arena. Why do they choose this line of work if it so upsetting for them? The entire exchange was extremely immature and one more wasted effort.

So here I am, back on the streets. As I walk out of the building I am instantly enthralled with the beauty of the sunshine and the clear blue sky. This is as good as it gets for the Seattle area. I mean it was gorgeous.

For those of you that don't already know, a manic state of mind can be a pleasant experience. Of course, it depends on the circumstances. Don't get me wrong, it can be hell if you're tied to a gurney and locked in an airtight cell. Pure Hell. But on a beautiful day, with the wind in your hair, and the smell of nearby flowers wafting through a simple mind, it can be heavenly. And that's how it felt in that moment, absolutely beautiful and as free as the soaring clouds. I wandered down the road, as happy as could be, without a care in the world.

Chapter 8

✣ heaven's gate ✣

All day staring at the ceiling, making friends with
shadows on my wall. All night hearing voices telling me
that I should get some sleep because tomorrow might be
good for something. Hold on, feeling like I'm headed for a
breakdown and I don't know why...

—Matchbox 20, Unwell

I just happened to be passing by a magnificent landscaped park-like setting that took up most of the block. It was captivating and I gravitated toward the gated entrance. It took me a while to realize that it was a cemetery.

Washelli is a big well-known cemetery right on Aurora Ave and not too far from Northgate. It was filled with blossoming flowers, decorative plants and beautiful landscaping. The overall impact was absolutely breathtaking. The grass was so vivid and green as the garden appeared to go on forever. It was like entering an etheric dimension of an alternate universe and I was blissfully mesmerized.

I'm walking toward the entrance as I notice a young woman who is walking out. She seems to be in deep thought with her head hanging low. Perhaps like most people that enter a cemetery, she is grieving the loss of a loved one. That's a pretty safe guess. So out of nowhere I come up with this deep philosophical question, something to do with Christ, and present it in passing. I don't recall what it was and it wasn't the question that struck me, it was the answer. Whatever she said in response blew my mind. My very alert and receptive state of mind was stunned and my consciousness was altered through the exchange.

I was deeply spellbound as I began to walk along the gravesites. I had entered near an Asian section of tombstones and I began to read them aloud as I passed. There was little thought involved and I was unaware of any underlying intention. It all seemed to unfold in a natural manner. The recitation of name after name morphed into a sacred chant. Yamaguchi... Nakamura... Takahashi.... The names and the sounds just flowed into a single stream of rhythm that absolutely launched me into another realm. It took me deeper and further down the line until I came to a stone that stopped me dead in my tracks.

I found myself captivated by a solo headstone that was sitting separate from the others and had only one name on it. *Jeffrey*. It was a red granite stone and appeared unique in many ways. The typical birth-death dates and the surname were not included in the engraving. My mind was transfixed.

What could this possibly mean? What is going on here? I found myself considering that perhaps this was God's gentle way of letting me know I had passed over. Was this my tombstone? Was I in Spirit form? That sure would explain a lot of my confusion. I sat there in the empty heaven-like landscaping and contemplated the possibilities of such a discovery. *"What are you supposed to do when you realize you're dead?"*

There was nobody else within sight. Just me, all alone in this heavenly garden scene, now sitting upon what appeared to be my own gravesite. Contemplating the mystery of the moment, I sat in silence searching for the meaning and the message that was here for me. Time was standing still. The line between life and death had vanished. Heaven is a very quiet place.

I'm not sure how long I sat frozen upon the red stone but something moved within and I was suddenly released. I walked up the hill to a section where row after row of little white stones stood before me. It was obvious that the Veterans of War had been laid to rest here. At least this was the location where they were being acknowledged, if not actually laying here resting in peace. Along the winding road, in front of the veteran's grave sites were two military canons.

I climbed up onto one of the cannons and straddled it like a horse. Still… there was not a soul in sight. As I was sitting in the sunshine I became aware of voices that were speaking to me. It feels inaccurate to say that I was actually hearing voices. It wasn't that obvious. It was more of a distant call from the angelic realm that abides far above in perhaps a neighboring galaxy. They definitely had a message and it wasn't one that I wanted to hear. I could sense and feel the voices gnawing at my soul. It felt like a calling, a request from beings that I couldn't put my finger on. They wanted me to do something. This much was clear. It seemed somehow associated with the whole Messiah trip.

The demand was for some sort of major rescue mission. A save the planet and heal the masses kind of trip. I could understand what they wanted and I didn't have an issue with that. I just couldn't see how I could be of much help in making it happen. Now I don't believe I was talking back aloud. It seems to have been more of an internal communication and I was most certain that they were barking up the wrong tree. The conversation continues on and on and I am becoming a bit upset.

It's like, "Hey… lay off man! There is no way I am going to heal humanity. I am a walking path of destruction. I am the destroyer! I can knock it all down… I could probably do that. But picking up the pieces and putting it all back together would take a great healer… and that ain't me." I suppose it was my default cocky attitude that emerged about then. I'm not sure what my options may have been in this situation but I decided to make them a deal. I mean these beings…. these angels… or demons… or extra-terrestrials …. were relentless.

I began to talk back to them. We were communing and it was certainly a two-sided conversation. I was doing my best to say, *"Hey... you've got the wrong guy here,"* but they weren't buying it. The nagging feeling remained as the streaming message continued.

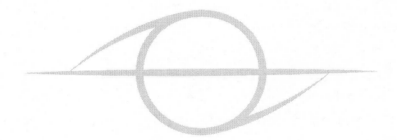

Chapter 9

❧ black elk speaks ❧

I think I have told you, but if I have not, you must have understood, that a man who has a vision is not able to use the power of it until after he has performed the vision on earth for the people to see.

— Black Elk

I had recently watched a documentary about a Native American healer by the name of *Black Elk,* so it was very fresh in my mind. As the conversation continued and the negotiations ensued I came up with a strategy.

I said, *"Okay... I'll tell you what. You want me to take on this preposterous mission of saving the world... right? So here's the deal. I need some help down here, and you're asking for the impossible. So try this one on. You send me the help I need, and I will consider this outrageous assignment."* I pointed to the matching cannon sitting about fifteen feet away. I said, *"You send me Black Elk. I want to see him right here... on this cannon. If you can send Black Elk, I will accept your rescue mission. I will tear it all down and he can put it back together."* So there you go. I'm thinking, *"Now the ball's in their court!"*

It seemed like a safe point of leverage to get these guys off my back. I've heard it a thousand times before but I wasn't remembering this very important piece of advice in that particular moment. *"Be careful what you ask for!"* I figured I had these guys up against the wall with at least a stalemate in the works. How wrong can a guy be?

As I sat on the canon in the stillness that followed, I noticed a very large cedar tree directly in front of me, overshadowing the tombstone that appeared to be my own. The white stones behind me seemed to have a hidden secret they longed to reveal. Out of the emptiness, I heard a distinct set of footsteps approaching from behind, that held a familiar rhythmic pattern. I counted them one by one as they came closer with each thump. I was trying to keep my eyes forward but the suspense was killing me. *"Was Black Elk actually going to show?"*

On the count of eight, I suddenly jerked my head around to see who was coming and there was nobody in sight. *"Damn it! I blew it!"* I quickly concluded. Somehow my impatience had impeded this noble and timely manifestation. I felt a deep disappointment as I cursed myself for turning around.

The next thing I knew my fascination with the cedar tree was becoming a mesmerizing dissolve into a mummified state of paralysis. As I peered into the tree I became entranced to the point of feeling a magnetic stream of energy between the tree and myself that left me incapacitated. I couldn't move a muscle. I drifted into a black out. I say that because I don't know how else to describe it. I actually felt my spirit launch into another world.

I lost consciousness in the scenario of being in the cemetery but was fully conscious in another realm. It's like a foggy dream in my memory and yet the events that unfolded left a permanent impression upon my soul. I was suspended, as if I was tied to a pole in the middle of an open field. The scene was one you might imagine for someone being burned at the stake. But it wasn't fire that was threatening my safety. There was an amazing assortment of animals coming out of the surrounding mist, biting me, and then retreating to form a protective circle around me.

Certain animals have remained in my mind's eye through the years. A ferocious Lion made his attack and took a big bite out of me as he turned to become my protector. This is basically what was happening with every animal that found its hungry mouth within my auric field. They each took a bite and after the first taste of blood were in turn transformed into a personal ally. Lions... bear... wolverine... jaguars... and many other wild animals participated in this bloody ritual. It was extremely bizarre and I was tormented to tears.

The most memorable segment of the attack was when my entire body was engulfed in a mass of bees. It was as if I was at the center of the hive and they were all stinging me simultaneously with venom that burned. This was the most painful part of this ceremonial event.

I have no idea what was happening back in the cemetery but I was screaming in pain where I was. The unrelenting torture was unbearable. God only knows how long this excruciating torment lasted. I can, however, tell you one thing for sure. It was for far too long.

I suddenly came back to consciousness in the cemetery, still looking deeply into the cedar tree. As I was returning to my body and becoming conscious of my surroundings, I noticed I was no longer sitting. I was standing fully erect on the skinny end of the cannon, and there was one other minuscule differentiating detail, *"I was as naked as a jaybird!"*

I looked around and about twenty feet away was a small congregation of police officers. They looked like they were huddled up for a football game but a bit more relaxed. As I was coming back to awareness and viewing the situation, I had this feeling that I was a mighty warrior. I mean, I felt like a full-blooded Indian. It's hard to explain but I was looking at these guys and thinking, *"White Men!"*... as if I wasn't one of them.

I was prepared and ready for a battle and yet I could see that they were holding back. I assumed that they recognized I was obviously not one to offend and that attacking me would not be a wise move. I felt strong and proud, and had no love at all for these *white men*, to put it mildly.

So I jumped down off of the cannon into a fighting stance and looked at them directly. They made no indication of interest in pursuing me as I turned to walk away. I trusted these officers knew better than to mess with such a noble warrior. *"Oops... perhaps a slight miscalculation."*

I didn't hear them approaching, as I suddenly felt the hand that grabbed my long hair from behind and slammed me to the ground. The rest of the gang swiftly jumped on and held me down.

I think that in that frightful instant I actually returned to my body. The shock of the violent attack served to pull me out of my altered state. I was stunned, frightened and crying like a child. I had no capacity for understanding what was happening. It was incomprehensible and completely overwhelming. They helped me into my clothing, cuffed me and put me in the car. I wasn't resisting or putting up a fight. It felt as though they were saving me from something far worse. What that was, I didn't know. I was still swimming in a deep, dark sea of confusion.

Chapter 10

⧉ jailbird blues ⧉

Blackbird singing in the dead of night. Take these broken wings and learn to fly. All your life, you were only waiting for this moment to arise.

—Beatles, Blackbird

I was unsure of the point or the purpose but I was abruptly delivered and escorted into a small building with a single cell. I don't recall any questioning or tests of any sort during that brief stopover. I was held for a short while before being transferred and transported to the King County Jail in downtown Seattle.

So there I was, sitting in the jailhouse waiting to be booked. I suddenly noticed a wiry, bald-headed black man with piercing eyes across the room. He was staring directly as though he could see right through me. It appeared to me that we were in a similar situation. As our eyes met, I got the distinct feeling that this guy had a special message for me. The eye contact generated an undeniable spark of recognition. The glimmer in his gaze zapped me right between the brows. No understanding... just a feeling. I was certain this man held a key to my quest if I could only discover what it was. Like me, he was being admitted and I guessed that he was a transient by the look of his clothing. Perhaps he was making the same assumption, looking at me. I couldn't begin to imagine what was flowing through his feverish mind.

They finally completed the paperwork and booked me into a cell. They put me in the E-sector, so I assumed this was where the crazies went. That was probably a safe guess. The moves in this matrix are fairly predictable. After being escorted into the cage, I was sitting on the floor staring out through the bars at the nothingness of existence. I wasn't terribly upset, nor was I extremely thrilled.

A short while later, guess who came shuffling in? That's right... It was him! I got a little excited, stood up and started toward him as he entered the cell. He looked me right in the eye from about a foot away and said, *"Don't fuck with me man!"* His tone was very serious and I was stunned and hurt, I mean really upset.

I'd held visions of a friendly encounter. I was steeped in the notion that our crossing paths would allow us to help each other in some mysterious way. I was struggling to believe that this guy would go straight to being an asshole, right off the bat.

I turned around and sat back down on the floor. *"Screw him,"* I thought to myself. *"His loss. I don't need a friend like that anyway. Two can play this game. I know how to be an ass too. Big news... right? Another dick head... big deal."*

This guy was black, so I just figured it was a racial thing. I was probably the wrong color to be his friend. I didn't really understand what his problem with me was and at that point I was too hurt to care. I was sure he could see that I wasn't glowing with joy after our initial encounter. It was rather obvious to anyone paying attention.

So... time kept drifting by. How long? Oh, maybe an hour or so. Suddenly, Mr. Nice Guy decided he wanted to play. I assumed he was trying to make up for being a jerk, but it was too late. My feelings were hurt and I wasn't ready for a make-up dance. After a bit of his own sitting and sulking, he got up, came over, and tossed a little white hand towel at me.

I couldn't believe it! I was instantly pissed off. I angrily grabbed the towel and threw it back at him. He threw it again, and this time I stood up and threw it back even harder. The pace picked up as the towel went back and forth, until we were standing within reach of each other. I don't remember who started it but we began bumping shoulders and butting into each other like a couple of rams. Apparently, about then I went unconscious, or through some kind of spirit metamorphosis. I had no sense of where I'd gone this time. There was no open field, snarling animals, or excruciating pain. I had no recollection of visitations to the other side on this peculiar occasion. I only knew that when I came back into consciousness, I was sweating profusely and breathing heavily.

My buddy who I now called Blackbird was sitting on the floor, up against the wall barking out commands in a foreign language. He looked tired, I mean really beat. With each yell, I shuffled across the floor, performing a martial art form that I held no conscious knowledge of. My body was responding as if I'd been in training for years. I was maneuvering across the floor in a very specific pattern and punching as if it were an advanced Kata.

Kata is the word used in Karate' to mean a *form*; a certain pattern of movement with kicks and/or punches that is pre-determined through a particular arrangement. It seems that my body knew the proper form that was intended through each verbal command. It was like he was flipping a switch with every order. My body responded precisely and without hesitation. Somewhere inside of me, I knew, *"This is utterly bizarre!"*

As I was just regaining consciousness and still in motion, a man in orange coveralls passed by the cell. These guys are the inmates that have achieved a level of status that allows them to do janitorial type work in the jail. It's considered a privilege to be allowed out into the common area.

This guy said to Blackbird, *"Teaching him... huh?"* Blackbird responded with a bit of an astonished tone, *"He already knows it."* I remember this so clearly because it was news to me. I had no idea what style of martial art this was or what language he was speaking. To this day, I have no clue.

As a kid I was introduced to boxing and wrestling. I stayed with wrestling through high school and I knew how to fight. My early years were filled with fist fights and being forced to be tough enough to hold my own. I had an older brother who was able to push me around pretty easily, so I was no foreigner to a bout of good old-fashioned fisticuffs.

However, what was coming through me in this bizarre moment was unreal! I mean I was completely astonished by what I witnessed my body doing. My teacher seemed to be just as amazed with the exhibition as I was. I was calling him Blackbird, he was calling me Blackbird, and this outlandish scenario somehow seemed perfectly fitting.

We finished up with the training and sat and talked for a short while. As with the initial anointing and the recent cannon dance experience, I had no reference for the passing of time. I had no way of knowing how long the "training" had gone on for. Neither do I believe my mind was in any shape to carry on a conversation that would make any sense to most folks. Blackbird didn't seem quite as lost as I was but he wasn't any shining example of normalcy either.

After the exchange it was quite obvious to me that this was my Master. He was my new hero and I worshipped the ground he walked on. That was the feeling that came over me as I sat down and massaged his feet. I remember looking into his dark eyes as I ate my baked potato with my bare hands, feeling like a couple of caged animals. He spoke of the hardships he'd faced as a child. His early life was filled with strict discipline and little in the way of comfort. It sounded pretty tough and that's about all I remember through our limited conversation.

In the midst of the mundane activity there was a spiritual war ensuing. A crazed and fanatically religious voice was echoing scripture off the walls of our overflowing jail cell. He was in the cell across the hallway, facing ours and his endless barrage of antagonistic shouting was becoming extremely annoying. The longer it went on, the more deeply disturbing it became, until it seemed that everyone was being drawn into the battle. New recruits continued to arrive and there were now eight or ten men in this cramped cage. It was feeling overcrowded with lots of yelling and agitated bodies in motion.

Now just about in the peak of the chaos they sent a new inmate into our cell. *"God no! This guy is just like the other one!"* He was ranting and raving about how he shouldn't be here. His talk and his energy were extremely disturbing and his message seemed to be that he was somehow better than the rest of us due to his self-proclaimed status as a Christian. He seemed to be in sync with the guy who was barking the deeply convoluted scripture.

I remember asking him what he was in for. He said, *"For carrying a gun in my car without a permit."* So I felt driven to make a point here, *"You mean to tell me that you are a gun carrying Christian? What about turning the other cheek? What about thou shall not kill? And love thy enemy? What the fuck kind of game are you playing here pal?"* and of course the unspoken question was, *"How are you any better than the rest of us?"*

So anyway… I think you get the gist of the general attitude is in this setting. It certainly wasn't what you would consider harmonious. The one guy was yelling some distorted version of biblical scripture from behind his own set of bars and the guy in our cell was right onboard with him.

The rest of us were pacing around, plugging our ears and not digging it at all. Our guy was just kind of stomping around, grunting, groaning and emanating a message that was deeply annoying. These two agitators seemed to be fashioned from the same mold. It appeared as though they were working together on a mission to drive us all nuts, as if we hadn't already crossed that line. The tension was building and the rest of us had launched our own counter attack of verbal assaults. It was getting pretty loud and out of hand.

I don't recall if it was day two or three but at a certain point I found myself with no shirt, a pair of shorts and Blackbird's socks. They were thin black socks and they felt as if they were filled with a magical power. I don't remember putting them on but I was suddenly aware that I was wearing them. I could feel the energy flowing through my feet, up my legs and into my body. They were energized and alive.

As the tension grew, and out of the blue, I reached a point of no return. I walked over to the groaning guy who was sitting against the wall. I very casually with my hands in my pockets reached out and gave this guy a little slap across the face with the top of my foot. It was certainly not a death blow by any stretch, but it was definitely enough to get a message through. With my hands still in my pockets, I turned and walked back to the bars of the cell, facing outward. I could hear this guy growling and rising to make his attack from behind. I could feel the spewing anger through his approach even though my back was turned.

Like something out of a sci-fi, my body whipped around and I caught his jaw with the back side of my leading fist. It spun him a hundred and eighty degrees and I watched my arms go into a rapid launch of strikes that appeared to be perfectly and strategically designed. The speed was quite unnatural. In my peripheral vision it looked as though I had four arms, and I recall being astonished by this. The motion was so fast that it was as if I was seeing double. To my knuckles it felt as though I was delivering a gentle massage. The blows began at the base of the spine and went upward in increments that seemed to leave no space between. This rapid fire motion was stopped mid-stream by the Master.

Blackbird grabbed my wrist in mid stride, looked me right in the eye as he shouted, *"That's enough!"* I instantly came to a halt, frozen by his intervention. In that same instant, the frazzled opponent screamed and puked a pool of blood onto the floor. Blackbird immediately snatched the towel and wiped up the blood as if he'd done it a hundred times before. There was no second thought. The scream set the guards in motion and they quickly came and pulled the bewildered man from the cell.

I watched him sitting in a chair in the hallway telling his story, and could only imagine what was coming next. This uncanny stream of events seemed extremely significant. Silence had fallen like night upon this lonesome cell and I was quite certain that the Master and I were about to clean house.

Blackbird went and crouched in the corner of the cell. I squeezed in behind him, also squatting, with only my toes on the ground. I envisioned the guards opening the gate and the two of us taking out the whole lot of them. I felt confident and certain that this was precisely what was about to unfold. I imagined us taking the keys and setting everybody free. The scene didn't exactly unfold in the way that I had foreseen.

The barred door came flying open, the guards came rushing in... and what the hell? Blackbird sat there frozen. They reached over him and grabbed me so fast that I didn't have time for a second thought. He didn't move a muscle. Faster than I could realize what was happening, I had six burly men that weren't the least bit pleased with me, hauling me out of the cell with a vengeance.

I was being carried out horizontally with one man on each arm, each leg, one around the waist, and the other around my neck. The guy on my neck had me in a stranglehold and was squeezing so tight that I couldn't get a breath. I was trying to speak but only a whisper came out as I muttered, *"You're killing me."*

Suddenly, an incredible strength came from deep inside that flowed up and out into my arm. Do you remember what I said about a manic state being amazing? Well my left arm was moving like a steel robotic machine. It was as slow as a turtle and against all the strength that one assigned man could muster up, it wasn't stopping. It broke his hold enough to grab the wrist of the man's forearm that was around my neck. I slowly pulled it down just enough to take a breath. That was all I was wishing for. I just wanted to breathe. It was a divine moment of relief as they took me around the corner and tossed me into a solitary cell.

I could still hear Blackbird talking to me as I settled into my new nest. He said, *"You know my voice..."* as he continued to speak in a calming fashion. I was definitely comforted knowing that my comrade was safe and sound and that I was not alone.

My visions went dark in my solitary confinement. I recall several strange occurrences but the timing is lost and the order is scattered. I remember taking my clothes off and trying to flush them down the toilet. The resulting clog created a small flood. This alarmed the highly unimpressed guard who quickly came and opened the cell door. When he did, I was standing at the entrance. He eagerly kicked me square in the chest which sent me flying across the room. The very strange part of this scene was that I slid perfectly erect across the floor like a solid piece of iron. I went sliding across the wet floor and banged into the frame of the bunks without falling or bending. It was a very bizarre experience that felt extremely peculiar.

I remember growling like a lion at the top of my lungs and raging like a wild animal. An inmate from the neighboring cell reached around the corner and threw a paper cup of piss right in my face. I could taste it. I remember yelling, *"Thanks for the lemonade!"* wanting with all my might to not let anyone know they were succeeding in hurting me any more than I already was. It was a direct hit and I was soaked.

I was given a woolen blanket and I threw it over my shoulders and wrapped it around my naked shivering body. I was standing there trying to get warm when I felt this little tug at the bottom edge of the blanket. I could feel a tug as if an invisible entity were pulling at the lower corner of my covering. I surrendered and began to move into the tugs that came in sporadic and increasing impulses. A little tug one way... and a little tug the other. I felt my body moving with the guidance until I was doing what felt like a Native dance in this wet and darkened solitary cell. I later wondered, *"Was this the long lost Ghost dance?"* It was a very weird feeling as though I was somehow being guided by invisible ancient spirits.

At another point during the solitary confinement I remember seeing with my eyes, four ghost-like images flying out of the cell. I watched them float under the bars like cartoon figures. Two were dark shadow-like entities and two others were light in color. I had no idea where these phantoms had appeared from or what this could possibly mean. It was all so bizarre and happening too quickly to make any sense of it. I don't recall being let out of the cell; in fact, I don't even remember being released from the jail. I can only guess that I was drugged and taken to a mental hospital, as my memory of the transfer is absolutely blank.

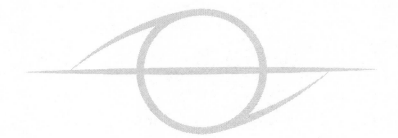

Chapter 11

∾ beyond the veil ∾

To raise new questions, new possibilities, to regard old problems from a new angle, requires creative imagination and marks real advance in science.

—Albert Einstein

I was never able to fully comprehend what took place during this lengthy and chaotic predicament. It stayed with me, in the back of my mind, replaying through the years as I continued to contemplate the possibilities and the meaning of it all. I would eventually find my way to a psychic reader several years later and ask her about this highly unusual occasion. Specifically, *"How did this guy instill these martial art skills into my mind... telepathically?"*

She informed me that this wasn't the case. *"You two were very close in another lifetime,"* she said. *"You have lived two entire lives that were dedicated to the martial arts in this monastery type environment. Your lives revolved around these teachings in a location somewhere near Mongolia. This man simply tapped into the cellular memory that is deeply ingrained in your being. The stored knowledge was drawn forth in his presence... however... you already contained it... before you ever entered this life."*

"Wow!" I thought. *"That's the best explanation I've ever heard!"* Well, the truth is, it's actually the only one I've ever heard, and whether or not the explanation was accurate or relevant would never change what I experienced during that three day stay in the county tank.

So here we go again. I'm being hospitalized once more and immediately re-administered those godforsaken nasty drugs. I'm thinking, *"Just what I need!"* as if my mind isn't clouded enough already. Round and round she goes as the vicious cycle continues.

I did my standard two week stint in the mental ward and soon after I was released I came to hear the hidden side of the graveyard story. The first hint of an alternative view of the cemetery scene emerged when I first saw my brother. He excitedly blurted out, *"You were on KZOK!"* My dad immediately tried to hush him up. It was obvious that he wanted to keep this *behind the scenes* story undercover.

KZOK was a local radio station and apparently there had been a special announcement regarding my trip to the dark side. Evidently, during the time period while I was being chewed on by wild animals, I reportedly performed a Native American ceremonial dance... naked. It made the Seattle Times and was broadcast on the local radio stations as well. *"What?... A dance? I don't remember any dance!"*

My neighborhood buddies got a real kick out of it. The mother of one of my friends even made a little wooden figure of a man standing on a cannon. It seemed to be inspiring in some strange way, at least enough to cause a sense of celebration in the ranks.

From what I heard, the police were summoned and showed up to the cemetery just in time to witness a naked man on a cannon performing some sort of Indian ceremonial dance. *"C'mon... man. I don't know any native ceremonial dance. This is nuts!"* The part of the report that was most baffling was when the police officers said they were unable to stop it.

"What? How could this be?" When I came to, they were all casually standing in a huddle. *"How were they unable to stop it?"* I began to wonder, *"Was there an invisible force field holding them back? Did I physically oppose them?"* I don't think so. There was

no report of resistance and besides, they had me outnumbered by a long shot. I couldn't imagine how they would be prevented from pulling me down. This puzzling question would keep me searching for answers for years to come. The other obvious question to me was, *"Who was doing the dancing?"* It certainly wasn't me. I wasn't even there. Besides, I don't know any Native American ceremonial dances.

My only answer was Black Elk. The voices, the ET's, the Angels... the ones I had communed with had answered my request. In my judgment, a spirit had entered my body and used it to dance on the cannon. I was somewhere else being chewed on by wild animals. Why? God only knows. I missed the fun part and I can only surmise that I had received what I'd asked for.

Black Elk came out of his resting place deep within the cedar tree and stood upon the cannon. He not only stood, but danced in what appears to have been a glorious manner. What I wanted was for him to materialize on the other canon next to me. I was looking for someone to stand by me, quite literally, like in the flesh. What I got, was him appearing on my canon... through me. I guess I hadn't been specific enough in my negotiations, but they certainly had delivered. Be careful what you ask for... huh?

My fear now was that I had just sealed the deal of the century. Was I somehow obligated to this precarious assignment of saving the world? *"Oh Christ, I'm right back where I started!"* Pure madness, along with a mission impossible... and no Black Elk, at least visible, to stand by my side.

The aftermath would take me back to my normal routine of trying to function and recuperate from the so-called drug "therapy." I continued to contemplate these strange scenes that repeatedly played like a sci-fi movie in the back of my mind for years to come. This simplistic idea that it was all due to a chemical imbalance in my brain was hard to swallow. I wasn't buying it. What about the astral realms? Where do spirits live? What does it mean to be possessed? Is the soul actually eternal? How does reincarnation work? These were the burning questions I wanted answers to.

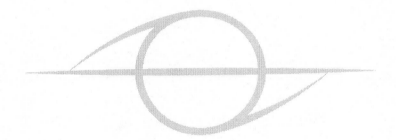

Part 3

Quest for Normal

"Here's to the crazy ones.

The misfits. The rebels.

The troublemakers.

The round pegs in the square holes.

The ones who see things differently.

They're not fond of rules. And they have no respect for the status quo.

You can quote them, disagree with them, glorify or vilify them.

About the only thing you can't do is ignore them. Because they change things.

They push the human race forward. And while some may see them as the crazy ones, we see genius.

Because the people who are crazy enough to think they can change the world, are the ones who do."

— *Rob Siltanen*

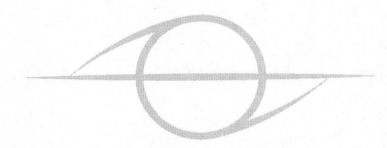

Chapter 12

❧ back to the drawing board ❧

The harder the conflict, the more glorious the triumph.

—Thomas Paine

When all the bells and whistles came to a halt, and believe me there are drugs that can bring anyone to a frozen cold standstill, I remained in a body that needed a place to be. At a personal level I just wanted a normal life. I had witnessed how normal people lived. I could recognize what it looked like. My parents had modeled what I accepted as "normal" throughout my childhood. I can see now that dysfunctional families truly are the norm.

At this point in my early adulthood, the understanding that was forming was still in an embryonic stage. I was reading and extracting bits of knowledge from many sources, but they hadn't gelled. The excessive amounts of incoming data often added to the confusion. Each new door that opened added one more stream of thinking to toss around in the mix.

The Bible was perhaps one of the most confusing and disturbing pieces of literature that I would ever put my hands on. *The Book of Revelations* received a great deal of attention in those days. The end of the world was coming without a doubt and the urgent need to bring about change was underlying an overwhelming wave of social dissension.

I felt as though I was surfing on the leading edge of that wave and crawling under barbed wire on the frontlines of a spiritual battleground. There was no favorable direction to turn toward, no safe place to hide. The best I could do was pretend I was doing okay for as long as possible. Like they say, *"Fake it til you make it."*

I worked in salons when I wasn't chasing demons or being eaten alive by invisible animals. I opened my own shop in '81 which proved to be a valuable solution to my ongoing trips to the loony bin. At least my job was secure. No reasonable employer could have endured the comings and goings, or the insanity that came with each departure and reentry.

My youngest sister, who has since passed, had followed in my footsteps and joined me as a partner in the salon business. She had encountered severe medical challenges of her own. Somehow we had developed the ability to hold down the fort for each other, which allowed for the regularly scheduled treatments we were continually receiving for these ongoing issues.

Cathy Jo was five years younger than me, and the baby of the family. She had been randomly born with underdeveloped kidneys, or so they said. Actually she had received a blood transplant at birth due to an RH factor that was not in sync with our mother's. Apparently, this issue is resolved with a pill nowadays, but back then they just pumped new blood in like changing the oil in a car.

I still believe this was the cause of her underdeveloped kidneys, but either way she was confined to a kidney machine as a means of survival beginning in her early teens. Three days a week, for six hours at a time, she would lay hooked up to a blood sucking machine. It was tough to watch and difficult to appreciate the technology that would ultimately extend her life. Her attitude would serve as an example of courage and steadfast love for the rest of my life. She underwent three kidney transplants through the coming years and her clients would have never known. She lived life as though it was a birthday party. She smiled and laughed more than anybody I have ever known since.

The salon was a fun place to hang out and I loved working with people and *doing hair*. I delighted in the artistic aspect of coloring, cutting and perming. It was an enjoyable way to get lost in something I could put my hands on. I also appreciated my sister's company immensely.

I never felt that she looked down on me for my strangeness. We shared a deep connection and understanding, and it appeared that somehow we had each been dealt a bum hand. *"Oh well... you can only play the cards you're dealt... right?"* She was a shining example of playing her hand to the fullest.

Looking back, I realize that I've always been a people person. I appreciated hanging out with and communicating with folks of every kind. I very much enjoyed the daily social interaction in the beauty business. The challenge and the difficulty came each time I was pulled back into that dark abyss and an underworld of confusion.

It was a constant embarrassment... that feeling of being incapable of consistently functioning as well as so many others were able to. My attempts to appear "normal" masked the deep agony of a misdirected anger and resentment. My immature mind held fast to the notion, *"There must be someone to blame for this!"* I didn't understand how this could be happening and struggled to accept that I should deserve such punishment in life.

The deep seated fear-based emotions continuously boiled like oil within my unconscious mind until it would sloppily spill over into my waking life. The insanity would creep up out of nowhere and drop me like a plucked feather. The standard pattern was fairly predictable. I would go off the deep end and then be either forced or voluntarily admitted into a mental hospital, drugged, and held captive for a couple of weeks.

Back in those days it was all about lithium carbonate. Lithium is a basic element, and if you look at an elemental chemistry chart you will find it there with the others, such as hydrogen and oxygen. This elemental component is considered a salt. It was even sold as table salt in the 1940s until it was discovered to be deadly at certain levels. This lithium is ingested in pill form. It is measured and monitored with the intention of keeping the level in the blood high enough to be effective, without reaching the toxic point. You are required to have your blood levels measured frequently which involves being stuck with needles for taking samples. An insufficient dosage has no beneficial effect while too much can literally kill you.

The first time I was put on lithium I gained forty pounds in thirty days. The salt caused my body to retain fluids beyond the natural volume and simultaneously increased my appetite significantly. Apparently, this was typical, and it was easy to see how a person would feel sluggish by way of the weight gain alone.

The idea of impacting the mental faculties was based on how lithium works in the brain. With a high enough level in the bloodstream it would act as an insulator to the neuro-receptors. The little flashes of lightening that were popping off at random all over this crazy brain, causing psychotic delusions of madness, would be insulated, calmed, and ultimately subside. According to my research, this was the general idea of how lithium was supposed to work.

It doesn't sound so bad on paper but the reality for me was a living hell. Along with the massive weight gain, I fell into a lethargic and foggy state of mind that felt like mental imprisonment. I was routinely dropped back into my world in somewhat of a stupor. I typically felt as though I had somehow been disconnected from life itself. I couldn't think or feel much in this condition. I was generally overcome with a numb sense of self, like being strapped in an emotional straightjacket where happiness was merely a foggy concept.

The whole program of checking blood levels on a regular basis, and having to watch the daily scheduled intake so closely, was a serious pain in the butt. I also had other drugs to monitor and take in addition to the lithium.

The doctors had me over a barrel and could withhold my medications if I didn't comply with their every demand. Once I was addicted and relying on a drug, it was frightening to have them threaten to take it away. I had a deep feeling of powerlessness in my life as this merry-go-round would spin for over twenty years, dumping me in the dirt on at least an annual basis.

When I couldn't handle the lithium blues any longer, I would stop taking the pills and eventually have another *episode*. I was then immediately ushered to the front of the circus line, once again, and forced back on to the prescribed medications. As ludicrous as it seems, this was the only solution offered.

My crazy spells were certainly wild enough to get the attention of the legal authorities, so I couldn't really blame them for wanting to make a zombie out of me. Obviously not for my sake, but just to take one more crazy off the streets. This seemed to be the true motivation behind the drug therapy, rather than genuinely striving to assist an individual in regaining their sanity.

The general perspective of the medical model was that the cause for the mental illness was a chemical imbalance in the brain. This set in motion the faulty conclusion that, therefore, the solution must also be a chemical one. The proposal was that a person could take drugs that would supposedly restore that balance.

Now keep in mind, they didn't actually have the technology to measure these brain chemicals, so this was all pure speculation. The ignorance in this simpleminded explanation, backed by a multi-billion dollar pharmaceutical industry, was ridiculous and insulting.

You could sooner master a tightrope juggling routine than attain balanced brain chemistry, while chasing drugs around in circles, using one to combat the side effects of the other. This is without mention of the ongoing damage being inflicted upon vital organs.

I already knew that repressed emotions and memories of traumatic experiences were an underlying cause for imbalance in the brain chemistry. Trauma can leave an impression on the physiology of the brain, and thoughts and feelings will alter that chemistry as well. The chemical imbalance was not *the cause* but rather *the effect* of software related experiences, impacting the functioning of the brain. It was also obvious that the drugs didn't transform the memories or dysfunctional belief systems lying dormant beneath the pain and confusion.

Sure, you might be able to drug a Vietnam Vet enough to have him sit motionless in the corner, but if you really wanted to help him with his mental health, it would take much more than that. It was plain to see that the drugs only masked the symptoms, and I was positively certain this was not the answer. The traditional medical community stopped short in the examination of cause, effect, and solution. They seemed far more interested in pushing expensive pills than actually solving a problem.

One of the things I came to understand through my trials and tribulations, is that once you've been diagnosed and labeled with a mental health disorder, you are marked for life. Having been stamped as *mentally ill*, it was as though I'd become property of the government.

Every so often I would be overcome with confusion and emotional upset that would make me undeniably mad. The insanity was simply too overpowering to hide and I would end up behaving in such a bizarre manner that I would be escorted, often times by the police, back into the hands of the doctors. This reaction to my urgent need became a default response by everyone in my life. It was a deeply ingrained habit that left no room for actually helping me with my present internal dilemma or underlying issues. I had been tagged, and the overriding system was set, as to how to handle a person with this label. *"Turn him in!"* That was the standard procedure and breaking this cycle had become one of my greatest challenges in life.

According to Einstein, this repeating pattern was precisely the definition of insanity. *"Doing the same thing over and over again and expecting a different result."* As expected, the outcome was always predictable. I was turned over to the authorities, and the drugs were forced upon me once more, even if it meant strapping me to a table and giving me an injection.

I hated being locked up in those little rooms as each recurring visit brought a new series of trauma. Whoever decided that imprisoning all of the crazies together was a good idea? If you had any sense of normalcy coming in, it was likely to be gone by the time you left. Screaming, fighting, and general chaos put Western State at the top of the *worst* list. It was very much like a prison, except the emphasis was on enforcing the drug treatments. It was clear that I had no choice in this environment and that my basic civil rights were no longer valid.

The only way I would ever get out of this nightmarish maze, was if I could heal my mind to the point of no longer being crazed enough to warrant the lock ups along with the forced drug therapy. Each time I was captured and *treated*, it was a major step backward that left me feeling like I was starting all over again. I would find my way to deeper understanding, feel my mind making incredible progress in the way of healing, and then suddenly it would all be stripped away.

Even though the fork in the road was clear, it was challenging to lead myself through the labyrinth that lay before me. When my madness spiraled out of control, my freedom to choose for myself was lost. My life path and the mandatory consumption of psychotropic drugs were dictated by the governmental forces that be. The cycle was vicious. Whatever I believed to be true became worthless in this grim situation.

Before the diagnosis I had been exposed to a variety of spiritual teachings and genuinely believed that I could be healed. The medical community didn't share this perspective. I remember hearing with my own ears, a doctor telling my parents, *"Your son will never have a chance of living a normal life without drugs."* Unfortunately, they believed her. It was difficult to blame them for their stance toward enforcing the medical treatments and even more difficult to educate them. My heartfelt quest for effective solutions was continuously interpreted as a lack of desire in receiving help. It all became "my own fault" because I wasn't complying or buying this highly ineffective drug therapy as *the cure.*

Beyond my reasoning, my motives were suspect. It appeared to the onlookers that I was simply exhibiting rebellious behavior that was merely a part of the illness. You can imagine the frustration this dynamic would stir, as certainly being disturbing enough to alter one's brain chemistry. *"Ya think?"*

It was a real catch-22 and only I knew that I would one day break free of this torturous mouse trap, and find a path to recovery. I was never given any psychotherapy through the conventional medical world. I remember asking one of my doctors, a full-fledged psychiatrist, why I wasn't being given any therapy. He said, *"I don't do psychotherapy."* The funny thing was, the monthly bill said *Psychotherapy* on the column next to the fee.

Within the first year of my governmental entanglement, my charges of schizophrenia were dropped to manic depression. The manic depressive label would later be renamed bipolar disorder, but the sentence remained the same. I continued doing time behind locked doors and being forced to take psychotropic pharmaceuticals that I wouldn't wish on anybody. Nevertheless, the state and federal laws dictated the treatment I was required to receive, regardless of how ineffective, destructive, or damaging it was.

The recipe was solely drug based, with a bit of periodic confinement sprinkled across the top. My struggle to finding a healthy and effective path to healing became a war with an entire governmental system that was apparently socially acceptable. The medical system was backed by the legal system, and even my family believed that the medical model was the only way to receive help. Once I was considered *off my rocker*, my rights were no longer valid, and this created a challenging dynamic as I rebelled against the entire paradigm.

I eventually came to realize that a great deal of the contention I was facing stemmed from an atypical belief system. What I mean, is that many of the accusations for being mentally *off* were actually ignorant prejudices by the medical professionals who were assessing me. My thoughts, beliefs, and philosophies on life and the universe, were not considered acceptable. To speak of beings in other realms or dimensions, was an automatic check in the "out of his mind" box.

I was undoubtedly suffering with mental health issues. However, many of my spiritual and metaphysical perspectives that were considered *out there*, held no correlation to an ill mind.

My beliefs and understandings just didn't fit into the mold they were trying to squeeze me into.

The majority of those condemned views have become commonplace in this current age. Our scientific community now confirms a multi-dimensional model of reality. Quantum physics has publicly opened doors to greater understanding, as well as shattered many *set in stone* theories about the nature of reality. What appeared to be *bizarre*, as well as topics that were commonly shunned back in those days, are now openly discussed on mainstream television.

Even in the early years, it was obvious to me that much of what I was being judged for was purely due to an overriding view of deep ignorance as to how this conscious universe works. My mission for restoring a healthy state of mind was constantly being undermined by the ongoing bureaucratic pressure to conform to a model of reality that I could easily see through.

I lived what appeared to be a fairly normal lifestyle, if you didn't look too closely. I married in '82 and we had two children over the next few years. My children gave me a new sense of joy and hope that carried me through the many miles of deep pain and sorrow. They also became the motivating factor that would drive me to change my course in life. Unfortunately, that change would mean living apart from my precious young family.

I knew I couldn't stay on the path I was on and ever hold my head up in front of them. The shame and guilt was far too painful to carry forward. I knew without a doubt that they deserved more than I could deliver.

I remember my children coming to me one day as I was sitting in the living room. My daughter was about five years old and as bright minded as a child can possibly be. My son was three and I am sure he was drawn into his sister's lead for the announcement as he enthusiastically stood by her side. My daughter approached me and said, *"Daddy... Daddy! We were angels before we were born and we came here to help you!"* My son, standing by her side, just nodded his little head with a big smile and said, *"Yeah!"*

Besides being the cutest thing I could imagine, it was very meaningful from my perspective. As the years slowly passed, I would come to realize the truth in those innocent words. My children were like little cupids, that brought a new level of love and joy to an otherwise overburdened heart. They have remained to this day, an angelic presence in my life.

It was fairly obvious from the get-go that the medical approach to my struggles would never bear fruit. It didn't seem to be about helping me. The general tone of treatment was seemingly directed toward protecting the rest of the world *from* me. The confinement and the drugs were designed to keep me down. Understandably so, this approach would never bring positive change to my troubled mind. The drugs could only mask the symptoms on a temporary basis. No drugs... no mask. The underlying truth of my darkest nightmares must be fully explored if any healing was to be expected. Somewhere at the foundation of my frantic and frazzled mind, I knew this to be true.

My relentless quest for understanding, and ultimately a solution, would prove to be worth the fight. The pressure to conform to the medical approach has been constant and horrendous. Although social values and understanding are always in a transitional state, the evolution of mental health care in this country has been slow in its developing. Pain and suffering have a powerful way of giving time a great deal of consideration.

In my early years it became apparent that doctors were seen as closer to God than the rest of us. You shouldn't dare question a doctor's diagnosis or subsequently prescribed avenue for treatment. You just don't go there. This appeared to be the general consensus that surrounded me. I, however, didn't have this program in place. It was consistently rejected by an overriding agenda of a deeper nature. The entire medical model of treatment seemed lacking from where I sat. As an experimental project, I was well aware of the short comings of the general perspectives of the A.M.A.

I remember sitting with my wife in the gynecologist's office during her first pregnancy, as he prescribed her a drug for morning sickness. When I asked the doctor for information about this particular drug, I quickly realized that he knew very little about it. He unwittingly revealed that it was a drug that the sales person presented as the answer of choice for this basic symptom. *"Wow... so that's how it works. The drug dealers are calling the shots and the doctor has no clue,"* I thought to myself. My trust level was low and I openly opposed his recommendation. My wife honored my request as she understood my concern for our unborn child.

I caught all kinds of hell from her family for daring to question the doctor. My wife's mother was actually working as a receptionist in the clinic, and was appalled that I had not complied with the doctor's advice. Her grandmother gave me a good chewing out as well.

The saving grace would come a year and a half later, when I came across an article in the newspaper that revealed an interesting story. Apparently, that same drug had been taken off the market due to babies being born with deformed stomachs! Suddenly I was a hero. Do you think I shared this documented evidence with the family? Damn right I did, several times with a big smile. I must admit it was a beautiful ending to an otherwise distasteful incident.

The western medical model seemed to be rooted in short-sighted perspectives that were designed to mask or repress the symptoms. It seemed the concern for side effects was typically minimized and quite often ignored in the overview of any given treatment plan. Even the uneducated mind could easily detect the obstacles to this faulty program.

Preventive medicine and eastern perspectives have since taken root in an otherwise half-assed approach to restoring health. Drugs tend to do a poor job when it comes to unraveling a deeply twisted mind. Holistic medicine is finally being recognized as valid, and making its way into mainstream America. Thank God.

The bulk of my experience with medical treatment was back in the day when spiritual teachings were held completely separate from scientific understandings. It appears to me that this bridge is currently being crossed with vigor. *The Tao of Physics* and *What the Bleep do we Know* are both great examples of the emerging evolution of consciousness in the world today.

The massive movement in education that is available online through independent documentaries is also incredibly inspiring. YouTube is a Godsend if you know what to look for. Science, and particularly quantum physics, is finally aligning with the truth in basic spiritual principles that were considered primitive not so many years ago.

My own family was a powerful force that opposed my efforts to find my way off the dead-end street of traditional medicine. They had no knowledge that could withstand the suggestions coming through the legally supported assignments of the doctors and hospitals.

My defiant attitude and opposition to the prescribed treatment was considered rebellious, and constantly judged as a lack of willingness to receive help. This couldn't have been further from the truth, as I was striving with all my might to find a path to sanity and a healthy mental-emotional state of existence. My need for moral support was constantly undermined by this overwhelming body of ignorance that ruled my world.

Fortunately, I was able to understand that my mind was deeper than what I was consciously aware of. Freud had been successful in introducing the idea of a *subconscious mind* to the masses. My personal search had acquainted me with many alternative approaches to working with these underlying realms of mind.

I was deeply intrigued by my hypnotherapy studies, and convinced that the unconscious aspect of mind was not only accessible, but reprogrammable like a computer. Just because a deep seated thought pattern was in place, and wreaking havoc in a person's everyday life, didn't mean it must remain intact. The answers were available. The solutions were apparent. They just weren't to be found in the standard, governmentally enforced path of treatment; and believe me, the treatments were forced.

The laws that pertained to my circumstances required that I comply with the prescribed methods of treatment, regardless of my oppositional views. I felt like a rat in a maze that held stale cheese as the reward for remaining in the game. The exit ramp would not easily or willingly present itself. My burning desire for sustainable inner peace would lead me through years of alternative pursuits. I took every class I could find that would bring the hope of tearing one more brick from those institutional walls that held me tight.

Chapter 13

∽ into the fire ∾

True wisdom comes to each of us when we realize how little we understand about life, ourselves, and the world around us.

—*Socrates*

In the early eighties, a high school buddy told me about an entry-level hypnosis class that he was taking. The idea of being able to reprogram the subconscious mind was compelling and I soon joined him. The teacher, Charles Tebbetts, was in his late seventies, and his speech was obviously slurred. His claim to fame was that he'd healed himself from the after effects of a stroke through self-hypnosis. He spoke candidly of his hardships and courageously shared the indomitable spirit that would bring him back to his rightful place in the world. His efforts and techniques prevailed and he was once again functional in his professional life. I liked Charles, and he provided me with a solid foundation for the understanding that would lead me forward on my own search for functionality. He had written a book titled *Self-Hypnosis and Other Mind Expanding Techniques* that was popular among the local seekers.

One of the most valuable lessons to remain in the forefront of my understanding, through all these years, relates to the basic functioning of the subconscious mind. Charles explained how this aspect of the mind worked with images or pictures; however it did not allow for negations. In other words, the subconscious is influenced by the images we hold in our mind. To negate that image is pointless. If a person is focused on something they don't want, they are actually creating the image that will draw them closer to it.

To quit smoking, it's counterproductive to repeat to one's self... *"I will not smoke"*... or *"I will stop smoking."* The subconscious mind only sees the image of smoking. It does not acknowledge the negation. Each time this statement is repeated, the image of smoking is flashing in the mind's eye, only strengthening this behavior pattern. This rule applies to every purposeful suggestion. *"I don't want to be poor"* instills an image of poverty, only allowing it to be more deeply ingrained in the subconscious mind.

The great lesson that made it so simple and clear was when he challenged us to NOT think of pink elephants. *"Go ahead... try it! Just say No pink elephant!"* and of course the only image in the mind's eye is a PINK ELEPHANT.

I came to a clear understanding of how positive imagery and affirmations are an effective way to bring deliberate change to one's mind, and ultimately to one's life. I began to focus on having a *healthy mind* rather than NOT being *mentally ill*. As small as this may seem, it was the foundation I set my ladder upon to climb out of the dismal cage I was floundering in.

I made tapes for myself that I listened to regularly. Charles had helped me in a deep way and when he spoke so highly of his teacher, I was immediately intrigued. His mentor had quite a reputation in the field and was stationed just outside of L.A.

His name was Gil Boyne, and when I finished the fifty hour beginning course with Charles, I signed on for Gil's intensive course that was presented as the next level. It too, was a fifty hour program, but it was tightly squeezed into a single week. I had the good fortune of being able to alter my work schedule to accommodate the training, and my semi-tolerant wife didn't put up too much resistance, so I went for it.

The course was intense all right, and so was Gil. He was well known for his instant induction technique. He would put his hand behind the client or student's head, give a good jerk and shout, "*Sleep!*" Apparently, through this point of imbalance, the subconscious mind is opened enough for the suggestion to slip in. He was highly skilled and very proficient with his rapid induction. Although I was hesitant to follow in his footsteps, it was hard to argue the point, given his reputation and success. He also held a certain sense of confidence that was more easily sidestepped than confronted.

During his introductory opening to the class, there was an announcement that one of the students was willing to work for donations as a way of paying his course fee. He did bodywork, and more specifically had trained with a man named Trager. It was a very unique approach, and I have since come to realize this Trager guy is a pretty heavy dude. His work is highly regarded and well known. I signed up for a treatment and was pleasantly surprised.

This young student was good! He seemed to use more of a wiggling method than any particular style of massage. No deep tissue work was involved. He would just kind of wiggle the joints in my toes, my knees, and my arms. He didn't appear to be doing much at all, but my reaction was profound.

I had a strong emotional response in a couple of instances that were linked to memories related to physical issues in my body. Certain events came flooding into my mind's eye as I felt the emotions that had occurred through the injury. Through my willingness to consciously feel the hurt, my tears and emotions were discharged along with the dysfunctional core beliefs. As this clearing took place, the tension in the injured area faded along with it. It was as though an act of forgiveness was taking place at a causal level in the body/mind, and the release created an extraordinary healing experience.

One of my concerns was a knee injury I'd received when I was about twelve. I was going up a rope tow and my ski had turned outward into the deep and heavy snow. It slowly twisted my leg around as I was pulled up the hill against the pressure of the ski in the sludge. I had cable bindings on, which are now considered ancient relics, and they did not release. I tore the cartilage in my knee, which was a painful and frightening event as a youngster. I was put in a full-length leg cast for several weeks, and it never quite functioned properly again. I just chalked it up to being a permanent injury.

As he wiggled the knee, the emotion came up in connection to the injury, and I realized that I was holding or storing the emotional trauma of the event in my body/mind, along with the physical restrictions of the injury. I was lying on the table crying as he wiggle, wiggle, wiggled the joints in my body. It wasn't a cry associated with physical pain, but rather tears that carried the stored emotion of hurt feelings to the surface.

The second injury was to my shoulder. It was during a wrestling practice that my buddy, who was a couple of weight classes heavier, had twisted my arm beyond its range of motion. It was done with enough force that it had damaged something in my shoulder joint. I was never officially checked by a doctor, so I didn't know exactly what had been torn or disjointed. Once again, I assumed that it was permanent.

The wiggling of the shoulder tissue sparked the memory as I relived the wrestling event in my mind's eye. I could feel the anger and resentment that accompanied the incident of the injury. I was very hurt that my friend would be so careless with his good buddy, and I was still holding this anger toward him for hurting me. *"We were literally on the same team for crying out loud!"* My deep unwillingness to let him off the hook was actually preventing my own healing from arising.

It was through letting go of the resentment that I was able to allow the injury to heal. The attached emotion was the energetic glue that was holding the trauma intact. It was all balled together. What I learned at an experiential level was how the emotional body can hold an injury in place. The Trager work facilitated my forgiving and the release of emotion, which in turn allowed the tissues to heal. Both of these injuries found relief, and ultimately healed to a point of full recovery.

It felt like I had experienced a strategically designed miracle. The experiential learning was deep and at a level of feeling rather than conceptual. I felt the process in action and it made perfect sense as I experienced the mental-emotional shift, the physical transformation, and the pain-free results. What I had recently learned *about*... I had now experienced firsthand.

It was becoming quite obvious that the road to healing the body and the mind was a single path. They were not separate after all. They were interwoven in an intimate fashion, and drugs were by no means the route to resolution on this major highway of healing.

Gil's program was awe-inspiring as we experientially learned the impact of a powerful induction, and how profound the results of this work could be in such a short time. It was eye-opening to witness rapid transformations through this direct work with the subconscious mind. Gil was a powerhouse.

Toward the final hours of the course there were rumors of a fire walk spreading through the crowd. It was scheduled for the upcoming weekend and some of the students were already signed up to go. It sounded like this might very well be another awesome experience emerging. I was fascinated by the idea and so high from the intensity of the hypnotherapy class that I didn't give it much thought. I quickly signed up.

It was taking place near San Diego and a classmate who lived in the general vicinity offered me a ride. We drove down and found ourselves in a remote and rural location. It was noticeably hot as a Washingtonian, but I could still see a beautiful snowcapped mountain range in the distance, which comforted me. It was truly a spectacular setting.

There were about twenty people in the class. We gathered to watch a film showing a tribal community of indigenous people walking on fire, as the teacher coached us on the proceedings. It was amazing to see their garments dragging in the glowing coals and not catching fire.

We were guided through an exercise that allowed each participant to get in touch with his or her fears, including the fear of burning, pain, death, and any others that might arise. We were instructed to write them all down, and later held a ceremony in which we threw the papers, along with the fears, into the fire. Those flames would turn the scripted fears into the red hot bed of coals we were soon to be walking over. We spent a few hours in deep contemplation of the overall ritual, in preparation for the fire walk.

As we hovered in line to walk on the coals, the teacher stood at the leading edge with words of encouragement for each person as they came forward. An older gentleman, in line just ahead of me, freaked out halfway across and fell down into the coals. It was frightening as he was frantically carried off in a big hurry. My guess was that he was being delivered to a nearby hospital, although we never did hear exactly what happened with him.

My turn had come and as I stepped up to the fire, I remember feeling let down with the teacher's role in launching me. It seemed to be lacking the inspiration I had hoped for. Even so, I made the heated trek. I walked swiftly across the bed of coals and was discouraged to feel a small point of pain in the arch of one foot. It felt about the size of a small thumbtack and I was disappointed that I had not succeeded in the way I'd expected to.

My understanding was, in the proper frame of mind, I shouldn't feel any pain whatsoever. I was slightly dissatisfied with my experience and quickly stepped back in line to request another turn. This time I wouldn't expect or depend upon a supportive launch. I gathered up my own sense of solidarity and confidently walked across the bed of hot coals without a bit of pain. I was content this time around and finally felt that I had fully succeeded. Unfortunately, not everyone felt so satisfied. Some of the participants were in pain and complaining of burnt feet. The situation inadvertently presented a splendid opportunity for the hypnotherapy students to do some healing work, which we happily did. It proved to be a very effective approach for relieving the pain. Once again, the level of misery was directly correlated to the emotional attachment to resisting the pain. There was an opportunity for choice available here, at a deep level. The more one resisted feeling the hurt, the more intense it became. As each individual was guided toward allowing the acceptance of going into, rather than away from these feelings of soreness, they readily subsided. *"Talk about counter-intuitive!"*

I mentioned the hot spot on my foot, in relation to the teacher, because later in the journey I had a chance encounter with a reflexologist. I told her about the fire walk, and when she examined my foot, she determined the position of the burned spot indicated a weak coach or guide. This information aligned precisely with my experience, which for me, validated her modality as well. Overall, the adventure was very productive and quite enjoyable. My greatest learning was coming by way of experience, and my intellect had some serious catching up to do. This appeared to be the prevailing theme of my entire life.

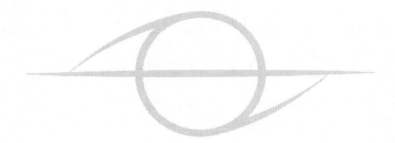

Chapter 14

ꙮ trials and tribulations ꙮ

The wild and windy night that the rain washed away, has left a pool of tears crying for the day. Why leave me standing here, let me know the way. Many times I've been alone and many times I've cried. Anyway you'll never know the many ways I've tried, and still they lead me back to the long and winding road.

—Beatles, The Long and Winding Road

When I returned home, I was flying high. My wife was not in any frame of mind to accommodate my exuberance. She seemed extremely angry and resentful for my being gone. The fact that I was so excited about my adventure didn't go over well with her. Her harsh attitude hit me like a two-by-four upside the head, and I wasn't prepared for the nosedive. It was a dramatic change, to go from a group of people so locked into positive thinking that they could walk on coals, to a negative attitude that could turn those burning coals into ice cubes. There seemed to be no point in discussing it and I was suddenly sinking into a pool of depression.

I sat up that night and drank the good portion of a bottle of whisky, quite determined to drown my sorrows. The next day I woke up angry and fed up with all of it, the salon, the house, my marriage, and the entire scenario. I needed to make a big change, and it needed to happen today!

I called the travel agent that day and booked a trip to Hawaii. It took most of our savings to buy the airline tickets, which were top dollar because of the last minute purchase. My wife, our year and a half old daughter, and I were soon bound for the friendly skies. I had pretty much drained the bank account and it didn't seem to matter. I desperately wanted out of this agonizing situation. My anger would soon turn to rage as my mind remained entangled in a sea of madness.

We packed our bags and flew directly to Hawaii, with no reservations for a hotel, and no idea where we were destined beyond Oahu. Upon arrival we hailed a cab, asking the driver to take us to an inexpensive hotel in Waikiki. He did just that, and we soon found ourselves in a semi-sleazy hotel room just after dark. It was definitely not a setting to get excited about, but we didn't have many options at that point.

I'd been noticeably agitated and angry on the flight over. I remember yelling at the woman sitting next to me for sticking her nose in my business. I can't even remember what she'd done to flip my switch, but I am sure it was minor. I was drifting into my other world... falling into the darkness. My insanity was returning with a vengeance, and I was bouncing off the walls. I had an overwhelming sense of gloom and doom with visions of a bloody battle ahead.

I became extremely manic as we settled into the hotel room, telling my wife that a big war was coming, and that we needed to be prepared to fight. I was trying to show her how to punch and kick, getting her pumped up for the battle. My mind had grabbed onto a dark vision of violence and revolution coming our way. It was crazy stuff and she was frightened, well aware that I was off my rocker. Fortunately, my daughter was too young to know what was brewing as she slept through most of the madness. My highly manic state was continuing to escalate as the darkness rolled on. I don't recall if we slept that night, but my guess would be little if any.

The next morning we went to breakfast in a nearby restaurant. Just as we were finishing our meal, I got up and went to the restroom. I returned to the table to discover my wife and daughter were gone. I instantly panicked and scurried about the room, asking the waitresses and other workers if they had seen them. Nobody had a clue, and I frantically ran out into the street, desperately searching for my family. I was so disoriented that I had no idea where I was. My mind was too far gone to retain a clear sense of direction. I ran through the city until I was completely lost. I inspected the many faces along the never-ending sidewalks until I could no longer manage my dismal frame of mind. In a crazed state I found myself wandering the beach.

I went for a swim and considered just floating out to sea. I swam out to a floating dock and contemplated heading offshore to the next island. My mind was swimming in a dark zone of unbridled fantasy. I drifted back to shore and meandered across the sandy beach. I sat on a nearby bench that was shared by a young man who also appeared to be in his own world. I told this stranger that I was lost and he eagerly offered to help me find my way back to the hotel. As we began to stroll through the nearby park, we passed a group of guys that seemed very antagonistic toward us. I had no idea why, and as we continued, my vision dimmed until I went completely blind. I closed my eyes, as I could no longer see with them open.

My newfound friend seemed just as nonchalant as myself with this peculiar event. I held onto his arm like a blind man as he guided me through the backstreets of town. We entered a few shops, asking for directions as we circled around the edge of the city. It was casual and yet blatantly bizarre. My guide eventually became weary and made a comment about needing to get on with his day. As we prepared to part paths, my vision returned, and I found myself standing directly in front of the hotel. We were both elated with the strange way the mystery was resolved, and I thanked him as we waved goodbye.

I went straight to the front desk and asked if my wife had been in. They told me she had returned earlier in the day and checked out a short while ago. She'd left a suitcase for me, but I had no wallet or money. She also left a note saying my return airline ticket would be waiting at the airport. I anxiously grabbed my luggage and headed back out into the streets. I carried the suitcase with me as I began to walk in the general direction of the airport. I hiked for miles without knowing how far I actually needed to go. I was walking past a gas station when a man stepped from behind a vehicle and yelled, *"Where are you going?"* I shouted back, *"The airport!"* He casually approached me and said, *"You can't walk from here... it's too far. Let me give you a ride."*

By the grace of God, another kind and caring soul had been sent my way. I took him up on his offer and he graciously followed through immediately. I was appreciative and grateful for the lift. It was very hot and my last drink of water had come from a rain puddle in the street. I was worn out and yet still highly energized. I was very moved by the kindness of this man as he delivered me to the airport. He was a compassionate and generous soul who was doing his good deed for the day.

Once I arrived, I went straight to the front desk of the airline that we'd flown in on and told the story of my wife leaving a ticket for me. They lazily looked around and muttered, *"We don't know anything about this arrangement."* I was very upset with this disturbing response and slipped into a fit of anger, which only made matters worse. When I realized I'd pushed these employees beyond their limit, I promptly walked away.

I continued to wander around the airport aimlessly and frantically until nightfall, searching for my next move. I don't remember sleeping, as there was nowhere to lie down. I didn't have any money which made it difficult to eat. There were drinking fountains, so at least I had access to water. My state of mind was growing more delusional by the minute. It's difficult to remember what took place, or in what order, but I do recall coming very close to entanglements with some of the locals who seemed troubled by my presence. My state of mind was disturbing to most everyone who was paying attention, including me.

At one point, I had the feeling I was being watched, and perhaps followed. I approached a young man who was standing with his back to the wall, watching me walk by, and I confronted him, yelling at close range, *"If you have something to say... just say it!"* He was as stunned as you might imagine and certainly not happy with my outburst. The next thing I knew, I was in a restroom, when this other local guy came in all amped up, looking like he was ready to fight. I assumed he had some connection to the other guy I'd just offended. There was a noticeable similarity between them.

A younger boy who was tagging along, quietly mumbled, *"No way... don't do it,"* and I could sense the older man's second thought. Even though I was aware of the extreme tension in the air, I remained centered and calm as we stood side-by-side facing the urinals. The guy never did make his move, and I figured his young companion had convinced him that it was a questionable plan. I was grateful for his youthful input, and avoided further encounters with the locals. Even so, my wake was getting wider, louder, and more disruptive.

I walked back out into the airport, still utterly lost and confused. Apparently, my presence was causing enough of a stir to get the attention of the security guards. Two of them approached me and asked what I was doing. I told them I was trying to get a flight back to Seattle and how the airline had lost my ticket. They escorted me back to the customer service counter, where the attendant was still unable to locate a ticket with my name on it. The longer I stayed in the airport, the more insane my thoughts became.

I haphazardly found my way to the second level of the terminal and was peering out over the airstrip. I had a very odd feeling come over me, as my mind was picking up strange messages from above. I had a clear and overwhelming sensation of an alien spacecraft overhead. It wasn't visible or even necessarily within the three dimensional reality that we perceive with our five senses, but I could feel its presence. It was trying to land but couldn't break through a certain energy field that was keeping it at a distance. The feeling was that these alien beings were good and could be of help, but they needed some serious assistance in being able to penetrate this dimension. I held visions of an extra-terrestrial spaceship hovering far above the land.

It was getting late and night was falling fast. The airport was open-aired with no windows, and I found myself standing near an opening that was two stories above the asphalt landing at ground level. I suddenly jumped out of the building from the second story, and landed on my feet like Spiderman on the asphalt below. It was extremely surreal and I was surprised to not be hurt. I anxiously ran out onto the tarmac and began to spin around in circles with my arms fully extended. I knew that I could create the frequency and the gravitational pull required to allow the ship to enter this morphic field. I was inspired and determined beyond my own understanding. I was spinning and spinning, and all of a sudden this jeep came flying up with two guys in it as a voice yelled out, *"Revert!"* I was stunned and shocked by the command and instantly stopped cold. Surprisingly, I noticed

I wasn't dizzy. The two guys seemed genuinely concerned and shouted, *"We've got to get you out of here... this is a military zone!"* I automatically jumped in the rig, and they drove me to a gate where a posted guard let me out. The guard quietly nodded to the attendants in the jeep as I strolled past the barriers of the exit.

It was getting darker as I wandered down the backstreets, out into the chill of the night. I crossed over to the other side of the street as I passed a small group of street people enjoying a fire ritual of some sort. It also could have been a drunken party from what I was able to see. I wasn't really sure what was going on, but I knew instinctively that it was safer to keep my distance. I wasn't on my own turf any more and stayed far away from the scattered groups of people that I stumbled upon. As I wandered through the dark alleys, circling back into town, I came across a stranger that seemed as rattled as I was. It appeared as though he'd been through a similar kind of day. He was headed in my direction and walking the same way, so we talked a bit as we trudged along the rugged road. It seemed that he had a score to settle with somebody. He was ready for battle and I went with him as he returned to the airport. I had nowhere else to go.

We split up once we entered the terminal and I noticed the guards watching me from a distance this time. I was beginning to get cold as I wandered through the open airport alone. I came across a few folks who were sleeping in bags on the floor, and asked one of the guys if I could wear his coat since he wasn't using it. He was agreeable and graciously handed it over as he allowed me to borrow it for a spell.

He and his friends were waiting for a flight to Sydney Australia. It looked like a letterman's jacket with all kinds of interesting patches on it. The one that caught my eye, had a pyramid with an eye at the top, like the image on the dollar bill. It was particularly outstanding to me, and wearing the coat felt like an honor and a privilege. I was also grateful for the warmth that accompanied me for that short while. As I continued to meander aimlessly, I forgot that I had his coat on. A couple of hours later, he came frantically running up to grab it, just in time to catch his departing flight. I continued milling around the airport and didn't bother to sleep that night, knowing full well that the next day it would start all over again.

I returned to the ticket counter first thing in the morning to discover that they had actually found my ticket. *"YES!!"* They had me booked on a flight to Seattle. I was so relieved! Finally I would be allowed to go home. I held that ticket like it was gold. When the plane arrived and we were allowed to enter, I was one of the first customers onboard. Shortly after I had been seated, a stewardess came over and asked me for my ticket. My immediate response was, *"No way!... I'm not letting this out of my hand!!"* as I clinched it tightly in my sweaty palm. *"Do you have any idea what I've been through... getting this ticket?"* I scowled. I was angry, upset, and in no mood to be hassled.

Apparently, the exchange was disturbing for the stewardess as well. The next thing I knew, a man in uniform, obviously in the position to have to deal with this situation, approached me. He told me I wouldn't be allowed to stay on this flight. He was very proficient and skilled as he talked me into coming with him.

He and a security guard professionally escorted me off the plane. They took me to an office where he suggested that I get some rest and perhaps something to eat. He said, *"Maybe you will be able to calm down enough to be ready to fly tomorrow."*

I could feel his genuine concern and became exceptionally cooperative as I quickly developed a deep sense of trust in this man. I told him that I didn't have any money. He explained that the airline was willing to give me a room for the night if I would agree to follow the recommended plan. I readily agreed, and they hailed a cab that transferred me to a hotel several blocks away. I checked in and was almost ready to settle down when the shit hit the fan. I still remember the room number on the key that I would, unfortunately, never have the opportunity to use. *"911... How appropriate,"* I mumbled to myself.

It was mid-day, and I wandered directly to the pool outside of the main entrance. It was almost empty except for one young lady who was lounging in the sun. Our talk began as a casual conversation about the universe and such, but quickly went south as I delved into some deeply philosophical notions about life and death. She actually seemed okay with my unusual ideas, until I presented the perfectly wrong question. I asked her, *"How would you feel about dying?"* She instantly flipped out! I mean she shot out of her lounge chair like a rocket, extremely upset and fuming with anger. I was stunned by the lunacy that had instantly transpired, but had no idea where the hell it was going. I was unfortunately about to find out.

As I began to walk back into the hotel lobby, I was suddenly confronted by her husband who was brazenly accusing me of threatening her life. With a red face and veins popping out of his neck, he screamed, *"You threatened to kill my wife!"* He was raging mad and ready to fight. I was dumfounded. I tried to tell him otherwise, but it was to no avail. He wouldn't listen to a word. The hotel manager was called to the scene, and desperately begged the man to calm down, as he did his best to intervene in the loud, aggressive conflict that was emerging.

I was trying to explain the misunderstanding but the angry husband was in no mood to listen. To top it off, this guy was a military man and his entire platoon was staying in the hotel. Pretty soon a whole flock of angry young men were huffing, puffing, and stomping about. There seemed to be no confusion around their clear intent to do bodily harm.

When the number of men involved became too large for the manager to handle, the police were called in. If it weren't for the prompt arrival of the local police, I think I would have been in deep trouble. Two police officers sat me down in a chair in the lobby, and stood guard over me as the men circled past, in what seemed to be a never-ending stream. It was a real circus. At one point I was actually laughing out loud because I couldn't believe the absurdity of the confusion. This only stirred the pot more and made the mob angrier. They behaved like a pack of bloodthirsty wolves.

Even the police seemed intimidated by the display of anger and threats of violence. One of the officers finally said, *"You can't stay here,"* as they escorted me out of the building. They drove me straight back to the terminal and casually dropped me off. Thank God the airport had a revolving door. As I entered the lobby I was quickly subdued by a couple of security guards who told me I needed to sit in a chair and not move. One man stayed close enough to watch me as I sat in the hard plastic seat. *"How long would this go on?"* I wondered. It felt like I'd been sitting for a couple of hours and suddenly I just couldn't take it any more. I had no idea what they were holding me for. I'd finally reached my limit and shouted, *"Hey ... you have no right to hold me! I am not going to sit here any longer!"* I got up and the guard argued with me briefly, but allowed me to walk away. I knew I was being watched and did my best to stay under the radar. I returned to the terminal gate, where I'd almost achieved my departure, and waited patiently. I guess it felt like I just might have a chance there. There was at least a slight sense of hope in that spot.

So, I was sitting for what felt like eternity, and my conscious awareness was suddenly blown wide open. I realized I was beginning to receive messages that seemed CIA related. I felt like I was picking up signals from an outside source, as if I had a transceiver in my brain, linked directly to the radio broadcasts of the secret service. I could see the entire plot being revealed as if I was listening in on a top secret channel. There was something crazy happening here and it related to international espionage and divisive warfare, with an association of several nations involved. My body was quivering as the images of sabotage ran through my highly receptive mind.

The intensity escalated until I found myself crawling out of a window, across the roof, and onto the top of the flexible tube that reaches out to the doorway of the plane. I'm not sure what it's called, but it's the retractable hallway you walk through when entering a passenger plane. I was eagerly crawling along the top of this bridge, and as I reached the end, I spotted stair-like handles going down alongside the body of the plane. I scurried down them and surprisingly discovered an opening into the fuselage. I crawled in and ran straight up into the cockpit as if I had done it a thousand times before.

What remains so bizarre about this entire incident is that I had no previous knowledge of these points of access, or the elements I'd used to enter the plane. I have no understanding as to how I acquired this instantaneous ability to navigate through these unknowns.

I entered the cockpit and there was a guy working with the wiring on an electrical panel at the foot of the cabin. He was on his knees, working diligently, when I came dashing in. Surprised, he barked, *"What are you doing in here? You can't be in here!"* as he moved toward me. I told him, *"I want you to show me how to fly this plane!"* as he continued forward even more aggressively. He grabbed hold of me and we instantly rolled into a full-scale brawl. My energy was high, my strength extreme, and this guy was giving me a serious run for my money. He was unbelievably strong, and it turned into a go-for-broke wrestling match. I finally got him in a headlock and started ramming his head against the wall. I said, *"I'm not letting you go until you show me how to fly this plane!"*

He finally conceded, *"Okay... okay,"* and I let him go. He instantly screamed, *"He tried to kill me!"* as he bolted out of the cockpit door. I immediately went over to the pilot's seat and began flipping switches and pushing buttons. I guess I was under the illusion that I could start the engines, taxi out to the runway, take off, and figure the rest out in the air. *"What else could I be thinking?"* I obviously wasn't thinking at all, as I was running on one hundred percent autopilot.

The next thing I knew, the cockpit door flew open as three huge Samoan sized cops came charging in. *"Freeze!"*... they yelled, as two of them already had their pistols drawn and pointed in my direction. One was chrome, one was black, and the guns were obviously custom fit to the officers, because they were gigantic. I had never seen such large guns, especially that close up. *"What a shock!"* I just sat there frozen.

All three of them simultaneously jumped me, one on each arm, while the third man latched onto my neck. I held my arms straight out from my body, like an iron cross. They remained in that position without budging an inch, while these enormous men struggled with all their might to bend them behind my back. I could see my arms in my peripheral vision, solid like a concrete statue. I still find it hard to believe that they were totally rigid and motionless. The two officers on my arms began to panic, as the third man commanded them to put my hands behind my back. *"I can't!"* one of them yelled. *"Choke him out!!"* they both exclaimed, *"Choke him out!"*

Those were the last words I heard as I faded into unconsciousness. The guy on my neck squeezed tighter and tighter until the lights went out. The next thing I knew, I was returning to consciousness, sitting perched in the same seat. There was nobody else in the cockpit and I could not begin to understand what had just happened. My mind was thrashed. This made no sense at all! What I'd just experienced seemed very real... but what actually happened? Was it a hallucination?

I was dumfounded for a short while, and then hastily went back to flipping switches and pushing buttons, hoping to God that something would come of it. The next instant, the door came whipping open as the same three guys came crashing in again, like an ugly déjà vu. *"Don't you try to get away from us!"* one of them yelled. This time, they didn't have their guns drawn, grabbed hold of me, yanked my arms behind my back, and easily cuffed me. They pulled me out of the chair, carried me out of the plane, and down onto the pavement below.

It was as if my super powers had vanished completely as they effortlessly subdued me the second time around. There was a handful of officers standing there waiting, and they encircled me as I lay on the ground. I was hysterical and crying, *"I don't understand what is happening!.. I don't understand!!"* I couldn't wrap my mind around the unfolding event. It was beyond my ability to comprehend. As I lay on the ground, an officer walked by escorting the man who I'd originally fought with in the cockpit. *"Are they taking him into custody?"* I couldn't tell. He looked a bit beat up and his head was hanging down. One of the officers made a comment, *"You shouldn't hit people like that."* It seemed like the appropriate advice for a three year old, and apparently I appeared like one in that miserable moment.

Chapter 15

❧ back in the tank ❧

They sat together in the park, as the evening sky grew dark. She looked at him and he felt a spark tingle to his bones. It was then he felt alone and wished that he'd gone straight and watched out for a simple twist of fate.
—Bob Dylan, Simple Twist of Fate

I was put on my feet and taken to a temporary holding cell. It was like a mini-jail located on the airport grounds. The cell was extremely cramped, even for one man. I was anxiously trying to make conversation with the guard sitting at a desk within eyeshot. I told him I needed to go to the bathroom several times and he completely ignored me. He was totally unreceptive to my request for assistance. My hands were cuffed behind my back and I was on the verge of peeing my pants. The tiny cell wasn't equipped with a toilet, as the only amenity was a half-sized sink, stuffed in the corner.

I stretched my hands down to the point of being able to pull one foot at a time through the cuffs. With my hands in front of me, I was able to undo the zipper of my pants. I was standing there pissing in the sink, when the officer finally noticed. He had a flipping fit! He grabbed the keys, quickly opened the door, and yanked me out of the cell onto the floor. I fell on my back as he jumped on top and began punching me in the stomach repeatedly until I went unconscious. I made no effort to protect myself or retaliate. I was pretty well exhausted by then and don't recall what exactly occurred beyond that point. A good beating can leave your mind in a stunned state of emptiness, and I'd finally reached that point.

My memories skip ahead to being taken from the little holding cell to be booked into the Honolulu Jail. They fingerprinted me in admittance and promptly locked me in a dark and God-forsaken hole with a mob of crazed and vicious animals. It was like a horror movie. Once again, I'd found my way to the designated cell for the crazies.

It was large and overflowing, with nothing but intense chaos streaming through this agitated swarm. One of the guys was parading around, waving his arms in the air, boasting of how he'd just killed three men. He cantankerously went on and on about his murderous activities. It's difficult to separate make-believe from real in a situation like that. Who knows? Regrettably, I was in a similar state of madness.

Another guy was muttering to himself as he secretly smoked a cigarette he'd somehow sneaked in. I went up to him, grabbed the smoke out of his hand, and took a couple of quick puffs. His trigger was cocked and the danger meter rising. The energy was intense and violent, and I was just as boisterous and cocky as the others. It felt like we were on the verge of a bloody battle. I stood my ground and made sure these guys knew that I wasn't willing to be pushed around. It's not easy to settle into a situation like that, but I soon found myself securely nestled in.

As I sat in a state of deep contemplation, I noticed the tile beneath my feet beginning to melt and swirl around as though it were liquid. The flooring looked like the glass top of an aquarium, and I imagined we were in a submarine, being taken underwater. My imagination stirred up many far-out scenarios as I pondered this impressive illusion. I knew I was in someone else's hands and realized they could take me wherever they wanted to. Perhaps we were being shipped off to Atlantis to be sold as slaves. Maybe I was experiencing an

LSD flashback; who was I to say? My mind was reeling in the shadows, and I had little choice but to wait for what was coming next.

A couple of hours later, the gate opened as a very timid man was pushed into the cage. He looked frightened and walked with a slight limp as if he had some sort of disability. It appeared to be a defect in his spine, or perhaps one leg was marginally shorter than the other. I felt an immediate sense of compassion for this guy and spoke up as he entered the pen. *"C'mon over here... and have a seat!"* I blurted out. He cautiously shuffled over and sat next to me. *"Don't worry about these loud mouths,"* I muttered, *"I've got ya covered."* I held a deep and sincere desire to protect this guy for some odd reason. It was cold, so I grabbed a blanket and placed it around his shoulders. I told him in a loud enough voice that the others could easily hear. *"Don't sweat these guys. They won't lay a hand on you... I promise."* He seemed relieved and grateful to have someone by his side. I asked what he was in for, and he said he'd been arrested for inappropriate conduct at the beach. I could only imagine that it was for being naked or somehow sexually related. I didn't pry. He sat with me for a couple of hours before a guard approached the cell and called his name for discharge. He thanked me with deep sincerity as we shook hands and said a quick goodbye. A short while later the guard returned and this time called my name. *"You are being released,"* he exclaimed as he opened the gate. I was utterly shocked! *"What!? Are you serious?"*

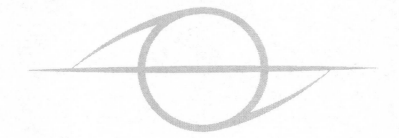

Chapter 16

⋟ monks like me ⋞

At any moment, you have a choice, that either leads you closer to your spirit or further away from it.

—Thich Nhat Hanh

The guy that I'd befriended had just paid my bail. When I exited the building, he was standing with his buddy who had shown up to bail him out and give him a ride home. I thanked him for getting me out and he said, *"It was only twenty five bucks,"* as if it was no big deal. I was very grateful and humbled by his generosity. They offered to give me a ride, so I got in the car and we headed back into town. The driver said, *"Just let me know where you'd like to go and I'll drop you off."* I told him, *"To be quite honest, I have nowhere to go. I've been trying to fly home for several days now and I have no money."* My newfound buddy realized that I was in a tight spot. He said, *"How would you feel about sleeping in a Buddhist temple tonight?"* I was very pleased and quickly responded, *"I would love to!"* Heck, I would have been happy if he'd offered a garage or a doghouse for Christ's sake. I was in a desperate situation.

His friend drove us through the backstreets of a nearby residential area. It was dark as the car pulled over to let us out, near what appeared to be a vacant lot. As we walked from the street into a grassy area, he pulled out a little white stick that looked like something a blind man would carry. I had no idea why he was using this strange object, nor did I bother to ask. It seemed to appear in his hand from nowhere. I took hold of the back of his shirt as he tapped his way through the overgrown brush and around the small trees. I blindly followed as I had no idea where I was or where we were going.

This night seemed especially dark, with no streetlight in sight. The little white rod looked as though it was made from fishing pole material and appeared to be glowing in the dark. This was one more bizarre incident that would leave me wondering for years. That unusual little walking stick still strikes me as so very odd.

We made our way through the bushes and tiptoed around the corner of a small building. Tucked beneath the overhanging trees was the front door of what appeared to be a typical home. *"Was this the Buddhist temple?"* As we took our shoes off in the entry, I noticed several pairs of sandals lined up on the floor.

The main chamber beyond the corridor was set up with an ornate altar that stretched the entire length of the room. It was fifteen to eighteen feet long and completely covered with an artistically designed formation that was delicately shaped and brightly colored. I noticed a centerpiece to the intricate mandala that appeared to be a little brass bell. The overall decor was aesthetically striking. There were burgundy velvet fabrics draped from the ceiling, and little wooden benches facing the altar. It appeared to be a place for gathering to worship, pray, or meditate.

My guide gave me a brief tour as it was late and the other monks were sleeping. He quietly showed me around and explained that this main room was the sanctuary. As we passed through the hall, he pointed out the pictures that lined the walls. There were many portraits of Asian men in Buddhist monk attire. He told me who they each were by name and explained that they were highly trained martial artists. I could easily recognize

114

that this temple deserved a high degree of respect. I was also deeply pleased to have a safe place to sleep on this mysteriously auspicious occasion.

We went into his room where he showed me a few of his personal items. He was living a very simple lifestyle. I remember questioning the bowl of white powder, sitting out in the open, which looked like cocaine. He explained that it was baking soda he used to brush his teeth. As we began to unwind from an anxiety filled day, he gave me a little pad to lie down on. The thin mat almost softened the hardness of the wooden floor, and as I began to settle upon it, he asked if he could cover me up. I don't recall what the purpose was or exactly what this ritual was about, but I readily complied. He then wrapped me like a mummy from the bottom of my feet to the top of my head, in a material that reminded me of cheesecloth. My face and head were completely covered, but I could still breathe through the fabric. It was very peculiar, and yet somehow seemed perfectly appropriate.

I slept very well and when I woke up I was charged with a new energy. The sun was peeking through the window shades and I instantly wanted out. I peeled off my mummy garb and was surprised to see the body next to me also wrapped from head to toe. I assumed this tightly wrapped body was the one that swaddled me so neatly the night before, but I couldn't for the life of me figure out how. *"How did he do that to himself?"* I wondered.

I was puzzled for a moment, but mostly anxious to get outside. I started pulling on the window screen to see if I could make a quick exit and about then the mummy awakened. *"No... Don't go out the window!"* he exclaimed as he freed his face from the linen. This sudden mug shot didn't appear to be the same face I'd seen before the mummification. I wanted to believe it was the same guy, but I wasn't sure. My mind was suddenly searching for practical answers. *"How long had I been in that darn mummy suit? Was it the next day or the next week?"* I pondered the possibilities as I realized I truly had no way of knowing.

I exited the sleeping room and wandered back into the sanctuary. I was definitely feeling hungry, or more appropriately, ravenous. I don't recall eating a meal in the jail or in the recent days before the lock up. My eyes scanned the altar in the prayer room as I optimistically imagined an offering being left for the Gods. Certainly God wouldn't mind sharing, considering the circumstances.

I couldn't spot any fruit or food of any kind and considered the little bell at the peak of the arrangement. *"That looks like the perfect place to hide an offering!"* I desperately hoped. I reached out, picked up the bell, and anxiously looked beneath it. As I lifted it from its perch, the entire display began to disintegrate. I hadn't realized until this moment that this delicate, beautifully crafted arrangement was actually rice that had been artistically hand molded. The bell's movement caused the rice to shift and crumble from the center outward, like ten thousand dominoes, *"Oh my God! What have I just done?"*

I suddenly envisioned martial artist monks pouring out of the walls, karate style, to punish me for such an offense. I panicked and rushed for the door. I put my shoes on outside, and raced down the street like a frightened rabbit. I kept running until I wasn't able to run any more. Even so, I continued to keep a steady pace until I was outside of the neighborhood and headed back into the city. In the meantime, my mind was reveling in the fear of this unintentional transgression. *"Was somebody after me?"* I had no idea as to the degree of this violation according to a sacred order I knew nothing of. I certainly didn't want to find out the hard way, so I kept moving.

Chapter 17

❧ on the run ❧

If you're going through hell, keep going.
—Winston Churchill

I soon came across a park-like setting with sidewalks and older buildings arranged like a military compound. I strolled around the site as if it were a museum and felt intuitively drawn to a particular entrance into one of the office units. I climbed the stairs to the landing and walked right in. A man in uniform was sitting quietly behind a desk, front and center, as I entered the room. I asked him a few off-the-wall questions and he seemed very puzzled by my presence.

Beyond his left shoulder was a doorway to an adjacent room. The door was closed and I could hear the distinct sound of large items being moved, and shoes shuffling around behind it. I could feel the vibrations through the floor and the peculiar noises sparked my curiosity.

It sounded like people were crashing around beyond the doorway and my imagination began to muster up crazy imagery. *"Was this related to the extra-terrestrial landing? Was somebody taking a classified beating behind that door? What kind of covert establishment is this?"* I thought to myself. The man sitting at the desk acted as though he didn't hear anything. For him, it seemed that beyond me, nothing unusual was happening.

I pondered this very strange situation for a while and decided to continue on my way. I left through the same door I'd entered; however as I exited, the surroundings appeared to have changed dramatically. These flowering plants were so brilliant and brightly colored. *"How could I have not noticed them on the way in?"* I was puzzled by the shift in my awareness of these surroundings. *"Where was I? What kind of uniform was that guy wearing?"* It appeared to be a campus-like setting, but for whom I couldn't tell. *"Was this the National Guard or some other military operation that I was unfamiliar with?"* I contemplated this mystery from my altered state of consciousness, as I found my way back to the streets and once again drifting into the city.

I came across a few kids waiting at a bus stop, and a brief but friendly conversation led to one of the kids giving me fifty cents to catch the bus. I appreciated his generosity and insight as I soon discovered this route would take me straight to the airport. I took a long, quiet ride back to what felt like a bad déjà vu. I don't recall much of what happened during this phase of the journey. I know the return of my presence was not appreciated, and the security guards were on me like white on rice. The only real memory I have in the airport is of dashing out of the front entrance to escape being pursued. As I was running through the city streets, it became quite obvious that the cops were engaged in a full-scale chase.

It was nightfall as several police vehicles raced my way. I was on a main thoroughfare that was directly beneath another highway. The one above was suspended between large cement pillars that stood central to the lanes below. These huge columns separated the south and northbound lanes on the level where I was on the run. I quickly realized the difficulty this structure created for the police cars, and I was taking advantage of the split highway by dodging back and forth through the traffic. When I spotted a police car approaching from one direction, I would run across to the other side where the traffic was reversed. The vehicles were unable to turn around with the one-way street being divided by barriers, which made it very difficult for them to catch me.

It was fairly dark by now, and I realized that my light colored clothing was giving me away. I had white tennis shoes on and a reflective decal on my sleeveless t-shirt that lit up in the headlights. I quickly ducked in behind a large bush and stripped off my shirt, shoes, and socks. I left the socks and shoes in the bushes and stuffed the shirt in the back of my jeans like a tail. I wanted desperately to disappear into the black of the night.

Just as I was ready to move on, I heard a very distinct, loud voice echoing through my being. It was emanating anger and carried a low, deep and ancient tone. This one didn't seem to be an internal voice. It sounded like it was booming from the sky around me. *"I am the one who called you here!"* it bellowed. It was strong, malicious and frightening, and I was baffled and bewildered by this strange, otherworldly tone. This was one of the rare moments in my life that I would actually hear an audible voice. The bizarre nature of the experience was due to this bellowing voice having no apparent point of origin. I couldn't tell if it was coming from within my mind or from a loud speaker, as it seemed to penetrate both worlds equally.

I started running again and the officers appeared to be gaining ground. The cars were passing by more frequently and I could feel that my run was nearing its end. In the midst of this escapade, I'd discovered that I could duck behind the shadow of a column as a car was approaching, to avoid being seen. It seemed to be a highly effective strategy.

As the next squad car approached, I crouched behind a pillar, but surprisingly this time the vehicle came to a complete stop. The officer got out of his car as I spontaneously came out from behind the pillar and casually walked toward him. *"Why are you running from me?"* he shouted. I immediately and naturally responded, *"I didn't know it was you!"* He seemed dazed by the response, and was exceptionally calm and unusually non-abusive. I felt safe with this man instantly and he seemed particularly at ease with this no longer out of control situation. He didn't even cuff me as he helped me into the back seat of his car, just in the nick of time.

In nothing flat, several squad cars came flying up to the scene, as a gang of officers swarmed around me, buzzing like a bunch of pissed off hornets. I felt very fortunate to have found this one kind officer who appeared to be protecting me from the mob. I was very grateful when the others were unable to take out their frustrations on me, and held a strong suspicion that given the opportunity, they would have beaten me to a bloody pulp. That was my best guess from what I'd witnessed from the back seat of the police vehicle. I felt safeguarded and comfortable with the doors locked, and actually had a chance to relax in peace for a minute. I don't recall ever feeling so appreciative of being locked in the back of a police car.

Chapter 18

❧ captivation ❧

I cannot think of any need in childhood as strong as the need for a father's protection.

—Sigmund Freud

When the upset and excitement of the other patrolmen had subsided, my personal savior returned to the car. I was then taken to the hospital and two officers escorted me from the squad car to an exam room, where the doctor soon followed to perform a psychological evaluation. They stood guard at the door as he asked me a couple dozen standard questions that I'd heard so many times before. The psychiatrist looked somewhat perplexed as he analyzed my frantically manic state of mind. I could understand his confusion and realized he couldn't possibly have a clue about the chaos I'd lived through in the last few days. I wasn't even sure myself.

I was bouncing off the walls with a surge of high voltage energy, and my answers were delivered rapidly, as if I knew the questions before they were fully stated. The guards outside the door were finding it entertaining as they burst into laughter at a point that literally dropped one of them to his knees. It must have been a humorous event from where they stood. My highly creative responses were extremely animated, to put it mildly. The doctor asked if I was okay with him giving me a shot, and by then I was more than willing to submit. I knew how badly my body needed a break. *"Sure... that would be perfectly fine."*

The next thing I remember is waking up in a strange location. Although it was a familiar setting, it took me a while to figure out where I was. My mind was struggling to find a solid footing. *"Am I alive? Is this planet earth? Is this a dream?"* I awakened to a couple of Hawaiian women with long dark hair, untangling my mane with a large-tooth comb. I was in pajamas in a mental hospital and these ladies were apparently patients that had taken mercy on me for some odd reason. It was a very strange way to return to conscious awareness. It was pleasant, nurturing, and a stark contrast to my most recent experiences. I was being held prisoner once more, yet I was being lulled into a loving embrace of acceptance and encouragement.

On about the third day of my stay, I was notified that I had a visitor. Apparently, my family had been contacted and informed of my predicament. My father flew into Honolulu and came to the hospital, expecting that I would be released into his custody. He soon discovered that it wasn't going to be as easy as he had hoped. He was called in to meet with a group of representatives for the airlines.

As it turned out, Northwest Airlines was the only one willing to make a deal that would allow me to board a plane. The agreement they proposed would be contingent upon a long list of conditions. My father was being required to sign a contract holding him liable for any and all costs that might result, due to an abrupt decision to abort the flight plan. In other words, if I were to freak out or cause a disturbance during the flight, they would turn around and come back to Honolulu. If this occurred, he would be responsible for the fuel, passenger tickets, and hotel accommodation costs. Along with this agreement, several rows of seating adjacent to our seats would be left unoccupied. It sounded like an overkill response from my limited point of view.

After finalizing the arrangement, they released me from the hospital and I joined him in his hotel room. I was now under the influence of some heavily debilitating drugs. I don't recall any significant events at the hotel, but by the time we were boarding the plane to go home I was beginning to feel severe side effects. This was quite typical and the outcome was also very predictable. Normally, they would have given me a drug to counteract the primary prescription, but on this occasion it was overlooked.

The symptoms are a tightening of the jaw muscles and a heightened anxiety level that jolts through the body in a way that makes it very difficult to sit still. Actually, damn near impossible. I was already squirming in my seat as we prepared for takeoff with two rows of empty seats in front of and behind me. How strange it felt to be perceived as such a dangerous person. *"Did they have any idea of the frightened soul that was trapped somewhere deep inside?"* It was so odd to feel like a child being escorted by his daddy, while caught up in a peculiar blend of a disturbing and dysfunctional mindset. It was strange to experience such a childlike mentality, taking place inside an adult body that was classified as threatening.

As bizarre as it was, somehow we made it home safely. My reaction to the pharmaceutical side effects culminated in a midnight run to the emergency room to stop the body cramps and the racing heart. I think it was the shot of Benadryl that brought me the relief whereby I was finally able to relax. I wondered if the trip home with no antidote for the painfully crippling drug was a deliberate form of punishment. Luckily, I made it back before it became totally unbearable. *"Thank you God!"*

I later thanked my dad for trusting me, and he laughed out loud and said, *"Trust? Are you kidding? If you would have made one wrong move... I would have cold-cocked you so fast you wouldn't have known what hit you!"* Those were his exact words and I couldn't help but laugh. They say Love comes in many forms and I guess it's true. Apparently, brutality with the proper intention is no exception. My father also eventually told me the stories of what he'd heard during the airline meetings. This helped me immensely to understand more about what had occurred, unbeknownst to me.

There was a missing piece of the puzzle in the 747 cockpit scene; a glitch in the matrix. I couldn't comprehend how I was being choked out in one moment, and in the next, sitting by myself in that same pilot seat. He said that when I was choked out, I had been taken out of the plane unconscious and onto the tarmac, where several officers gathered around me. I suddenly came back into consciousness, took five of them out, and ran back up the stairs into the cockpit.

The thing is... I had no conscious awareness of this whatsoever. When I returned to my body, I was sitting in the same position as when I'd checked out. *"What was going on? Was this connected to the Black Elk episode?"* I had no idea. *"Was it a part of my subconscious mind... or another possession of some sort?"* I would never know. *"How was I able to skillfully climb over the bridging tunnel and into an access hole in the plane body... that I didn't even know existed? How did I run straight to the cockpit... as if I had been in a 747 a thousand times? What was the guy doing with the electrical panel? Was he sabotaging the plane?"* These perplexing questions would remain unanswered and haunt my mind for decades. *"Had I psychically stepped into some CIA operation... or was I having an acid flashback?"* Perhaps it was both. The greatest curiosity underlying this enormous and overwhelming sense of wonderment was, *"Had any good come from it?"*

These endless and circular questions would continue to pour through visions, like a sci-fi movie replaying in the deepest stratum of my mind, for years to come. *"Why was I not faced with criminal charges?"* I could think of several possibilities. *"Assaulting an officer? Resisting arrest? Breaking and entering? Malicious behavior?"* Nothing. *"Why was my bail so low?"* When it was all said and done, my mind was filled with one enormous *"Why?"* Once again, these questions would remain unanswered and I would come to abide in a mystical state of uncertainty for decades.

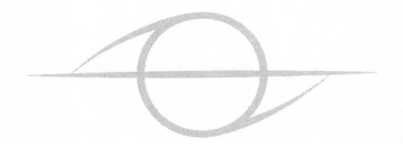

Chapter 19

๛ psychic warriors ๛

The ultimate value of life depends upon awareness and the power of contemplation rather than upon mere survival.

— Aristotle

My lingering curiosity would only be stirred further as the years passed. I was hanging out in a library on Orcas Island, almost twenty years later, when something rather strange occurred. *"Have you ever seen a book jump off the shelf?"* As hard as it is to believe, I witnessed one do just that. I wasn't looking for anything of the sort when *Psychic Warrior*, by David Morehouse, literally fell from the top rack into my hand. It was a true story of a man's experience in the CIA as a remote viewer. He was one of several people that worked in a special operations department that did psychic espionage. It was extremely fascinating and revealing as well. Several years later I would end up in training with one of his colleagues. I ultimately discovered that my wildest imaginings were not so far out of line with reality after all. The government actually had an undercover program that was designed to do exactly what I was trying so hard to avoid... psychic espionage. *"Were we on the same team?"* It was difficult to tell.

As my questions began to settle, and once again my mind had become comfortably numb, I returned to my routine of cutting hair and earning enough money to make ends meet. I always seemed to find my way back to my usual routine at the salon. I could quickly and easily regain the appearance of living a normal life once more. Appearance was an important piece of the pie. Unfortunately, my life was disintegrating from the inside out, and apparently I was the only one able to see it coming.

It was like carrying a time bomb on your back, knowing that it's bound to go off sooner or later. The lithium became the insulator that held back time, like water behind a dam. The pressure would build until I couldn't take it any more. Usually at about that stage of the game, I would stop taking my medication and feel relieved for a short while. Somewhere in the depths of my mind I was well aware that another manic episode was brewing like an incoming storm. Of course the doctors from their very limited point of view would say, "See... *the problem only comes when he's not drugged.*" It was all so obvious to them and of course they had such a simple solution. Just stay drugged for the rest of your life and forget about the underlying issues. *"Easy... right?"*

Nobody seemed capable of understanding how I found this approach totally unacceptable. I felt like I was in a closed-circuit that included a wild rollercoaster ride mounted on top of a merry-go-round, with an exit line that melted right back into the entrance. It seemed to be a never-ending loop, and I struggled to hold onto any hope of ever breaking out of this vicious cycle of suffering.

This roundabout cycle, of dragging me in and throwing me out of the nuthouse, continued for the next twenty years. The episodes varied in intensity and consistently appeared as rather bizarre, not only to me, but to my loved ones who were close enough to observe behind the scenes. My resistance to the drugged life kept me consistently framed as non-compliant, and even my family perceived me as unwilling to receive the help they believed the drugs offered. What I was rejecting, was a non-working model that apparently they could not see beyond. At the same time, I was holding tight to my deep and genuine desire for effective solutions to this haunting dilemma.

I consistently complied and basically tried every drug that was put in front of me, paying the price for each one along the way. At one point, I was offered a new drug that was guaranteed to be just what I was looking for, according to my psychiatrist. My doctor had made a childish comment as he persuaded me to try it. He said with a big grin, *"If you don't like it, you can punch me in the face."* Honest to God, he actually said that. The drug was called Stelazine. It was an anti-psychotic drug often used for schizophrenia. Apparently, he believed it to be the latest, greatest answer to problems like mine.

It actually turned into one of the worst nightmares of my life. I was unable to stop walking for almost twenty-four hours. I would come pacing into the house, absolutely exhausted and try with all my might to sit down. Without exaggeration, as soon as my butt hit the chair, I would bounce back to my feet and be compelled to continue walking, even though I was dead tired. My heart was racing and it seemed to go on forever.

My brother and a few buddies had met at a local bar that was inside a nearby Chinese restaurant. I cruised through the bar to say hi a couple of times during the night, but was unable to stop walking long enough to sit down and relax. I walked throughout the night, crying in the pouring rain, totally exhausted. It was utterly torturous.

I was taken to the emergency room the next day and given an antidote drug that finally relieved the anxiety. When I went back to see the doctor, I said, *"Okay, hold still,"* as I approached him with my fist in the air. He acted shocked as he replied, *"What is the problem?"* I responded, *"You told me I could punch you in the face if it didn't go well... remember?"* He didn't even want to talk about it. His immediate reaction was, *"I am going to have to drop you as a patient."* His absence from my world was no great loss, but still I asked him why. He replied, *"I can't have a patient that wants to punch me in the face."* I still find this entire exchange unbelievable. I had no intention of hitting him. I wasn't even angry at that point, and certainly not out of control. I just wanted to call him out on his stupidity. If I actually wanted to punch him in the face, I would have just walked up and clocked him; after all, he'd given me permission. In the recesses of my mind, I was wondering, *"What kind of games are these folks willing to play with my life?"* Ultimately, I would surrender to the fact that recovery was not possible within the conventional Western medical model. I eventually came to realize that it had not been designed for that purpose.

By the time my son reached his fifth birthday, my inner world had become such a mess that I made the conscious decision to throw my life into the wind. I did so without any further consideration. My drinking, pot smoking, and womanizing had led me directly to a point that would ultimately bring my marriage to an end. My sister pulled out of the salon and my business collapsed beneath my feet. It all came crashing down, and I was finally at the end of my false-hearted attempt of living a normal life.

My inability to show up in person for a psychiatric evaluation brought my Klonopin prescription to a halt, and the consequential withdrawals would lend me a firsthand experience of a living hell. Although the salon was closed, I was temporarily living in the back room. The place was a total disaster and so was I. Desperation was begging me to escape this torturous circus ride and find my way out of the fairgrounds. At this point, even death would have been considered a relief.

I laid in that black hole, perspiring my way through nightmarish journeys in and out of consciousness for several days. In the middle of one particularly frightening night, I awoke with a certain awareness that time was standing still. There was nobody in town and no cars passing by. I was lost and alone, locked within my own isolation, cut off from all contact with others.

This was a clear and pure taste of the state of hell. The fear that arose in me as I pondered this as an eternal predicament brings tears to my eyes. I understand the fear of hell now, as I was frightened beyond explanation or description. I was truly experiencing a living hell and the scary thing is... it was just as near as heaven. I discovered that fine line between the two, and came to fully realize that either way; it's purely a state of mind. The truth became clear, that the state of mind, whether it is heavenly, hellish, or somewhere in between, is what fully dictates one's experience of life every minute of every day. *"Now, if I can just find a way to control it!"*

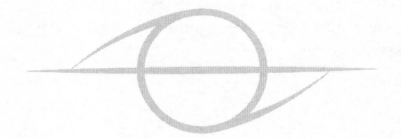

Part 4

Unraveling the Mystery

"You're so afraid your life is over,
And nothing I can say can change your mind.
How can anybody be so selfish,
And treat you all so cruel,
The woman screamed at me and cried.
I'll always hold you in my soul,
And I'm never going to leave you all alone
But your daddy doesn't live here anymore.
I did it for you, and the boys,
Because love should teach you joy,
And not the imitation,
That your momma and daddy tried to show you.
I did it for you, and for me,
And because I still believe,
There's only one thing,
That you can never give up,
Never compromise on,
And that's the real thing you need in love."

— Kenny Loggins

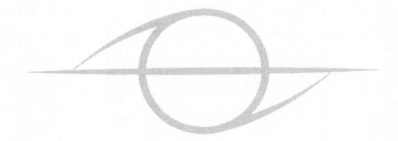

Chapter 20

∽ the times, they are a changin ∼

If the path before you is clear, you're probably on someone else's.

—Joseph Campbell

I've heard it said a thousand times that a person has to hit bottom before they'll turn their life around. As much as I'd wished this wasn't the case, it was certainly proving to be true for me. This juncture was painfully devastating beyond measure, and yet overall the best thing that could have happened. My entire life had been completely torn apart, and I was left empty-handed with nothing but a burning desire and every reason to change my ways. I knew too much to hang onto a victim mentality. Everything that I had ever learned was pointing to me as the responsible party. Regardless of how I had been taught, trained, and conditioned by society, I was the one responsible for straightening it out and getting it right. As much as I'd wished for a doctor to devise a magical pill that could solve all my problems, I knew this wasn't a realistic solution. I was certain that the answers were out there somewhere, and it was ultimately up to me to find them. The radical changes in my world left me searching and seriously reviewing what had occurred thus far on this magical mystery tour.

My experience of falling into the Light was undeniably the axis of my life path. It seemed to me that it was a gift from God, and yet it felt to be a terrible burden with a dark and heavy curse. My life was graciously redeemed on one hand and undoubtedly devastated on the other. My spirit had clearly been awakened, but my *real world* living was intolerable. It was such an enormous transformation and so instantaneous that it was like stepping through a gateway into an alternate reality overnight.

My way of perceiving had shifted dramatically and a major adjustment was in order. It felt as though a protective door to my soul had been viciously ripped off the hinges. What I was once shielded from was suddenly saturating my awareness of the world around me. That door appeared in my visions as the hatch on a submarine being torn violently from the vessel and vanishing. I was now swimming in a realm that I had previously been safeguarded from. I could frequently feel, hear, and experience another dimension of reality. I would sense beings, feel their emotions, hear voices, and receive messages from the other side without cease. I remember watching *The Sixth Sense* with Bruce Willis and thinking, *"That's how I feel!"* except that it wasn't visual. It was primarily kinesthetic, as though I could feel the other side. I wasn't seeing bloody dead people walking around, but I could sense their presence.

I eventually came to realize the heart of the problem was actually in the interpretation of what I was experiencing. It was frightening in the beginning as I often found myself imagining demons and evil beings battling for my soul. I suddenly wished I'd never seen *The Exorcist*, or a handful of those other spooky movies. They fed the fear and shaped my dark visions. I could scare the heck out of myself with such a wild and active imagination.

My lack of understanding and experience in dealing with this level of awareness made it a living nightmare. I couldn't seem to find anyone available with any relevant understanding. Nobody stepped forward to guide or assist me as my mind was spinning out of control. It was certainly worthy of being labeled ill, and the institutional system that did respond was far from helpful. The pressure from outside was almost as stressful as the tension churning within. I desperately needed to find an effective strategy for dealing with this madness. My hunger for knowledge was insatiable. I was compelled and obsessed with finding a path to freedom whereby I could take my healing, as well as my life, into my own hands. The intense suffering left me open to every possibility that would dare present itself. My radar was constantly in search mode.

In my early years, shortly after *the fall*, I had turned to religion with the hope of finding solutions and possibly safety. I remember going to church after church begging for answers and coming up shorthanded every time. The theological nonsense that was structurally foundational to each and every avenue I bumped into left me more upset and confused than the one before. I was baptized too many times to recount, hoping and praying each time that I would be lifted up and out of the chaos that lurked deep within my psyche.

As for my spiritual upbringing, my mother had taken us as small children to church and bible school. I didn't pay close attention to what was being taught, but I did enjoy the arts and crafts projects. I had also inadvertently come to believe in *God* and that *Jesus loves the little children of the world.* I was taught to pray and enjoyed my prayers at bedtime. I believe this was perhaps the strongest factor in my turning to God in my crisis situation. In my young mind, God was somewhere *out there.* I called out into the universe for God's help and to this day I believe that heartfelt petition saved my life.

Along with that divinely appointed rescue, came a drastically altered state of consciousness that forced me to do my time in the mental institutions as well. I came to intimately understand what Thorazine was all about and held deep regard for the other side of a strong dose of Haldol. These drugs were like chemical torture devices that made the normal waking madness feel like a relief. These primitive psychotropic pharmaceuticals were a guaranteed pathway to a living hell. I remember being drugged up and shuffling down a hallway in the Western State Psychiatric facility with cramps throughout my body. My hands were clinched like crab claws, my legs were charlie-horsed, and my face was doing some kind of a lockjaw response. Just one of these issues can be painfully overwhelming, but imagine all of this simultaneously. It was extremely agonizing, to put it mildly.

I felt locked inside a pain-ridden body as a prisoner who was chemically bound. My tongue was swollen to double its size, my eyes were watering, and I was drooling profusely as I shuffled toward the light at the end of the corridor. A nurse stepped out of a room about ten paces in front of me. She turned away as she moved in the direction I was headed. I began screaming for help but I couldn't get the sound to come out through my tight throat and past an unusually thick tongue. With all my might I shrieked, and finally a yelp came out. The nurse turned her head, and for that split second I was hopeful. She turned halfway around and as she gazed back at me, casually declared, *"It's all in your mind!"* She abruptly spun around and walked away. Boom! What a slam.

Beyond the staggering pain in my body, it felt like a knife to the heart. Of the many heart-wrenching memories still with me, this one stands out. It was a nightmare that would echo through my wounded soul for decades. However, on the bright side, it was a deep-seated and powerful lesson in compassion for the suffering that so many mental health patients have endured.

A few years later, I heard a story about a good friend of mine from high school that was being drugged in a similar fashion. I'm unsure as to what exactly he was dealing with, but another buddy had gone to visit him. Like the mentality I exposed a short while ago, the visitor thought it might be fun to take some of his friend's drugs. He popped a couple of his pills with the anticipation of getting high. The next thing we knew, he wound up shuffling into an emergency room, swollen tongue, lockjaw, and a rubber hose hanging out of his mouth. He ended up sprawling his body across the front counter and groaning with all his might for assistance. He had stuffed the hose in his mouth in response to the fear of his teeth breaking off under the pressure of his constricting jaw. Apparently, I was the only buddy within this circle of friends capable of relating to his frightening experience. I was utterly dumfounded by the notion that he'd done this to himself voluntarily. Like I said, I wouldn't wish it on anybody.

I did my best to have a life in between the semi-annual mental ward visitations, but it was like living in two worlds. There was a gnawing from within that wouldn't let me go and simultaneously it seemed the entire governmental, medical, and judicial system were grinding at my back door. In addition to this torturous ordeal, I was supposed to be making a living. As difficult as it was to maintain a state of mind capable of working, this was also a gift.

Thank God for this piece of the puzzle, because basic survival mode can be an effective way to forget about what is eating you on the inside. I actually appreciated the time and space for focusing on something other than my personal issues back then. At the time, I didn't know how to deal with them appropriately anyway. I easily recognized this perspective on life as nothing unique. It's actually a form of escape that is strongly supported in this capitalistic society. As acceptable and supported as this avenue was, I eventually discovered its fatal trap as I continually felt the repercussions of using work to avoid my inner conflict. I could only last so long until I was suddenly faced with everything I was trying so hard to avoid. The dam would break and the walls come tumbling down.

This approach certainly wasn't uncommon by any stretch; in fact, it was the most socially acceptable form of avoidance available. *"He may have some serious issues in life, but you can't knock a guy that's making money!"* This was a strong voice in mainstream America, and one that powered my father's path as well. I'd discovered another classic pattern etched deeply in the collective psyche and could now understand the attraction.

How many people become engrossed in their work as a way of avoiding having to deal with the feelings of hurt, shame, and inadequacy that are more easily stuffed into a dark closet in the recesses of a busy mind? How many folks use their work as a way of ignoring relationship issues? These would be difficult numbers to unveil and most likely shocking. In the extreme form, we call this behavior pattern a *workaholic.* In a lesser form, it is just considered being a good taxpayer. The truth is… it can be almost as effective as heavy drinking or taking drugs to numb the brain. The combination of alcohol and excessive work is a powerful approach to holding back the hurt, at least for a short while.

Emotional pain can be a real bitch; relief often comes by way of closing the heart and putting your nose to the grindstone. All too often, this becomes a default mode and habits take hold. It's easy to find something more pleasurable to do than facing the inner agony of a hurtful state of mind or an unfulfilling life. When the upset reaches a noticeable level that can no longer be easily hidden, we call in the label makers and they declare it a *disorder*. It's usually pushed under the radar and not tagged as a *mental illness*. Only certain cases are acknowledged openly with such a strong label, even though the milder forms do qualify. It's a tricky program.

140

Those proficiently experienced with self-medicating get shuffled down a separate aisle. They are labeled *alcoholic, drug addict,* or both. *"If you are using the drugs we supply... stand in this line. If you are supplying your own... line up over there."* They have created two entirely separate departments according to where you get your drug of choice. You get the label *addict* if you buy from the street and you're on your own. You're tagged *mentally ill* if you've been captured by the highly profitable medical industry, and you'll never need a street dealer again. You will receive plenty of support in keeping the drugs flowing. The system would rather see you as *mentally ill* because this channel feeds a much more acceptable and distinguished cartel. They find a fitting box to put the paperwork in, and assign the appropriate pharmaceutical remedy for suppressing that particular type of upset. These mind-altering drugs can energetically dam up the emotional system for years. As you'd likely expect, the overriding side effects are gruesome, but hey, *"What's a guy to do?"*

Mood disorders and mental illness really suck; yet the unraveling of such a distorted structure of false and destructive beliefs is far more laborious than simply walling it off. Ignoring... repressing... denying... staying busy.... these are the easy steps to temporary relief and long-term avoidance. Drugs are great for that. Sex, money, alcohol, and every other addiction that ranks on this growing list, can support the same approach. There are a million ways to divert the mind from dealing with the basic issues that stand in the way of progress, development, and growth. They won't get you anywhere, but they will allow a short-term form of escape that can make coping a little easier, at least for the time being. *"Sometimes that's the best a person can do... right?"*

Just about the time I was groveling in the gutter of this circular insanity, I was asked to take one more test to evaluate my mental state. It was a very involved examination that included a wide variety of questioning and mental puzzles. Although I thought I'd done quite well, they generously decided to give me one more label… "Gravely disabled." Apparently, this was the one to tip the scale. I was put on SSI, a form of government assistance, and restricted in my ability to work. I felt a sense of relief at first, because I thought I might get a break in which I could stabilize myself. However, even though there was a paycheck involved, it wasn't even close to being enough to live on, so the basic struggle for survival continued.

I learned a priceless lesson through this transition. I would have never believed that there were people who would come to your home, give you food, and treat you with loving kindness just because you needed it. Thank God for the Mormons. They came knocking on my door one day, discovered a man in need, and helped me immensely in many ways. I'll get to that story in a minute, but for now I have another important piece to share.

An unbelievable reward that came through the *gravely disabled* label was hidden in the fine print of the accompanying paperwork. I discovered that I had become eligible for educational financial aid through Medicare. I promptly dove into the research and quickly discovered a local community college that had a program which appeared quite fitting. It was a two-year certification course in Alcohol and Chemical Dependency Counseling. I anxiously jumped through the required hoops and soon found myself enrolled. This would prove to be the most transformational choice I would ever make, besides my crying out to God. The education that followed, laid the groundwork for all of the intellectual understanding I would ever need. It was absolutely a dream come true.

Chapter 21

❧ back to school ❧

The saddest aspect of life right now is that science gathers knowledge faster than society gathers wisdom.

—Isaac Asimov

Ibegan to unravel the mystery of the diagnosis and to look deep within myself for the path to wellness. I remember getting a look at the DSM-IV, which is a diagnostic manual for mental disorders. It listed the pre-disposing factors for bi-polar disorder; I had all of them, including the child sexual abuse and head injuries. I realized that both software and hardware issues could be at the base of my overall predicament. I also soon came to recognize the role of drugs, both pharmaceuticals and street, as predisposing factors to many of my symptoms.

I wondered and worried about the hardware issues that came by way of physical head injuries. By the time I was in second grade, I had so many scars on my head that my teacher questioned me about it. I had cracked my head open a dozen times and had stitches put in on several occasions. The school counselor set up a meeting with my parents to discuss the possibility of abuse. The truth was, I had received these injuries through wild child play, from football in the streets, to bicycle accidents and rock fights with the neighbors. We didn't wear helmets on bicycles back then. Heck, we didn't even have seat belts in our cars! It was a rough and tumble childhood.

The worst head injury I would endure came at about age 18. I had a Yamaha 175 dirt bike, and I was warming it up for a ride. My friend had backed his van into the driveway and opened the back doors for me to load my bike. He set the ramp in place while I was taking a quick test run before we headed out. He was standing in the driveway talking to my dad when I had this "brilliant" idea flash through my mind. *I should just ride the bike up the ramp instead of pushing it in!*" As quickly as the idea had arrived, I found myself flying up the ramp; suddenly realizing that the opening looked a lot higher from the ground. I ducked my head down, hoping to clear the upper edge, as I was violently peeled from the bike. The top of my head hit squarely into the upper frame of the door, throwing me into a back flip that ended with me flat on my back on the concrete driveway. The motorcycle went shooting into the van and crashed against the front seats. I was knocked unconscious for a moment and *came to* as my dad and buddy were dragging me into the house. My show-off move had failed miserably, and I slowly came back to conscious awareness, after lying on the living room floor for a couple of hours. I felt like a cartoon character with his head pushed down between his shoulders. It was pretty traumatic, but I eventually got up on my feet and appeared to be okay. There wasn't any obvious need for a doctor visit so I never had a formal evaluation of the injury.

My on-going mental health challenges would prompt me to seriously question the impact of that particular brain injury. In considering my course toward recovery, I felt deeply concerned that the consequences of this lifelong list of multiple head injuries might pose a serious obstacle to my quest for healing. This department seemed beyond my ability to deal with. I had no understanding at the time, of the brain's ability to regenerate tissue or rebuild neurological pathways. I still believed that most of the causal patterns associated with my symptoms were software based, and held a clear understanding of the subconscious as accessible and reprogrammable. I knew that the software patterns could be altered, and felt confident that my mind could be psychologically repaired and restored.

The medical approach was presenting just the opposite. Their answer was the use of drugs to suppress and counteract the symptoms. This approach didn't seem to consider healing as an option. There was no discussion, consideration, or effort to address any underlying issues responsible for creating the symptoms. The medical position was obvious and to the point. Drugs were the answer to everything.

"If you have anxiety…Take a pill! Depressed? Take a pill. Don't concern yourself with the beliefs, thoughts, or feelings that are creating it. Why defuse the bomb when you can simply buy our drugs… forever! Don't worry about side effects… we have pills for that too!

And don't forget… you can trust us… WE ARE THE DOCTORS."
Wow, as sick as this is, it seems to cover it.

It was frustrating and difficult to understand how so many thousands of highly educated individuals could fall prey to such a dysfunctional approach to mental health while a first year college student could easily decipher this clear equation. This wasn't coming from a genius mind; it was a very simple, straightforward observation. The answers were in the 101 level college textbooks, and they simply weren't being implemented.

As I continued to study the DSM-IV, I came to discover another classification called, *Chemically Induced Mood Disorder*. The symptoms were very much the same as the ones listed for *Bipolar Disorder*. The only difference was that one was induced through drug use, while the other occurred without ingestion of chemicals or mind-altering substances. This was a huge breakthrough for me. I had smoked pot regularly since I was fourteen, and had also been known to drink alcohol to excess. I had experimented with cocaine, LSD, psychedelic mushrooms, as well as many other pills, including amphetamines. I was a '70s kid, and I was not secretive about my drug use. I couldn't comprehend how this factor was missed in my diagnosis.

I soon came to understand that a proper mental health diagnosis could not be given to a person under the influence of drugs or alcohol. This made perfect sense to me. How could you evaluate somebody's mental health accurately while they were intoxicated or on mind-altering drugs? It turns out that a person should be clean and sober for six months to do a proper evaluation. This certainly wasn't the case for me or anybody else I'd ever seen diagnosed for mental health issues. *"Why was I misdiagnosed in such an obvious manner?"* The deficient methodology seemed to result from something much deeper than ignorance. It was as if the system itself made no allowance for an effective approach.

So here I am, stepping into being my own physician and making huge advances in my understanding right from the get go. At times I would actually find myself feeling like, *"This is ridiculous... it's too easy. The errors are so incredibly blatant that it blows my mind."*

I took a Pharmacology 101 class that helped me understand a great deal about drug abuse, particularly the impact of long-term marijuana use. My ears perked up with this subject, because it related very directly to my personal issues. My pot smoking began at age 14, and over the years developed into a serious habit that I relied on, for sleep, as well as getting through the day. What I hadn't realized was how it contributed to psychotic thinking, which was exactly what I needed relief from.

The active ingredient, THC is oil based. The oil tends to store in the fatty tissues, unlike a water soluble substance like vitamin C that passes through your system. The largest fatty

146

tissue in the body is the brain, which becomes the primary dumping ground for storing the THC. It is cumulative and after many years this stored oil becomes an observable white coating on the brain. My pot smoking history was severe, and I felt certain that this could be a powerful contributor to my psychotic thinking. This was like a neon sign flashing in my mind's eye, and a major piece of new and valuable information. It was easy to see the correlations and exciting to discover answers to questions I'd carried for years. It was also scary to consider the changes I would need to make to utilize these discoveries.

One of my doctors had actually said to me at one point, *"Just between you and me, you are probably better off smoking the pot than taking the pharmaceutical drugs."* This may have been true, but did he understand the nature of the long-term repercussions? I was already well aware of the fact that the psychotropic drugs were damaging, but I now knew that marijuana was also an obvious part of the problem. I was convinced that this might very well be one of the most obvious and significant contributing factors to my on-going mental health issues. If this self-evaluation was accurate, the conversion was within my reach, and I was driven to discover the truth. The obvious approach to fully comprehending this significant factor was to experience life without weed. My sheer determination won out, and when I quit *cold turkey* I came to a deeper understanding of this slang term. It was definitely not a party. I've heard folks boldly proclaim that pot isn't addictive. Well, I beg to differ, my friend. It was a miserable and tormenting experience to stop after 22 years of habitual use.

After a week of night terrors and cold sweats, you would have believed I was coming off heroine. Going through withdrawals was painfully torturous, but I finally made it through the suffering, and soon found myself feeling better with each passing day. It can take up to a year to completely flush the THC out of your system; as the year crawled by I gradually discovered deeper peace of mind and greater clarity in my thinking. The psychotic thought patterns subsided to a large degree and it proved to be an enormous step in the right direction. I had friends that continued to smoke pot regularly without any obvious issues involving psychotic thinking, and I realized that everyone's system is different. I wasn't trying to heal the whole world... just me.

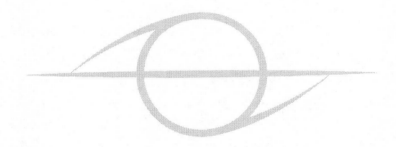

Chapter 22

❧ the gate ❧

Your vision will become clear only when you can look into your own heart. Who looks outside, dreams; who looks inside, awakes.

—Carl Jung

My next major revelation came by way of a class called *Being Man*. It was focused on the Men's Movement, of which I had no previous awareness. There were two books for the class, *Iron John* by Robert Bly, and *King, Warrior, Magician, Lover* by Gillette and Moore. The enthusiastic teachers, as well as both of these books, guided my path toward healing in an entirely new direction.

One of the primary teachings I came to appreciate, was that men had developed the habit of experiencing initiation into manhood over thousands of years. Every tribal or primitive culture preceding our so-called civilized society had incorporated some kind of ceremony and intentional experience of moving from being a boy, to being seen and recognized in the community as a Man. It was suggested that the need for a ritualistic event to trigger this psychological shift was deeply ingrained in the collective psyche, and might very well be encoded in our DNA. The symptoms, presented as a by-product of not experiencing this much needed event, fit me to a tee. As I was approaching forty, I still felt like an immature boy inside. I was thrilled to see that the emotional maturity I was seeking might very well be attainable after all.

I was introduced to Jungian Psychology in a grand fashion through the *Gillette and Moore* book. The main archetypes that were being presented were the King, Warrior, Magician and Lover, and they would eventually evolve and rise to rule my inner kingdom. These archetypes were a blue print of sorts within the collective unconscious of humanity. They each held certain patterns that were characteristic of a particular aspect of the mature male psyche. This book served as a guide to understanding the ways that the immature patterns showed up, and like a road map, pointed the way to the healthy psychological model. The practice and process for developing these immature patterns into healthy ones was referred to as *inner work,* and this would soon become a focal point in my life for many years to come. The term that was used to delineate the immature and dysfunctional splits from the ideal archetype was *The Bipolar Shadow.* This was a new, brightly shining star in my night sky, and it seized my attention immediately. It was the first reference to the term *Bipolar* that had made any sense for me at a deep psychological level. It would take me years of study and experiential learning to fully digest what I could see hidden in the pages of this literary treasure.

Carl Jung had effectively introduced the idea of the *collective unconscious* and *the shadow* to the masses, and these incredible concepts became central to my understanding of the psyche and how it was, once again, interrelated with the whole of humanity. I was fascinated by the potential for emotional healing through this hidden portal, and anxiously set out to find a men's group.

My teacher was enthusiastic and helpful as he directed me to a local *gathering of men* that was explicitly created for this approach. I attended a few meetings and found it rather refreshing, as well as comforting, to sit with men that were focused on inner work. It was very much about embracing the shadow; the part of us where all that we had suppressed, repressed, ignored and denied was hiding out. The focus was on becoming conscious of the many thoughts, emotions, and dysfunctional beliefs that were running behind the scenes. To discover a dysfunctional or immature pattern in the shadow, and bring it into the light of conscious awareness, would frequently lead to discovering what had set that particular dynamic in motion. Oftentimes, the event through which the emotional wounding initially occurred was revealed as we practiced facilitating processes that ultimately delivered deep resolution and healing. It was generally easy to see how a dysfunctional pattern had been supported through the years. I was fascinated by the complexity of how each man's life played out.

The work was utterly amazing to witness and extremely uplifting to experience. I signed up for and attended the group's initiation retreat weekend. It was a powerful transformation that brought an enormous shift to my life. As odd as it sounds now, I finally had the sense of being an adult. It was everything and more than I had hoped for. Something deep within my heart and soul had entered a new territory. It was notably enjoyable to be in the company of caring, intelligent men, including older men who I respected. The idea of Elders who had wisdom to share was a foreign concept until now. I was not accustomed to being in the company of wise elders. This was certainly new territory and a highly unusual experience.

Most of my emotional wounding had come by way of being raised by a very emotionally immature father that was more interested in teaching his boys to fight than to love. My conditioning began very early and much of my work would fall within this department. I remember at age five, coming home from my first day of school. I was crying to my mother and telling her how the other kids had been mean to me and were pushing me around. When my dad got wind of this, he came stomping in and gave me a strong scolding. I remember looking up at this six foot one, two hundred and some odd pound, enormous figure looming over me and shouting, *"Don't you ever come home whining again! If somebody pushes you... push them back harder! If they hit you... punch them in the nose! You fight your own fights!! I don't want to hear it again!"*

As a five year old, I was terrified, and the trauma obviously left a powerful impression to leave me with this vivid memory so many years later. I took the scolding to heart and never came home whining again. I did, however, spend many hours with school counselors and was often sent to the principal's office. I was kicked out of classes and even out of school several times for fighting, but never again came home complaining. In credit to my father, he was consistent. He seemed quite content with the fighting and never judged me as wrong for it.

The other prominent male figure in my family was my brother. He was two years older, bigger, stronger, and smarter than me in those days. We shared the same aggressive, emotionally abusive, and often downright mean dad. My punishment and abuse was only magnified through being the second son. My brother seemed to take the brunt of our father's abuse and like him, was more than willing to pass it along. I guess I made a good punching bag, so when they say it rolls downhill, I can attest to that perspective. My mother would cry and make it obvious that she didn't approve of the abusive nature of my father, but never did anything to bring it to a halt.

I remember being kicked repeatedly from behind, as I fearfully scrambled on my hands and knees toward my room. I recall being grabbed by the scruff of my shirt and my little body pounded against the ceiling as the floor appeared to be twenty feet below. A backhand to the face was standard practice, and being welted with a leather belt was customary in those days. This is a strange way to treat a child you claim to love, and certainly not easy for a kid's mind to translate. Hell, even the teachers at school would beat our butts with a wooden paddle. They went as far as drilling rows of holes in the board to get a good swing while preventing the air from cushioning the blow. It was also quite common to have the paddle displayed on the wall in the classroom. These common practices seem absurd and bizarre, looking back from a day when this behavior is considered a crime. I was being beaten into submission and forcibly molded into the macho character my father had come to idolize in the movies. It seemed I was destined to become a custom-made version of this John Wayne persona, which after all, was my namesake.

Chapter 23

❧ pandora's box ❧

The fact is that people are good. Give people affection and security, and they will give affection and be secure in their feelings and their behavior.

— Abraham Maslow

To sit among a group of men who were compassionate, caring, and focused on modeling emotional maturity was a one hundred and eighty degree turn for me. A deep sense of relief and hope came along with the many great insights and personal revelations delivered through this work, and believe me, it was definitely work. It took a great deal of courage and serious effort to look within, and be willing to experience these feelings that were so unpleasant to reclaim. I was led to recall memories and to feel the associated pain that had been repressed and stored in the far reaches of my troubled mind. It was as though we were deliberately opening channels for the fiery lava to flow out peacefully, rather than waiting for the volcano to blow. I came to understand intimately through experience, *The Shadow* that Jung spoke of.

This ugly stuff had been shoved into Pandora's Box for a reason, and the layered pile was high. It wasn't easy to open the lid and face the barrage of demons, skeletons, and ghosts that lurked in the darkness of this unconscious mind. The support and guidance was a necessity, and I couldn't imagine being able to do this work alone. With professional training, I learned the art of facilitating another man's process, and found it equally rewarding to realize I could be of help to others, who each suffered in their own unique way. I enjoyed weekend retreats that were specifically designed for training facilitators. It fit well with my hypnotherapy background, and it became obvious that the answers to healing these deep emotional wounds were embedded within this work.

Ironically, the hurt and confusion that I intentionally accessed was exactly what the drugs were designed to hide. The drug therapy was supposed to numb the mind and suppress the feelings, so as to bring relief from the emotional pain that was overflowing and spilling out into the conscious mind. The medical model was a very shortsighted approach to dealing with the hurt that could no longer be contained or repressed. The alternative approach that I had stumbled upon made much more sense and became my greatest hope for salvation. It brought forth healing in the deepest stratum of my psyche and continued to expand for years to come.

Through this exploration, I discovered an international organization that was focused in the same way, and entered the community through their own version of an initiation weekend retreat. The next few years allowed me the opportunity to attend various trainings and retreats affiliated with this community. They primarily focused on relationships and leadership training, which introduced an expansive opportunity for continued growth and healing.

A core element in this highly disciplined men's work was *conflict resolution*. It became apparent through my years of training that this was the most important lesson to be found on this crazy planet. I was humbled to realize that conflict was inevitable, particularly in intimate and family relations. If conflict was a given in this world, it wasn't the real issue. The obvious problem was the lack of knowledge and inability to create healthy resolution. That problem was extremely common, due to the neglect in understanding the importance of this essential step. I'd never heard of anything relating to *conflict resolution*, except a fist fight, growing up. Apparently, it wasn't recognized as important enough to mention.

The equation that was flashing before me now was that... conflict plus resolution equaled a deeper connection, or intimacy. It was a solid mathematical statement. Conflict actually represented an opportunity for deepening intimacy with someone that cared enough to pursue it. To recognize the benefits that could come through dealing directly with the conflict, made it obvious that it was a gift, when followed by healthy resolution practices. It no longer appeared as a negative.

However, it was easy to see the impact of the overwhelming social ignorance in this department, and how it commonly developed into *neglect* on a grand scale. From marriages to families, social groups, and all the way out to deadly and devastating wars between nations, our collective ignorance and neglect were creating a costly toll. Conflict resolution was, without a doubt, the key to healthy relations of every nature, and a required stepping stone on the path to peace.

There were weekly group meetings in this growing community that allowed for a fairly constant focus on inner work of a personal nature. This was helpful for integrating new perspectives and allowing the healing to settle in. I spent six years of consistent involvement in the men's work, which I began in 1996, just before I turned forty. It seemed that I was twenty years behind schedule in finally being able to experience life as a mature adult. This was an enormous shift that brought a deep sense of inner peace, confidence, and mental clarity.

Ten years earlier, at age thirty, in a mental hospital I had finally cracked open and admitted to the sexual abuse in my childhood. It didn't happen through any therapeutic process, but rather came as a natural psychotic breakdown. The secret had finally been revealed. It was one of the dark demons that had been locked away, and I'd somehow been able to contain it until then. I still remember the blank look on my parents' faces when the counselor had convinced me to tell them in person. I couldn't tell if they were in shock, didn't believe me, or already knew. It was deeply disturbing to feel such a lack of response. It troubled me for years to come. I found myself wondering if it was all some evil scheme that had been knowingly allowed or set up.

Terrible scenarios like this can take a confused and psychotic mind even deeper into mental illness. It was no wonder that child sexual abuse was considered a pre-disposing factor to so many mental health disorders. It was an overwhelming and obvious central theme to my inner work. The guilt, shame, and deep confusion left an imprint that worked like a computer software virus, eating at the core of any sense of well-being or stability.

One of my initial processes in the men's work was dealing with the deep-seated anger and hurt that emerged through not being protected by my parents. I also held a deep anger around the fact that my father had instilled such fear in me as a child, that I was unable to approach him with my dilemma.

The sexual abuse had begun when I was seven, and I had no idea that I was even a sexual being when the first offense occurred. My brother and I had set up a tent in the backyard and were given permission to take sleeping bags out to spend the night. We had settled in as night fell and were already drifting off to sleep when our "good friend" came crawling in between us. There were no words exchanged as he casually and slowly reached his hand down into my bag far enough to touch my genitals.

The most remarkable aspect of the event was the stunning effect that it had on my mind. I was utterly and literally dumfounded. What physically took place seems minimal. It was perhaps a few minutes of fondling at most. I wasn't mature enough to be sexually aroused. However, I was old enough to feel stunned into a state of bewilderment. My mind was unable to process what had occurred and my feelings went completely numb.

I recall my state of awareness the following day as being lost in a dense and heavy fog. This traumatic experience left an impression that was reinstated repeatedly for several years. That blank mind and numb sense of being, would overcome me many times as I frequently found myself stupefied in a pool of confusion and shame. Sexuality was foreign territory to me at that time, and the incestuous abuse secretly continued for years. The accompanying guilt and shame that was continually generated was buried so deeply that it became the background and foundation for my general sense of being in the world.

When I was old enough to hear derogatory comments like *faggot* or *homo*, I found myself secretly wondering if I was one of them. After all, I couldn't deny that I'd been in sexual relations with a man. The hateful tones that accompanied the name-calling made it clear, this was a despicable form of humanity, and I already knew what it felt like to be that. *"How long could I keep my secret hidden?"*

I was grateful and felt fortunate that my experience had been one-sided. His compulsion as a pedophile was toward oral sex and by the grace of God never persuaded or forced me to do anything to him. I believe it might have been more traumatic and difficult to face had it been otherwise. Even so, my mind was severely twisted in the area of sexuality.

As a young teen I had doubts about my pose as a heterosexual. Was I actually gay? I had been homosexually tainted long before I'd touched a girl sexually. The truth of the matter was that I had been masterfully groomed to the point where I actually learned to enjoy it. That's where the serious challenge with deep-seated guilt came into play. To accept that it actually felt good was a disturbing position to admit to, and even more difficult to deny.

The confusion was very ingrained, and it would take years to fully comprehend that my natural attraction had always been for women. It also took time and effort to accept that some men were just wired differently, and that I had no reason to feel threatened by them. It was a serious stretch for me to finally realize and accept that there was a big difference between a homosexual and a pedophile.

In my teen years I saw them as one and the same, and my wounding came out as a hatred for all homosexual men. I would eventually discover that a great deal of the hatred was a compensation for the shame, upset, and insecurities I had around my own homosexual history. As I successfully healed my emotional wounds related to sexuality and the confusion subsided, I was able to accept others as they were, regardless of their sexual preferences.

One exception has remained when it comes to the acceptance of others' preferences. To this day, I am unable to view adults that want to have sexual relations with children as acceptable. Through my wounding, I have come to believe that children are not equipped mentally or emotionally to deal with sexuality, and to violate this innocence is criminal in my eyes.

Through many hours of devoted introspection, I came to realize that my deepest hurt and confusion revolved around the primary wounding associated with my lack of trust for my father. After all, the sexual abuser was his best friend, and he'd been intimately involved with the family long before I was born. This undercover pedophile was a friendly and loving figure in my early childhood that ranked right up there with Santa Claus and the Easter Bunny. He would bring us gifts and make us laugh. His gentle, kind, and loving manner would be the ticket to the trust required for the success of his sexual advances. He was quite the opposite of my stern and generally abusive father.

My lessons in trust would run deep as the realizations came to light around this twisted dynamic. The abusive father figure would eventually turn out to appear as the one truly out to protect me, while this loving, kind, and gentle male figure would inflict the deepest wounding of my life. As I came to look closely at this distorted view, I realized how I'd grown unconsciously fearful of gentle, sweet natured men, who represented the seductive and secretive abuser. At the same time, the loud, aggressive, and outwardly mean individuals would bring me a false sense of security. This was a stunning realization. Looking even deeper, I could see how I had taken on abusive behaviors, in an attempt to fit into the trustworthy category I'd unconsciously created. I did not want to be affiliated with the gentle, loving, and caring character that appeared suspect, according to my unconscious calculations. What a complex mess I was discovering!

How sad to see so clearly how my development had grown twisted while my behavior had become hurtful and destructive. I realized that my heart and mind had flip-flopped intermittently, between my aversion to gentle spirited men, and my fear of the combative ones. I was confused in a highly contorted way, and it seemed to align well with the overall recipe for a bipolar mind set. My psyche was compartmentalized, fragmented, and quite obviously, I had some serious work ahead of me. I was so grateful to have found a path to resolving the underlying issues that wreaked havoc in my life and could see the potential of eventually defragmenting my emotional hard drive.

Chapter 24

❧ what a human needs ❧

All the evidence that we have indicates that it is reasonable to assume in practically every human being, and certainly in almost every newborn baby, that there is an active will toward health, an impulse towards growth, or towards the actualization.

—Abraham Maslow

My studies in college continued to open doors to new areas of learning. I was exhilarated to hear of Abraham Maslow's hierarchy of human needs. It was an enormous relief to realize that many of the needs I felt in my personal life were not unique to me. There was no longer a reason to blame myself, or feel bad about having a strong desire for a sense of love and belongingness in my life. It was easy to understand that this was a human need, and I just happened to be one of them.

I also came to recognize self-esteem as a reflection of the esteem of others. This was a major shift in my awareness. I had not realized that my feelings about myself had any connection to how others felt about me. I could suddenly see how my self-esteem was heavily influenced by the judgments, opinions, and emotions that others held. It became obvious that I could impact my own feelings of esteem by seeking out people that viewed life in a positive light, while avoiding those that held onto hurtful negative perspectives. This was a long-term challenge as I found my own family to be among those that held many undermining views, especially when it came to my personal circumstances.

Much of the resistance was due to the prevailing judgment of me as *non-compliant* from a medical perspective. Even my best friends were influenced by this overriding and faulty viewpoint. The idea that they shared was, *"If you really cared about yourself... you would just take the drugs and be content."* This wall of ignorance overruled any logic, as it was backed by an entire society that trusted in the unquestionable position of the so-called medical experts. It felt like an enormous cosmic comedy, but the joke appeared to be falling on me for decades. There is great power in numbers regardless of the ignorance or insanity those numbers stand for.

The more intently I studied this twisted dynamic, the more obvious became the need for a marked change. I used this knowledge to intentionally find my way into groups of people that were primarily positive, as well as genuinely loving and caring. Unfortunately, it isn't as easy as it sounds. I also came to realize that people, in general, seemed to carry optimistic or pessimistic views on life as a whole. Whether a person influenced my self-esteem in a positive or negative manner often had absolutely nothing to do with me. Although, it did very much relate to my choices in the company I should keep.

I never did find the courage or the strength to break away from my family of origin completely, nor did I feel that this was an essential step in finding my own path of healing. I did, however, discover that distance could be extremely valuable, and I was able to create new dynamics within the family relations by way of separation.

Through the self-esteem teachings, I could understand how my father's dysfunctional and hurtful ways of treating his family were merely a reflection of his own low self-esteem. His lack of self-love was projected out upon the rest of us, and his personal issues had been allowed, or enabled, to radiate out through the family circle. My mother's inability to stand up to him was a reflection of her esteem issues, and also served as a mirror to the children. We, in turn, had been impacted directly by our parental influence, and reflected their combined esteem issues, each in our own way. This was a grand example and a beautiful display of the domino effect, *"Line 'em up… and watch 'em fall."*

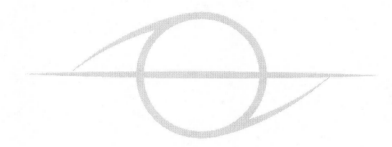

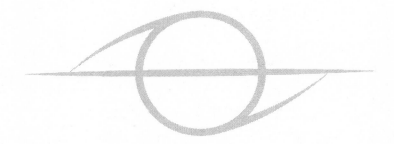

Chapter 25

✎ the ultimate goal ✎

If you plan on being anything less than you are capable of being, you will probably be unhappy all the days of your life.

—Abraham Maslow

P erhaps the most powerful lesson that came through the Maslow teachings was the realization that the ultimate goal in life is to *self-actualize*. The recognition of self-actualization as a need, rather than a luxury, was a real eye-opener for me. I was absolutely fascinated by this revelation. No wonder the general population seems so disappointed in life. How many folks, like me, were unaware of this monumental requirement? To have a genuine and innate need to fully develop, without an effective way to pursue fulfilling it, would certainly leave a large number of folks discontented, to say the least. I now had a new goal in life, but a daunting question overshadowed this brilliant lesson. Why was only two percent of the population expected to attain this level of personal development? Perhaps this question relates to the number of people who realize the importance of this target, and actually choose to aim for it. I was determined to be among that two percent.

The theoretical model was laid out in pyramid form, as so many human models are. The physiological needs for basic food and shelter were at the base. The second level was safety and security, and the third was love and belongingness. The fourth was self-esteem, or the esteem of others, and self-actualization as the fifth level, was the cap. The many layers of need, preceding this ultimate goal, were foundational to this quest for optimum development. Once a person had secured the first level of food and shelter, they could move their primary focus to safety and security. From there, the love, belongingness, and esteem could be put in order to ultimately place one in a position to achieve a state of self-actualization. This state of *self-actualization* appeared to be the pinnacle of personal development. I imagined it as the *flowering*, or the completion of an individual's full *blossoming*, into the unique being they were designed to be. It sounded a lot like the state of *self-realization* that Paramahansa Yogananda spoke of, as well as the state of *enlightenment* that was encouraged through the Buddhist teachings.

The overall philosophy was totally captivating and seemed to line up quite nicely, except for one little glitch from where I stood. I'd been shown a similar model at a seminar in Seattle back in the mid '80s by a man named Joseph Dominguez. The problem emerging for me was that these two formulas appeared to be in perfect opposition. Joseph's oral presentation was called *Transforming your relationship with money and achieving financial independence*. He eventually put this course into a book form entitled *Your Money or Your Life*, and it became quite popular. It was a new perspective and applied directly to many of my money related struggles.

The model he presented was also in pyramid form, like Maslow's, but reversed. He had spirituality at the base, followed by mental, then emotional, with the cap being physical, or the material realm. His theory suggested that if a person were to establish a solid spiritual life, along with a well-balanced, healthy mental-emotional sensibility, the physical realm would easily fall into place. In other words, the financial aspect of modern day living could naturally manifest, given a strong healthy base to place it on. His message was powerful and undeniably indicated the spiritual foundation as a top priority.

I was a bit confused as I intuitively compared this model to Maslow's teachings, which were standard college course material. I was beginning to doubt the opposing model until one day it hit me in a deeper way. I had a sudden realization that this model held a direct correlation to the teachings of *Christ*. Specifically, *"Seek ye first the kingdom, and then shall all else be added unto you."* This teaching also held the inner spiritual kingdom as the top priority. *Seek ye First* made the priority level clear, and this teaching also suggested that the rest of life would easily fall into place, once the spiritual kingdom was in order. *All else* was pretty darn inclusive.

It was evident that Joseph and Jesus were saying the same thing, yet Maslow's oppositional theory seemed equally valid. *"How can I feel balanced... or at ease mentally, emotionally, or spiritually... if I'm homeless and hungry?"* Having had experience with not having my basic needs met, I could relate to the obvious challenge in being spiritually centered from such a position. I did not see myself sitting comfortably in prayer or meditation, or even *at ease*, with a gnawing sense of starvation and a deeply disturbed mind. Certainly, I would need to find food, shelter, and safety, before I could concern myself with personal development. I could see how Maslow's model made perfect sense, and at the same time recognize the truth and value in the opposite view. The most obvious issue with Maslow's view, was that folks could spend a lifetime caught in the vicious cycle of getting material stuff in order to feel good about themselves, and never quite get to the neglected spiritual piece at the core of their life experience. The person who was sacrificing their spiritual wellbeing, to gain ground in the material world, could easily be on a path of destruction. There was an obvious split in this continuum, and the confused society that surrounded me appeared to be caught up in the mix.

Chapter 26

❧ a material world ❧

All the gold which is under or upon the earth is not enough to give in exchange for virtue.

—Plato

The priority of the masses, like Maslow's teachings, appeared to be focused on the material realm. Most folks were centered on working for money with the primary purpose of getting the physical aspect of life in order. Beyond food and shelter, it was easy to get caught up and ultimately lost in the game of buying happiness. This out of balance approach to *making a living* supported and aligned with a capitalistic society, that played a powerful role in maintaining this highly materialistic perspective.

The mental, emotional, and spiritual aspects of life seemed to be secondary for the standard American. Sacrificing the inner kingdom, and even happiness, to make a buck, was terribly typical. On the other hand, there were rebellious folks that totally sacrificed the materialistic world of striving for the almighty dollar, in pursuit of sanity and perhaps even joy. Some of them were fortunate enough to find their way into a monastery, or a communal situation where they were free to pursue a spiritually based existence while still having food and shelter provided. Others ended up living in a cardboard box under a bridge in the middle of some highly polluted metropolis. Still, I fantasized that somewhere on the planet, people had created a community which was thriving off the grid, in alignment with the highest model for healthy living. I've never seen it but firmly believe in the potential of this possibility.

As I contemplated these two models, they continued to appear as opposite ends of the spectrum. Each was extreme in its own way. They both seemed out of balance from the opposing perspective. I felt certain I could find a happy middle ground that capitalized on the value of both paths. It became obvious that the solution was in following these two models simultaneously, and I soon wrapped my mind around this complex mission. *"I will create my own bipolar path, down two roads that lead in opposite directions. Perfect. Right up my alley. This is the answer!"* My journey thus far left me accustomed to being yanked from one world to another. I was either taking drugs to numb my mental, emotional, spiritual being while working for money, or I was dealing with a flighty spirit that would break free, in search of something beyond the mental-emotional pain I encountered in the *normal* work-a-day world.

I needed to integrate these opposing approaches, and this inclusive two-fold path was the only solution I could see. I would keep my spiritual focus and my mental-emotional health as a top priority, while pursuing the means by which my basic bodily needs would be covered. One was an inner focus, while the other was outward, as if I were two separate beings. The physical body had obvious needs, but so did my heart and soul. This appeared complex in the beginning but was really quite simple as I gradually pulled it together. I soon came to the practical realization that it was a lot easier to draw on paper than it was to implement in my life.

I discovered that most of my daily living was an unconscious routine; not just the doing, but the thinking as well. Looking back, it seems that I was generally half asleep, and even more so when I was drugged. A primary challenge that frequently pulled me off course was an underlying resentment I carried for living in such a highly dysfunctional world. I struggled to let it go. *"What did I do to deserve this? How did I end up here? How could I ever find a peaceful mind and a happy heart, immersed in a world revolving around greedy children sitting at a monopoly board?"* I was very angry for feeling forced to play a game that I found so distracting and pointless, not to mention globally destructive. I recall an appropriate saying that came to me just when I needed it most, *"Holding resentment toward someone... is like taking poison and waiting for the other person to die."* I knew this wall of resentment was only hurting me. I was determined to find my way to forgiveness. Recognizing and accepting that I was the only one responsible for my choices, and truly not a victim, was the key to letting go of the undermining negative feelings. As usual, I could see that I had a lot of work ahead of me.

I carried these teachings with me through the many years to come. I gradually found myself moving in a good direction with the process of integrating these oppositional models. I focused on maintaining spiritual integrity through prioritizing my mental-emotional state of wellbeing, while continuing to take the physical actions required for meeting my basic financial needs. This effort would ultimately bear fruit, and I was grateful for both of these comprehensive perspectives.

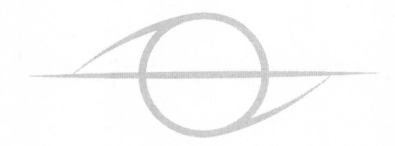

Chapter 27

❧ systems ❧

The strength of a nation derives from the integrity of the home.

—Confucius

Another powerful shift in my understanding came through a family therapy class. It was here that I was introduced to the systems theory. This approach fit nicely with the Maslow teachings and appeared to tie directly into the self-esteem lessons. The idea behind this modality was that an individual's symptoms were actually indicative of dysfunction in the family system or larger group. Rather than looking to the individual for the cause, the entire system or group interface is considered.

The theory appeared to me as a visual model much like the electrical system in a home. Each person is wired into the family dynamic that is completely interconnected. What happens within that system impacts every individual, whether they are consciously aware of it or not. It is a deep energetic connection that includes the unconscious realms that are shared. If an individual within the system is displaying severe symptoms, this is the equivalent of a fuse being blown. When a fuse blows, it means there is an issue somewhere in the electrical system. The fuse is designed to blow out and break the current, to ensure that the entire system doesn't go up in flames.

In the same way, within a family system, the individual that blows the fuse achieves the same result. Here too, the overall system is begging for a thorough evaluation. If you don't understand the systemic view, it's easy to blame the fuse and naturally pinpoint it as the problem. The old school approach did just that and set out to treat the individual patient, while disregarding the family as a whole. That's the equivalent of attempting to fix the fuse repeatedly without considering the contributing factors on a larger scale. Imagine your electrician using this method on the wiring of your home. It is certainly not a very professional approach. A temporary fix on a fuse lasts until it blows again, and each incident risks further damage to the system. It also does nothing to change the dysfunctional dynamic that is creating the issue.

When it comes to family therapy, the systems theory is the solution to this drastic oversight. I had witnessed and experienced this model in real life through basic electrical wiring. It was easy to recognize this correlation in understanding through such a practical premise, and I was elated to make this discovery. I expected this knowledge would be the catalyst to educating my family, and together, finding the therapy that would allow us to alter the patterns which were so painfully destructive. I wasn't the only member of the family suffering with mental health issues. Those are not my stories to tell, but it seemed to me that we were very fortunate that I had stumbled upon this precious knowledge.

I was soon to discover an enormous obstacle to this otherwise beautiful proposal. This plan would require my parents being open to hearing this theory for starters. Secondly, it would depend upon their willingness to follow through and implement this knowledge. It would realistically take some sort of effort, and most likely, time and money. Although it was not terribly shocking, it was disturbing and disappointing to find another brick wall where I had hoped for an open door.

The general tone of the response, which appeared as an insurmountable hurdle, went something like this, *"You mean to tell me... that you think your mental illness is our fault?"* How's that for a brick wall? My parents had absolutely no interest in taking responsibility for a dysfunctional family. There wasn't even a hint of willingness to explore the possibilities. What a heartbreaker to feel that you've found the solution to a life threatening issue, only to discover that your cohorts are not willing to listen to reason. They were not interested in attempting to understand a theory that would hold them accountable, let alone make any effort toward creating the change that was so desperately needed. *"Damn!!!"* Once again I was faced with beating my head against a stone wall, or accepting the reality of the situation and moving on. *"This is my problem now, and I will find the solutions, in spite of the uncooperative system that cooperatively created it."* I was frustrated to the core, and it seemed so unfair. *"Who said life is fair... right?"*

There was a deep irony beneath this dreadful family dynamic. Through my schooling, I would come to understand a core principle that made it clear as to what created the difference between a healthy family system and an unhealthy one. In short form, the bottom line was *honest and open* communication. The extent to which these communication channels are open, authentic, and flowing freely, is the degree to which the family system is healthy. Ironically, due to the closed communication channels, I was unable to get the corrections into the system.

As I continued to study, I came to understand that this little family system was connected to, and an integral part of, an ever-expanding network of groups and systems. The systems theory did not stop with one small group. It was all-inclusive. According to Carl Jung, there is a collective consciousness that we all share, and the whole of humanity is a larger system that we're each plugged into. My family was extremely influential in my personal life due to proximity, but it was actually a minuscule factor in the grander scheme of things.

Within the larger system are millions of varied groups that each form smaller systems, intertwined as one. People are grouped by religion, race, nationality, and cultural upbringing. They are grouped by age, gender, sexual preference, socio-economic status, language, fashion, and about every other way that people can be segregated. Within every grouping are sub-groupings, such as denominations within religions, and churches within denominations. In the same way, there are states within nations, counties within states, cities and towns within counties, neighborhoods within cities, and families within neighborhoods. The systemic view is certainly not limited to a single family system.

In my eyes, most groups I'd encountered would show up as dysfunctional. I hadn't witnessed a great deal of healthy functioning when it came to any form of grouping. It seemed that families, churches, cities, and nations were all struggling to function in a healthy way. This world displayed far more upset and chaos than peace and cooperation. A holistic perspective left me with the vision of an endless web of insanity that spanned the globe. The entirety of humanity was included in this mess, each of us contributing to the madness in our own unique way, regardless of our good intentions. It was difficult to be at ease with this unsettling viewpoint, *"Was there no way out?"*

Chapter 28

❧ scout's honor ❧

*We can easily forgive a child who is afraid of the dark;
the real tragedy of life is when men are afraid of the light.*

—Plato

Fortunately, I had grown up with the Scouts playing a major role in my childhood. I started early in the Cub Scouts and transitioned through the Webelos on my way to becoming a full-fledged Boy Scout. The training was serious, and I knew I could survive in the wilderness if I had to. I did have the final word on how I chose to live on this planet. That beautiful truth made me feel much better. I had learned from the best, in the Badger Patrol of Troop 407 in Kent, Washington. This wasn't your typical scout troop. We were at the top of the charts, with ongoing survival training and fifty mile hikes throughout both the Cascades and the Olympics as regular treks. We participated in National, as well as local events that tested our skills in many areas. We were hotshots and the experience was outstanding.

I often toyed with the idea of moving into the wild. It offered my disturbed mind temporary reprieve as I imagined such a soothing escape route. Just knowing that there really was a possibility of getting off the game board gave me a deep sense of relief. I also knew that, realistically, it would mean parting paths with my entire family and every other friend I'd ever known. It would mean walking away from the only lifestyle I was familiar with while adjusting to a whole new way of surviving. Still, it held a powerful attraction that carried me through countless nights of being at the end of my rope.

As sad as it is to admit, I had already developed a suicidal point of view by that stage of my life. It comforted me when I felt completely hopeless. The idea of being trapped forever with no way out was my definition of hell. To realize I always had a way out brought great consolation, as I faced this immense entanglement before me.

I tried not to consider the disturbing notion that beyond the veil might be just as screwed up as here. *As above... so below.* That frightful predicament was more than I could deal with. I held tight to my visions of peaceful and heavenly realms beyond this world. I desperately needed this alluring imagery to carry me through. Survival was more important than dickering about the ultimate truth. My vision of the beyond as glorious was necessary for my continuing this escapade, and I clung to it like a security blanket. My immediate area of focus was in this little three dimensional realm, and my hands were full. With a new awareness of this all-encompassing web of systems permeating humanity, I became attentive to the various influences that I was conscious of, and felt through the many connections I encountered. Some were brighter than others, and it was becoming apparent that sound discernment was essential.

Chapter 29

❧ mind over matter ❧

The world we see that seems so insane is the result of a belief system that is not working. To perceive the world differently, we must be willing to change our belief system, let the past slip away, expand our sense of now, and dissolve the fear in our minds.

—William James

Living in America and being influenced by the media was a huge factor in my life. It was quite obvious this powerful impression could alter one's life experience tremendously, particularly in comparison to someone growing up in a third world country without it. I gradually came to realize how negative the impact of syndicated television was for me. I had been raised in a family that held onto the idea that watching the news on a daily basis was a normal way of keeping up on what mattered in life. We also watched certain TV shows religiously. The toxicity level of television had definitely increased substantially over the years. *Leave it to Beaver, My Three Sons*, and *I Dream of Jeannie* had transformed into violent and sex filled replacements that would have been considered obscene and pornographic a few short decades ago.

The general anxiety level of the characters had shifted away from calm and at ease, to agitated, angry, and violent. The commercials had also become a form of mental sabotage that could bombard anyone into an unconscious state. I suppose that's an effective approach if you want to slip subliminal suggestions in. There was certainly an obvious motive behind this madness.

I turned away from the news reports when I realized these disturbing announcements held no benefit for my immediate life experience. It was obvious that it was a form of mental poisoning, and taking it out of my mind and my life was a major relief. Even so, I still found myself watching other meaningless and mindless garbage. One day, I caught myself cursing the TV, going on and on about how stupid the program was that I had just spent a couple of hours watching. I suddenly recognized the ridiculousness of my accusations, and just as quickly realized that I was actually the stupid one for wasting my time in this way. I finally had to admit that the addiction factor was more than I could handle. I was hooked on this stimulating form of mental trash that filled my mind with ugly thoughts and a hopeless feeling about the world. I came to fully recognize how disturbing it truly was to my overall peace of mind when I finally experienced life without it. This drastic revision brought an enormous sense of ease to my life. I also discovered, as I adjusted to breaking through this addiction, that I had plenty of time for more enjoyable things. The overall impact of taking TV out of my world became immeasurable and extremely beneficial.

Since then, I've been in other people's homes with the TV blaring and quickly remembered how overwhelming the advertising is. I actually believe it is growing much worse as time goes by. Along with noticing that every other commercial was pushing a drug of one sort or another, I was shocked to experience how disturbing it is, being bombarded with such fast paced, flashing imagery and sound. Every bit of incoming stimulus is strategically designed to influence a person's mind to buy a particular product. What a drain on the brain, not to mention the pocket book!

Today's advertising is scientifically advanced and intentionally designed to send the desired message deep into the subconscious mind of the viewer. It is so effective, that there are literally millions of people wandering aimlessly through shopping malls, buying certain products that they just *need* to have. They may not know exactly why, but by God they are going to buy them. The use of sexuality to sell is also obvious and can be overwhelming to the unfamiliar onlooker. God only knows the impact that our covert sexual approach to advertising has had on our youth in the last couple of generations. I would imagine the overflowing statistics on sexual crimes, teen pregnancy, and mental illness would be a good indicator.

My personal mission became one of doing my best to completely unplug from this constant source of upsetting news and consumer based programming. I recognized the AM/FM radio to be another form of unnecessary propaganda and quickly turned away from it as well. I stopped reading the newspapers, and made no effort to keep up with the daily updates of dilemmas, atrocities, and tragedy. I rented movies that I had consciously chosen to watch and listened to CDs that I'd also selected deliberately. The joy of watching movies that I actually wanted to see and listening to music I truly enjoyed, without advertising, was wonderful.

Keep in mind, this was long before Netflix, YouTube, and Pandora came along. It's a total cakewalk today and an encouraging sign of the direction we are headed in. Back then, this transition alone brought an immense sense of freedom and peace to my life. It was strange to see how this choice had never occurred to me before, as I was weaned from the obnoxious advertising that had plagued my frazzled mind for decades. As for the news reports, it was shocking to discover that just interacting with the public was bad enough. It was amazing to realize how informed I was, merely by way of gossip and idle chitchat. *"Did you hear about the hurricane? What did you think of that vicious murder in New York? How about that political scandal?"* Wow! People love to jabber about the horrendous events happening on a daily basis. It's like another form of addiction, being hooked on bad news. Even so, my mind became much more peaceful and at ease, as I shut down the instruments that kept me in a constant state of agitation and upset for so many years.

Chapter 30

❧ god or no god? ❧

God is dead. God remains dead, and we have killed him. Yet his shadow still looms. How shall we comfort ourselves, the murderers of all murderers? What was holiest and mightiest of all that the world has yet owned has bled to death under our knives; who will wipe this blood off us? What water is there for us to clean ourselves?

—Friedrich Nietzsche

I continued to learn and grow in my understanding of the complexities underlying my ill mind. There were many times when I would still find myself unable to cope with the overwhelming sense of insanity. My trips to the mental hospital had become routine. It seemed that every year I would experience being hospitalized at least once. I began to see a pattern that indicated my most difficult time was consistently around the holidays, and I focused accordingly.

I discovered S.A.D. (Seasonal Affective Disorder), and living in the northwest made this an obvious possibility, considering our dismal gray winters. This certainly seemed relevant to my seasonal mood swings toward depression. I happened upon light therapy and looked further into the science behind it. The pineal gland within the endocrine system is impacted by the light entering the optical nerve to the brain. This appeared relevant to my issues. The functioning of the pineal gland also corresponds to the circadian rhythms of the sleep cycles. It was obvious to me that my sleep patterns correlated directly to the bipolar symptoms. This seemed to be another avenue to support my cause. I purchased equipment and found the light therapy to be extremely effective for counteracting the winter blues.

As I pondered this seasonal pattern in connection to the systemic approach, I could easily see how dysfunctional family relations were also a powerful source of my underlying upset. The holidays presented a repeating situation where the energetic exchange was abruptly magnified. This family, that was typically scattered and interacting from a distance, would suddenly come together for Thanksgiving and Christmas. There was a serious lack of healthy connection in the family, and the actual meaning or purpose for the celebrations seemed far from the heart of our gatherings. Our focus was not on gratitude at Thanksgiving nor was the focus on Christ, God, or anything sacred at Christmas.

The childhood years had established the holidays as a *food centered, gift receiving* event. The primary purpose of Christmas was to *GET STUFF*. There was very little acknowledgement in our home of any deeper meaning. As the years rolled by, it became more of an obligation, than an occasion motivated by a genuine desire for loving celebration. You could sense the discomfort and see the uneasiness on our faces. The pressure to *get stuff* and please one another had become more stressful than enjoyable, and the very idea of Christmas had become a serious source of anxiety.

As I explored the history of these family dynamics in relation to religious holidays, I realized that my mother had always conveyed a subtle hint of her faith in God, as she quietly, secretively carried her inner convictions of believing in Jesus. My father, on the other hand, had turned the family away from church and religion before I'd reached the age of being consciously aware of it. There was a prominent and monumental piece missing in this family. Our spiritual foundation was non-existent, and I felt a strong desire to understand how this had transpired.

As a small child, I knew we had attended church regularly, so I wanted to know what had changed. I questioned my dad one day, and he told me a story of how he'd turned away from church when they requested that he pay a tithe. I didn't get the impression he'd put a great deal of thought into this landmark decision, but I recognized it as an enormous turning point for the family. My father's dominant position had shifted the family's religion without any conscious awareness of the impact, and my mother's passivity had, just as unintentionally, fully supported this detrimental move. The influence of the church, which appeared to be healthy and supportive, was no longer a part of our family's development. The choice to leave was supposedly due to financial priorities. The value systems that I associated with this fundamental decision appeared to be extremely important to my quest for understanding the root of this impasse.

Something here had been traded, and I desperately wanted to understand what had created this costly exchange. As young children, we had been exposed to teachings that introduced Jesus as a central figure in our lives. The awareness of God's divine nature had been planted in our receptive, young minds, along with the idea of us being his beloved children. This was a simple platform that provided the opening for a spiritual foundation. What followed was a model with no obvious God involved. I guess the actual cold, hard truth, is that the God that ruled the world I would grow up in, was the almighty dollar bill. This approach appeared to have a label as well, and *Materialism* seemed to cover it.

Living my entire life in mainstream America, I came to recognize that materialism is actually a covert religion of its own. In fact, it's an exceptionally popular religion that appears to be rapidly spreading across the planet. It is so well disguised, that it avoids any sense of competition to the unconscious follower. You can easily maintain your status as a Christian, Muslim, Hindu, Buddhist, or whatever you choose, and have no need to change temples. Very few people ever realize they have succumbed to the cloaked religion of materialism. It is so neatly camouflaged in a modern day lifestyle that it typically goes unnoticed.

Millions of churchgoers bow more deeply to the money game than to a divine, all-powerful, loving God. I hear many words spoken about *faith in God* through a variety of religions, yet collective actions speak in a way that show the greater faith of the majority is still in what money can buy.

The voice of America calls out, *"Maybe those Lilies of the Valley can get by on God's grace, but get real man ... We have an American lifestyle that requires a serious cash flow!"* It is so deeply ingrained, and society is so accustomed to this model and belief structure, that it's rarely acknowledged or even recognized. It takes a serious focus of attention, clear intention, and great effort to break out of such an overpowering mindset. We are drowning in it!

My definition of materialism is when we believe the material or physical realm is more important or valid than the nonphysical realms; where thoughts, feelings, and spirit reside. To place more value in what one accumulates in the material world, than the peace, joy, and love one can experience in the heart and soul, is to bow to the monolith of *Materialism*. This value system recognizes little worth in the spiritual aspect of living, as spirit is not regarded as relevant, applicable, or valid. Love and Joy are considered by-products of this material existence, rather than the bedrock.

We can easily observe our decaying social environment, and recognize the consequences of greater value being placed on profit, than the wellbeing of humanity. This sick and twisted perspective has progressively saturated the collective consciousness of mankind. Many enormous profit-based corporations are willing to sacrifice the health and wellbeing of the people for financial gain. The confused and ignorant masses continue to allow and support these blatantly devastating maneuvers. Our natural earth environment is being sacrificed for financial purposes, and the ramifications of this primitive value system are now threatening our basic survival.

As business entities, it is easy to be programmed to value profit over and above any mission to serve humanity. *We the people* and *taxpayers* inadvertently support this powerful force in the world, even though it is obvious and easily recognized on a grand scale. We are observing this exploitation in the form of social disaster on a global scale, while our planet is being devastated as a direct consequence. The big picture is undeniable and plain to see.

Where it all hits home, and yet is not quite so obvious, is on a personal level of functioning. When an individual chooses that which is financially profitable over what they know to be *for the highest good,* in their own heart, there is a violation of spiritual integrity that carries a heavy price. The inner balance and wellbeing of that poor soul is sacrificed for a temporal, material purpose. On a smaller scale; this is where the global issues begin. Every individual is a cell in the organism we call humanity, which is either thriving spiritually or contributing to the disease. Each individual has an influence and collectively the scale is tipped. Observing this grand matrix we live in, it's easy to point the finger *out there* at *them.* The truth is, every one of us is a part of creating that bigger picture. We all carry a portion of responsibility in the overall movement of humanity toward healthy living.

There is a profound delineating factor between these two religious platforms. One considers the spiritual aspect, or heart and soul of humanity, and one does not. One suggests that personal choices should first and foremost align with *the highest good for all*. The other proposes decisions be based primarily on profitability. From this point of view, it seems there are two distinct and separate value systems. If these opposing perspectives were assigned Gods, one would be from the heart, and the other backed by gold. One creates health and happiness, while the other devours all that is good, for the illusion of profit and gain.

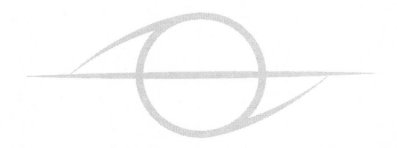

Chapter 31

❦ truth and success ❧

It is health that is real wealth and not pieces of gold and silver.

—Mahatma Gandhi

As I explored these opposing views, I felt as though I was swimming in a sea of madness. It was so obvious that this materialistic value system was backward. The idea of putting your attention and priority on attaining financial wealth, over and above your personal wellbeing, growth, and development, seemed absurd; especially in relation to Maslow's teachings. I had been fortunate to have witnessed the fallacy in this destructive approach firsthand, and perhaps this is how I was able see this misconstrued notion so clearly.

My father had followed the *materialism* path religiously. I'd watched my entire life as he made costly sacrifices to our family, in order to gain the monetary wealth that was supposed to signify *success*. He actually fully succeeded in what he'd set out to do. He became very financially successful, and yet never delivered his family to the Promised Land. Through those many years of *financial success*, the joy of healthy and loving family relations were sacrificed like bloody lambs. The money failed to deliver the happy family that was promised in the fairy tales. It turns out that a healthy, happy family wasn't to be found in a mansion, behind the wheel of a fancy car, or in a shopping mall. The façade that money could buy was merely a disguise that gave the appearance of something that didn't exist.

True success emanates from within and requires no disguise. The suffering that comes through the neglect of the

191

heart and soul of a family is not extinguished by the purchase of prestigious wrapping paper. The real heartbreaker in this story is that this wasn't even my father's idea. He had not designed the value system or the upside down list of priorities he was operating by. He wasn't doing anything unique; he was playing follow-the-leader like so many naïve consumers, as one more lemming in line for the circus ride that appeared to be the only game in town. Our family was *normal*. This outrageous error was merely one of a hundred million scattered across the nation. We didn't stand out in the least. It just hurts more when it's happening in your own home.

The truth is, this is the predominant religion of America today, and perhaps the world. Like a disease, it is spreading at astronomical proportions. We often call it consumerism, capitalism, or Western Civilization, but more often than not, it goes unnamed. It has become such a default mode of operation that it's just considered business as usual. This prevailing perspective is unknowingly taught and the invisible philosophy indoctrinated into the innocent minds of the children of this nation. Those children become the next generation, and the baton has already been handed off. Fortunately, many advanced souls are awakening to this obvious, yet well disguised reality, and discovering or remembering a better way. Will it be soon enough to save this world from total devastation? That is the big question.

If we could really see clearly and understand the ramifications of a value system that promotes war because of the financial advantages, we could begin to grasp the true cost of this underlying tragedy. To recognize the big money connection to the heroin epidemic sweeping this nation, reveals the evil hidden within this socially acceptable mindset. We are living in a world that could easily remedy our most atrocious issues, were we to shift our collective values. This appears to be the major jump in the evolution of consciousness required to survive this god-awful mess we've created for ourselves.

I look to my own father as I ponder this tremendous misfortune and try to understand why a man would hold fast to a sinking ship. To this day, he refuses to acknowledge any error in judgment or consider the possibilities of a higher path. The obstacle seems to be in accepting that he took a wrong turn and failed in the department that matters most. Consider how difficult that is to admit, after a lifetime of devotion to this socially promoted path; having tried so hard to succeed and wanting desperately to believe that you did. The financial statements will verify success if you're small-minded enough to subscribe to such a shortsighted value system. How many worlds would crumble, if those countless subscribers were to face the honest realization, that the love and joy sacrificed along the way were the main ingredients of *true success*?

This astronomical sacrifice often shows up looking like mental health issues within a family. It comes in many subtle forms, such as depression, anxiety, confusion, or a general sense of feeling empty and unfulfilled. In the more extreme forms, the personal overwhelm can appear as a serious form of insanity. Somewhere inside, we know when we are feeling miserable, just as we inherently know the feeling of success. These two postures are not meant to sit in opposition. We are not designed to be fragmented beings that succeed on one level and fail on another. We are created whole and capable of a unified experience as one integrated being that fully thrives. We can either experience happiness and a genuine sense of wellbeing, which is the core essence of true success, or feel the misery that marks our failed attempt at healthy living.

True success is confirmed in the heart. To measure one's success by way of numbers relating to material acquisition, rather than how one feels about the life they are living, is absolutely ludicrous. This is the crux of the exorbitant sacrifice that is undermining the mental health of humanity. We have been collectively sent on a snipe hunt, searching in the wrong place for something that doesn't exist. In the meantime, we've become so preoccupied with this faulty mission that we fail to recognize how strategically we have been misguided.

If we really want to promote mental health and healthy living in our society, perhaps we should begin by teaching our school children the true meaning of *Success*. It's easy to decipher that a life devoid of joy and inner peace has missed the mark, regardless of material or financial achievements. On the other hand, if a person achieves a peaceful and joy-filled life, regardless of financial achievement, would any wise person stand up to call them unsuccessful? I think not.

My journey into the depths of my family's predicament had uncovered a pathway deep into the darkness that undermines a healthy mind. It also made it quite obvious that this was not just a personal dilemma. Perhaps between Sigmund, Carl, Abraham, Jesus, and Joseph, we could collectively find an applicable strategy for healthy living.

Part 5
Out of the Box

"Your children are not your children.
They are the sons and daughters of Life's longing
for itself.
They come through you but not from you,
And though they are with you yet they belong
not to you.

You may give them your love but not your thoughts,
For they have their own thoughts.
You may house their bodies but not their souls,
For their souls dwell in the house of tomorrow, which
you cannot visit, not even in your dreams.
You may strive to be like them, but seek not to make
them like you.
For life goes not backward nor tarries with yesterday.

You are the bows from which your children as living
arrows are sent forth.
The archer sees the mark upon the path of the infinite,
and He bends you with His might that His arrows
may go swift and far.
Let our bending in the archer's hand be for gladness;
For even as He loves the arrow that flies, so He loves
also the bow that is stable."

—Kahlil Gibran

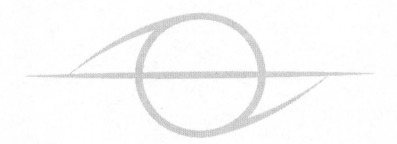

Chapter 32

❧ batter up! ❧

The best and most beautiful things in the world cannot be seen or even touched - they must be felt with the heart.

—Helen Keller

My brief college education was absolutely exhilarating, and I knew without a doubt that I was on the right path. This two year crash course had launched me into a new orbit, and I held an expanded vision for healing my mind and my life. I was wide-eyed about the many variables involved and striving to integrate each of them into the cosmic fabric that lay before me. The *Men's Work* was a powerful foundation that provided a solid footing for disentangling the back-lashed reel I was fishing with. It was effective and potent. Even so, I often found myself needing more than I could get my hands on. It was an absolute gift from God and yet, like a much appreciated stepping stone, it was time to leave that secure position behind and step forward upon a new path. Many beneficial revisions had developed over the years as my life gradually transitioned into a more fitting phase.

I had gone from being married with children, to divorced and disabled. I was doing my best to remain involved in my children's lives but it wasn't easy. My life was in deep disarray, and it was a challenge to function at a level that made our interactions healthy. I am grateful for having had a sense of what healthy was and for caring enough to strive for it. The kids were active, like so many at that age, and keeping up with the sporting events, school plays, musical performances, etc., was challenging. My regularly scheduled weekends were the primary point of connection with my children, and it was central to my life's purpose. Even so, I struggled to keep pace with all of it.

Looking back, I realize that a great deal of my angst was created through the self-generated expectations of what my life should look like. I was severely self-critical as I continued to fall short in my own eyes. My struggle to accept my lot in life was burning deep within my soul, and it didn't make for an easy ride. I did my best to rise to the occasion when my angels were onboard. They have reassured me many times since, that they felt loved and cared for deeply in those days. It was primarily an inward dilemma.

Fortunately, there were many occasions in which I could see how blessed I was by something beyond me. My faith remained, in spite of my continuous follies. As difficult as my daily living had become during that travail of darkness, I knew deep within that I was being carried through.

One of the outstanding events, that hit me like a slap upside the head, was when my son was about 11 years old. He was playing little league baseball, and I was in the depths of my drugged up despair. I had done pretty well with making it to the games, but when I missed one I felt such deep remorse that it was literally painful. I had recently missed a couple of them, not back to back, but within a fairly short time frame. He was experiencing a temporary batting slump, and the two times I'd missed were the games when he'd had a couple of decent slams. He would excitedly share the recaps of those solid hits, and then when I'd show up, he couldn't seem to connect with the ball. It was noticeably upsetting for him, and I was well aware of the frustration he was feeling. I honestly didn't have any need for my boy to be a hotshot on the baseball field; I just wanted him to feel good about himself. Like any red-blooded boy, he wanted his dad to see him hit the ball.

There was a big game coming up, and I was determined to make this one. The opposing team was leading the league, and the pitcher had a reputation that preceded him. Even with my best effort to make the game I still showed up late. I was just getting there as my son was stepping up to bat. It was still the first inning; I hadn't missed anything thus far. I shouted to him as I climbed into my seat in the stands behind the plate. *"Knock it out of the park!!"* I yelled. He heard my voice and turned his head with a smile to acknowledge my arrival. A few pitches and a couple of swings later, he'd been struck out in short order. I felt so bad because it seemed that I'd thrown him off by popping in at the last minute and diverting his attention. He was so angry that he threw the bat, kicked the dirt, and mumbled a few choice words as he basically had a temper tantrum on the long walk to the dugout. It was deeply disturbing to say the least. The coach came over, chewed him out, and pulled him out of the game. I couldn't believe it. *"Dam it! Why couldn't I have just kept my mouth shut?! How did I manage to show up just in time to throw him off... when I so badly wanted him to be inspired by me being here? What a mess!"* I muttered to myself, as I crawled into my self-made pool of guilt and shame.

I went over between innings and talked with the coach. I explained how badly he wanted me to see him get a hit, and the way I had contributed to the moment of upset. He was understanding and yet still needed to follow through with the appropriate consequences for the unacceptable behavior. I couldn't argue with his straightforward thinking. I went back to the stands and sat there dealing with my heartfelt sorrow. My inner dialogue of dragging myself through the mud soon transformed into a solemn prayer; I was pleading with God, *"Please don't make my boy suffer because of me."* I was begging for his chance to have this simple dream fulfilled, by allowing his father to see him get a nice hit.

Overall, the game wasn't lining up the way we'd hoped. The team score was down several runs, and the boys weren't hitting much against this sharp little pitcher. He was fast and had excellent control for this age of play. The coach let a couple of innings go by before he brought my son back in. When it was his turn to bat, and he began to move toward the plate, it was as though the entire earth was caught in my envelope of communion. My heart and soul were devoted to my prayer for his heavenly support. I purposefully yelled again as he approached the plate, *"Hang your tongue out, Jordan!"* I was purposefully diverting his attention this time around. He was a big Michael Jordan fan, and we had discussed the way Michael played ball in such a relaxed manner, that his tongue would hang out of his mouth. I wanted to remind him of that relaxed state and connect his mind to his highly successful hero. He smiled and stepped up to the plate.

What occurred next blew everybody's mind, including mine. The pitcher took the mound and wound up for his first pitch. My son looked as calm as could be as the fastball came burning toward the catcher's mitt. He swung the bat and hit the ball so hard that it cleared the heads of the left and center fielder by a mile, as they went scurrying after it. The crowd came alive again as we all jumped to our feet and cheered. It was an outstanding and memorable milestone.

The most magnificent slice of this momentous occasion was the look on my son's face as he crossed home plate. He looked like he'd seen a ghost! He'd just power-slammed a standup homerun and was in total shock, alongside the rest of the team and the fans. It was utterly phenomenal. It felt like our own little *Angels in the Outfield* encounter. Beyond the initial thrill, he'd also knocked a couple of runners in, which tied the score. The team was so pumped up that they started hitting the ball with a vengeance, and went on to decisively win the game. It was an absolutely magnificent event from where I sat. I was so happy for him and humbled by the power of this prayer that was answered beyond my wildest imaginings. It was an enormous and meaningful turn around for both of us. His attitude continued to reflect that spark of self-worth that had been lit through that simple incident. He had proven himself beyond any shadow of a doubt as a winner in his father's eyes, and I knew how important that was to a young boy. I too, was inspired to feel the self-worth associated with the entire affair. We were both winners now, and I could only thank God from the bottom of my heart. I continued to hold tight to the knowing of the devotion that was behind the veil, waiting to support our deepest needs, and was graciously humbled to the core.

Chapter 33

∽ home sweet home ∾

Peace demands the most heroic labor and the most difficult sacrifice. It demands greater heroism than war. It demands greater fidelity to the truth and a much more perfect purity of conscience.

—Thomas Merton

Along with my endless struggles, challenges, and utter failings there were some pretty big wins. One of the most rewarding endeavors I would ever take on was when I built the home that my kids would eventually grow up in. We had been renting a home in the north end of Seattle during the salon business years, preceding the split-up. During that phase, I discovered a piece of property on a small lake out in the far reaches of the county, and picked it up for a song. Later on when the shit hit the fan and I was sent back to Western State, my wife decided to leave me.

I don't recall the details of the episode, or her upset, as they had all gelled into one big, foggy mess. Her formal reasoning was based on my unwillingness to stay on the drugs. Although I couldn't surrender to the request, I could certainly understand her well-articulated logic. At one point, she'd gone to the minister who married us and asked him if she had an acceptable reason for divorcing. He assured her that she did and even though I didn't approve, it did my heart good to know that she had taken our vows seriously.

When I was released from the loony bin, I found her and our children in an apartment in south Everett. It was not in the best part of town and it troubled me deeply. I was visiting the kids regularly and even though she had been openly dating other guys, the split-up was somehow tolerable. I didn't have a leg to stand on as my chasing around had been in no way acceptable to our marriage agreements. We had not yet established a formal separation, and at one point she made it clear that if I wanted to give it another go, I had better speak up. She let me know that there were other interested parties. It wasn't long before I offered to build a home on the property I'd secured a few years back, and she agreed to us giving it another shot.

That was when the magic began. The project fell together like there were divine beings pulling strings from heaven. It was quite remarkable to go from being drugged up in Western State, to designing and building a home, in the blink of an eye. Every friend and acquaintance who was associated with construction was on board and available to help. I hired a buddy who was willing to act as the general contractor on the project for a flat fee. He allowed me to hire sub-contractors for whatever I chose, as long as he got the framing job. It was a sweet deal and all the subs fell into place, like peas in a pod. Some of my closest friends came through with a level of generosity that was beyond honorable. The completion of this three story waterfront home was perhaps the greatest material feat of my life. The timing was such that the market escalated shortly after beginning to build, and the equity was nearly double the investment as we moved in. It was an outstanding and lucrative maneuver, and I was quite proud of my efforts, as well as my good intentions.

I had close buddies who questioned my thinking when I first mentioned the plan. *"Are you sure you want to build a home for the woman who just left you? Have you considered the odds of this marriage actually surviving?"* and of course I had.

It wasn't about the marriage making it. It was about my kids growing up in an environment that they deserved. I longed for the day I could look honestly into the mirror without being thoroughly disgusted. It was one of the wisest, most rewarding moves I would ever make, and still my buddies were right. The marriage lasted another three years before it crashed hard.

How did I feel about the predictable split-up and inevitable divorce? Terrible... but the subtle twist in the outcome for my kids was colossal. My children weren't confined to a shabby apartment in the ghetto this time. They were in a beautiful rural area with nice schools and a decent neighborhood. They were enjoying fishing, swimming, and canoeing around a secluded country lake, instead of loitering in the back alley of a broken down strip mall. I was well aware of the enormous impact this major shift would have on their future. I thanked God for what I perceived as a rewrite of the script.

A significant portion of my research for understanding the map of my psychological struggles, pointed to the parental influence in my childhood. I couldn't recognize this so clearly for myself, without considering the influence my choices would have on my own children's lives. It felt like I was working from a deficit, but even so I was passionately driven to do my best.

I moved into the city when we first parted paths, but it wasn't long before I found my way back into that scenic rural neighborhood. I didn't move into a new home this time, but rather a beat up old trailer. The contrast was striking, and I can't help but wonder now, if the upgrade I saw fit for my family didn't quite feel appropriate for me personally. It seemed that somewhere deep inside I wasn't finished punishing myself. The wife and children might deserve a new home on the lake, but I wasn't so sure about me. The downgraded situation was sufficient in my eyes, as I knew the nearby location was the most important factor in my children's lives.

This is where I lived when I attended the two year college program. I very much needed for them to know that I wasn't drifting away. For the same reason, after completing my schooling, I opened a hair salon in the local town as they were moving into their high school years. I wanted them to know what I was doing and where they could find me. I had learned through the psychology teachings that these were important elements in a child's life. It appeared to hold true, as they both seemed genuinely pleased with my presence in the community.

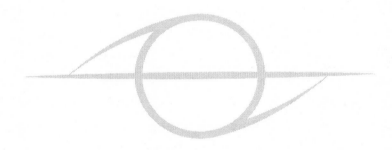

Chapter 34

❧ phoenix rising ☙

The priest wore black on the seventh day and sat stone faced while the building burned. I waited for you on the running boards, near the cypress trees while the springtime turned... slowly into autumn.

— Bob Dylan, Idiot Wind

This salon was not your typical beauty parlor by any stretch. It was a full-scale hair and nail salon with tanning units, massage, and an incredible retail area, front and center. I had modeled the retail portion of the salon after a store in Port Townsend that I was absolutely in love with, by the name of *Phoenix Rising*. It was a dream come true to emulate an environment that I felt so cleansed by and connected with. The salon was also a gracious way for my new wife and me to casually reenter the business world. We named it *Sacre' Voeu*, (which means *sacred vow* in French), *A Salon for the Soul*. It was basically a bohemian, New Age, metaphysical head shop/salon. The funny thing was, we'd opened it smack dab in the middle of one of the most white bread, fundamentalist, redneck, hick towns you can imagine.

We had a large selection of books that ranged from Shamanism and Wiccan, to Hinduism and Buddhism, and everything in between. All of the New Age popular titles were in stock from Deepak to Zukav, and every other kind of spiritual teaching available. We carried channeled work from *Kryon* and *Abraham*, to *Ramtha*, *Seth* and *Bringers of the Dawn*. We had an enormous array of Native American music playing in the background, and an awesome selection available to listen to, as well as purchase. We displayed Native American masks, trinkets and jewelry of an eclectic nature, as well as a wide variety of candles, crystals, and stones of every sort. We had an impressive selection of incense, Celtic tapestries, runes, and knick knacks by the truckload. It was over the top cool.

The quartz crystals had become a cornerstone to my personal work, and having a store to distribute them was more than I'd envisioned. I had been fascinated with crystals from a very young age. My parents bought me a build-it-yourself radio kit as a birthday gift when I was about ten. It was a simple project that involved wrapping copper wire around a small wooden thread spool and connecting it to a dry cell battery. The focal point was a little quartz crystal that acted as a frequency modulator as it moved over the bundle of copper wire. It became the instrument that allowed me to tune into a particular station. This presented an astonishing transmutation to consider as a youngster. *"How could a little crystal, moving over a spool of copper wire... magnetized by electricity running through it... dial in a specific frequency?"* I had no idea, but I was listening to the music as I pondered this mystical event, and it was obvious that it worked.

Later on, when I discovered a connection between the healing arts and quartz crystals; I was already well aware of their distinct and special nature through my exposure to electronics. Through commercial development, they had become standard equipment in radios, clocks, computers, and many other electronic devices. My crystal influence in my childhood allowed me to easily recognize their innate qualities and capabilities. I worked closely with a cherished collection of quartz crystals over the years and found powerful benefits as I broadened my area of play. (I'll share some of those stories in another chapter.)

As I floated between my hairdressing work and managing the store, I discovered there was more going on behind the façade of this storefront than I had consciously considered. I hadn't fully recognized the shadowy feelings beneath this business maneuver until a client questioned me one day while I was cutting his hair. He blurted out, *"Can I ask you a personal question?"* I naturally responded, *"Of course!"* Sincerely, he asked me, *"Is this kind of a big 'fuck you' to the community?"* I pondered his serious question, and casually replied, *"You know, I hadn't really thought about it like that... but now that you mention it, YES... I guess, in a way... it is."*

The only reason I was doing business in this town was to be here for my children while they were engaged in the local school system. I actually despised this place at a personal level. I figured if I was deliberately choosing to be in such a location, it was going to be in a manner that suited me. I was willing to be true to myself, but unwilling to concern myself with fitting into a mold I had absolutely no respect for. At one point, I'd asked a fellow shaman how he felt about the local area, and his response was, *"It feels like a small-minded redneck community .... that was founded on killing Indians and raping the land."* *"Wow"*... I thought, *"That's a strong and vivid response! With that kind of energy, it's no wonder I feel repulsed."*

My feelings were deep and not necessarily based on what I could put my hands on. I knew I wasn't alone in my sense of disgust for the local vibe. Perhaps it was my empathic nature that was picking up on something I couldn't define. Maybe it related to the fact that this town was home to one of the oldest penitentiaries in the state, established in 1910. The city center had formed around the old prison, and I can only imagine that the stagnant juju turns sour after a hundred years or so... ya know. I knew for certain that I didn't resonate with the energy in that town in any way, shape, or form. It definitely wasn't a place where I would hang out without a good reason.

Regardless of the stark dichotomy, our presence had a powerful impact on the community and there were, surprisingly, a good number of folks who were delighted with what we had to offer. We held meditation classes and brought in Native American artists and local Shaman to enact the desired blessings we promised to deliver.

During a ceremony of blessing the salon with my daughter and a dear shaman friend, we looked out the front window to witness a rainbow across the parking lot that was utterly breathtaking. It was so striking that we wondered if we had been mesmerized into a trance state that had us all hallucinating. This brilliant rainbow looked solid enough to climb on, like a golden gate bridge. It was extremely bright, and I had never stood this close to one so luminous. We opened the front door and yelled out to the passersby who didn't seem to notice, *"Hey! Can you see that rainbow?!"* as we pointed it out. Some of the bystanders turned their heads, responding with an emphatic *"YES"*! Even so, none of them seemed as stunned by this spectacular apparition as we were. The timing was too precise to be taken lightly. I'd never witnessed a rainbow like that in my entire life. Apparently, the store had been formally registered with a higher council than the local chamber of commerce.

Many divinely inspired encounters would come through the interactions that randomly took place in Sacre Voeu. One that stands out was when a young woman had come to me and asked about how she should handle her recently deceased mother who was continuously accompanying her. She was looking for a way to release her mother's attachment to her, and it was obvious that this unanticipated issue was bothering her deeply. She felt her mother was better off moving to a higher plane, but unsure as to how to proceed. I agreed, and as we discussed the situation, a piece of jewelry fell inside one of the display cases. It caught our attention, and as we examined more closely, we discovered the piece to be a necklace with an *Eagle* pendant. She shockingly exclaimed, *"That is my mother's totem!"* as she expounded with a few stories of her mother's spiritual adventures. It was a profound incident, and the physical manifestation of this close encounter seemed to have rattled her a bit. She departed the salon a short while later, and to my dismay she'd left something significant behind. Her Mother had undoubtedly remained with me, as her presence was unmistakable. I sat quietly for a moment, astonished by the bizarre situations encountered on a typical day in this mystical theater.

Fortunately, I had acquired some useful tools and a few clues as to how I might assist in a situation like this. That evening, a few of us gathered for a well-designed ritualistic ceremony. With the help of some Epsom salts, rubbing alcohol, and a little fire, we assisted our Eagle spirit friend on her migration beyond the vibrations of the earth plane. Our efforts were successful and our high-minded intentions accomplished, as she crossed over the rainbow bridge into more heavenly realms.

I recall another breathtaking moment that occurred one day as a young woman came bursting through the front door in tears. She was so deeply thrilled to find this type of storefront that her emotions had overwhelmed her. She was from out of town and our sacred presence assured her that she was not as isolated as she had imagined. She spoke of her feelings of disconnection in this new territory, and openly expressed her sincere gratitude for the sanctuary we had created. It was like watching somebody stumble upon a pool of fresh water after crossing the Sahara desert. She was thirsty! It really did my heart good to know that we had provided this space for her and that it carried such a powerful impact.

I also remember a couple of not so pleasant occurrences, even though I must admit I did get a kick out of them. One day, a woman came marching in as though she owned the town, and boldly declared, *"Well... You have crossed some boundaries here young man!"* She looked at me as though I should react like a child being shamed. I thought about it for a second and responded, *"Well thank you for noticing."* She was speechless and far too flustered to consider a second thought. She furiously marched right back out with a few obvious moans and groans. I did have a good laugh over that humorous display. It reminded me of an old *Andy Griffith* show, with *Aunt Bee* scolding one of the guys for misbehaving. It was sweetly hilarious.

Another entertaining incident occurred when a young boy was poking around and inadvertently pulled a paperback from the shelf on *witchcraft*. He was undoubtedly flabbergasted and about shit himself as he scrambled for the exit. I'd have donated a pint of blood to have captured that little escapade on video. It was evident that his upbringing had created this extremely fearful response. Keep in mind, this incident occurred slightly before the outburst of popularity for *Harry Potter*; I guess marketing carries a powerful persuasion.

The greatest blessing to come through this business related adventure was in witnessing other *alternative* healing stores beginning to appear in town during our brief sojourn. It was as though we had broken the bubble of energy that kept this backward town enveloped in a chrysalis state. I maintained this outpost for four years before moving on, which synchronized well with the kids' high school years coming to a close. It was a good run; I felt my time had been well spent, and that I'd accidentally accomplished something much needed at a local level.

Chapter 35

✺ circular insanity ✺

It is better to conquer yourself than to win a thousand battles. Then the victory is yours. It cannot be taken from you, not by angels or by demons, heaven or hell.

— Buddha

During those years between school and running the salon, my general state of mental health had moved largely up the scale, to a more settled and stable position. Even so, my struggles were still disturbing and often times devastating. Much of the difficulty I faced, even though I was making incredible progress, was that I felt pitted against the clock. I wasn't able to resolve the many layers of hidden issues, lying deep within the stored memories of my body-mind, fast enough to prevent the periodic visits to the mental hospital. Each visit felt like I was being dragged back to square one.

I remember reading that mania, or the manic state, was actually the result of a deep denial of depression. That was one of the layers. I had also come to recognize that depression was often a result of unexpressed anger being turned inward. This was an even deeper layer. I could see, like reading a roadmap, how caught I was in this multi-layered predicament. Understanding the dynamics in theory did not, however, override this deep-seated, unconscious, emotional response that repeatedly emerged.

When I was unknowingly holding back my anger to avoid the difficulties that came through expressing it, the contained rage was curiously transformed into depression. When I then decided at an unconscious level that I wasn't willing to experience the depression, the resulting ecstatic mood developed into a manic state. *"Holy Cow!!... What a merry-go-round!"*

All of this theory-based learning seemed to correlate with my experience, as I definitely didn't enjoy the feelings of anger, pain, or depression that I carried in the depths of my psyche. Typically, I would do anything to avoid them, which usually meant internally running from those dark feelings, right back into the egoic mind of the left-brain. This emotional detachment would generate a mania, which was an energized, anxiety-filled version of a self-created façade. I was desperately grasping for at least the appearance of happiness. It was a strange way of acting out and saying very loudly, *"I do not have to feel bad and I can prove it... just watch this!"* This very confused and immature ego-based display was extremely limited in its scope and certainly its longevity. It was a temporary escape from the anger laden, heavy depression that was guaranteed to end with a crash landing.

It was merely a conditioned response, originally designed as a form of avoidance, which had been strengthened through repetition. The neural pathways had been well established. This created a last resort strategy for feeling good, from a very unconscious and shortsighted perspective. Let's just call it emotional immaturity. This major loop on the never-ending rollercoaster ride came at a horrendous price. I felt like Bill Murray in the movie *Ground Hog Day,* as I experienced this repeating pattern in what felt like an endless cycle.

I can't count the many times that I contemplated suicide as the only way out. It truly was a recurring nightmare and I wanted desperately to be free from this closed circuit I was caught in. My children were often the only reason I could find for not checking out. I just wasn't willing to hurt them like that. They didn't deserve a life of wondering why their love wasn't enough to keep their father around. The truth is... it was. At the same time, it was embarrassing to have my children see me in a locked down facility for crazy people, as they consistently did. Their Mother was understanding and responsive, even after our divorce, and did her best to bring the kids to visit when it was appropriate. My children remained loving, caring, and supportive throughout those many years of madness.

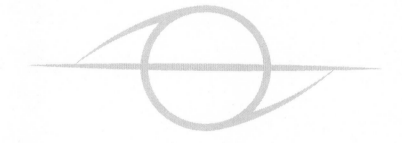

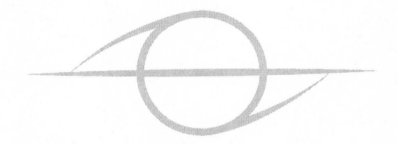

Chapter 36

❧ angels and past lives ❧

The natural desire of good men is knowledge.

—Leonardo da Vinci

I n my eyes, they were living angels. There was no judgment hiding behind their loving little hearts. As they grew older, I would often see them as parental figures that gave me loving advice and held sincere compassion for my struggles. This incredible blessing gave me a secure feeling that God loved me. It seemed to me that only an all-powerful divine love could have delivered such a gift. I do not believe I could have made it through without this sacred jewel to pull me forward. I was like the donkey following the carrot at the end of a stick tied to his back. For this immeasurable gift, I am so deeply grateful.

The spiritual bond I experienced with my children seemed to be rooted deeper than anything in this lifetime. I was intrigued by the general notion of living more than one life, and felt drawn to explore the soul connections that kept us together. My unconventional experience with *the other side* was like an enormous portal to the unknown. I had read books of every kind that related to the astral realms and life beyond death. I was moved by the *near death experience* stories I'd encountered and constantly searching for greater understanding.

I had taken a weekend past life regression therapy course back in '80. During that phase, I was immersed in my hypnotherapy studies and a great deal of understanding had come through this intensive training. This particular program was profoundly unique in that it was led by three individuals with varying backgrounds. One man was a hypnotherapist, another a psychologist, and the third teacher was a female psychic. It was a powerful combination and they worked well together. I was fortunate to have my first direct experience with a past life regression when I volunteered to be a model for the class presentation.

It was life changing to receive guidance in the depths of my subconscious mind, while discovering an alternate life experience in another place and time. I was obviously living a native lifestyle and exploring my daily habits through the regression. *"What are you experiencing now?"* she asked. *"I'm chewing on a piece of bark,"* I replied, as I felt myself handling the bark and putting it into my mouth. *"Why are you doing that?"* she inquired further. I recall thinking, *"What a stupid question... I am cleaning my teeth of course,"* as if this was such normal behavior. The details were interesting as I mentioned my family and the nearby tribal village setting. The storyline, however, was hazy and yet the gift that would ultimately come from this brief session was unfathomable.

I was presented with a simple question that sparked an event in my mind that established the groundwork for a transformational process that remains in motion to this day. She whispered, *"Where is your home?"* The fascinating nature of my response was that it was non-verbal. In fact, the therapist didn't think I'd answered at all because I remained silent. In my inner vision I replied by getting down on my knee and drawing an image in the dirt with my finger. It was simply a circle with a line through the middle of it. As the person I was in the regression, this simple drawing felt like a definitive response. To the rest of the students observing, it wasn't so clear. I was the only one to actually witness the dirt drawn symbol, and I didn't understand its meaning any more than anyone else. However, it stirred my curiosity.

During a previous exercise, I had envisioned myself laying on the ground and watching the clouds swirling in the sky overhead. They were spinning, as if I was looking through the eye of a tornado, and they gradually slowed, came to a halt, and formed a symbol. This image also had a circle at the center with a split tail spin off to the sides, like a galaxy spiraling through space. I left the weekend training with these two distinct images etched in my consciousness. With the central circle in common, I was naturally compelled to overlay them into a single form. The symbol had come from within my own psyche as far as I could tell. It took form, like a thorn in my sandal, as I found myself constantly pondering its deeper meaning. I continued to explore its significance and essentially developed a personal relationship with this symbolic expression that had come to me from somewhere deep inside. This symbol would soon become a cornerstone to my ongoing personal path of study. There was something powerful hidden in this image, and it called to me like a lighthouse to a vessel lost at sea. The message was profound, and it continued to expand as the years slipped by.

My interest in past lives grew, and I ended up spending many hours studying *Edgar Cayce's* work as I developed a profound awareness around reincarnation. He was known as *The Sleeping Prophet* and his life story is told well through a book called *There is a River* by Thomas Sugrue. In brief, his work began by accident. He had come down with a health issue that left him unable to speak at an early age. A friend had taken him to see a hypnotist who was doing a show in their small town. The hypnotist discovered that Cayce could speak when he was in a trance. They were intrigued and went on to find that Edgar was able to diagnose his own issue. Not only could he diagnose the problem, but he delivered an effective remedy as well. Another hypnotist pushed forward to discover that Edgar could diagnose other people's health issues just as readily and also present an effective remedy or cure for each of them. Cayce, although he was a photographer by trade, went on to do thousands of readings over the next couple of decades. Many of his unorthodox treatments have impacted the medical world in a powerful, beneficial, and lasting way.

A peculiar thing happened in the midst of his psychic servitude. One day he was doing a reading for somebody, and while in trance explained that their current issues were connected to a past life. This freaked Edgar out because he was a devout Christian and didn't believe in reincarnation. His family upbringing was religiously centered, and he was known to read the Bible from beginning to end every year. He suddenly turned away from his trance work and refused to do the medical readings. He considered the connection to reincarnation must be of the devil. After praying and gaining counsel from his church family, he eventually came to the conclusion that a great deal of good had come through his efforts. Many people had regained health and received amazing benefits through his personal services. He finally concluded that this good work could not come from the devil, as he continued on with his readings.

The big shift that followed was that every reading he did from that point forward was a *past life* reading. He did over 14,000 readings that I am aware of, and the majority of them were past life related rather than medical readings. His reputation is impeccable, and the history of his work is beyond reproach. He did an extensive volume of teaching on *The Akashic Records,* which is the subtle etheric dimension where each life of every soul leaves an imprint. Edgar Cayce was masterful at reading the Akashic vibrational library and his work is a treasure. After exposure to his comprehensive volumes of work, I wasn't even able to imagine living just one life. It didn't compute in any way that my mind could grasp. My personal perspective made a solo life experience seem pointless and absurd. *"What could a person learn in one lifetime?"* Not much. *"What would be the point?"*

The purpose in living seemed to be about soul development, individually as well as collectively. Weren't we here to learn, grow, and evolve into the spiritual beings we were meant to be? That's what *Abraham Maslow* was pushing to the college students with *self-actualization* highlighted as the highest NEED of humanity. Even Christianity was begging for an answer to this question. After all, had Jesus modeled an example that simple folk had the ability to follow or was he just showing off? Why would a divine being or enlightened soul bother to lead the way if we didn't have the capacity to reach this level of consciousness? From this standpoint, it seemed obvious that we are all capable of maturing into loving beings. Certainly humanity has many lessons to learn, but given the timeline, we appear to be destined for perfection. With this perspective, it seems inevitable that we will eventually rise to the occasion, even if it takes ten thousand lifetimes.

According to Cayce, our lives are interlinked. We tend to come back to the same families, circles of friends, and soul groupings. This ideology was similar to the systems theory I was so taken by. Many times, the group incarnations were wrapped up in relationships of varying sorts that needed healing. I read a book by Gina Cerminara called *Many Mansions* that gave a distinct impression of the way we change positions within a family. It seems that this shift in position provided multiple opportunities to learn and develop from different stations in life. For example, a family with a mother, father, son, and daughter in one life, could reincarnate with totally different roles in the next.

The mother might become the son, or the daughter the uncle, each incarnation bringing a unique perspective from which to learn. Her explanation came through in depth studies of the Cayce readings, and her theories included experiencing lives as women and men, as well as living in a variety of racial and cultural backgrounds. The changes seemed designed to bring a greater understanding of life, by way of experiencing it from every angle. *"I suppose that would be an effective approach to getting over yourself."*

After finishing Gina's book, I recall about a two week period of being at total peace and acceptance of every walk of life. No matter what situation or circumstance a person was in, I could see the perfect manner in which the universe was providing the ideal path to growth and learning at a soul level. The reasoning from this viewpoint didn't hold anyone as a victim. The entire universe was designed to teach each of us precisely what we need to learn through the optimal method and means. It is in perfect order. This was a beautiful window to look through, and I wished it had remained a permanent fixture as it gradually faded away.

Edgar also pointed to nations of populations having collective lessons to learn. I was intrigued by one notion in particular that he spoke of in depth. He suggested that the current influx of souls in America were the return of a soul collective that had previously occupied Atlantis. *"How fascinating does it get?"* Apparently, they or we... blew it the last time around. The story was that technology had advanced more rapidly than the spiritual awareness could handle, and through the imbalance, society self-destructed, taking the continent with them. *"Sound familiar?"*

Was it a nuclear weapon that sunk Atlantis? I'm not sure, but this gripping hypothesis lined up with much of what I was witnessing in the world, including the sudden advancements in modern technology. My grandfather had witnessed the invention of radio, telephone, the automobile, and airplane. Two generations later I was reviewing holographic keyboards on TED Talks, whereby I could observe the galaxy through the Hubble telescope, by way of the Internet, from my hybrid car that was digitally linked via satellite, without any physical instrument in my hands. Certainly a profound influx of advanced technology had emerged in mainstream America, as far as I could see.

The fundamental premise was that the progressive knowledge had followed this family of souls into this realm. In other words, they were born with it. The technological advancements of Atlantis had been retained in the collective unconscious, and had returned with the souls incarnating in this present age. It seems that as a whole, we are being given another chance to see if we can learn to live in harmony with each other and the planet, without sinking the ship this time. I guess the answer to this monumental question is yet to be seen. *"Can we?"*

In a vague and general manner, this seems to be how it works. Every system and every soul is born to learn and grow, and the opportunities just keep coming. Kind of like that Kenny Loggins song, *"You get endless second chances... so take it one chance at a time."* Edgar's ideology considered us each to be an eternal soul, destined to live into the next chapter of this endless book of life.

As for my personal experience with previous lives, I was fortunate to encounter a rare view into the past through what I came to recognize as a *spontaneous* past life regression. After my divorce, I had developed an intimate relationship with a girlfriend who was quite spiritually oriented, and our bond was strong. One night as we crawled into bed, I had a spontaneous vision occur, and I was fully conscious as the movie played in my mind's eye. It was very vivid, and played out as though I was watching a television program while she was around the corner unable to see the screen. I had my eyes closed as I was sharing with her what I was seeing.

The storyline revealed a time when our paths had crossed in what appeared to be a previous life. Alone on horseback, riding through the forest, I happened upon a very disturbing scene. I unexpectedly discovered an isolated cabin in the middle of the wilderness that was on fire. I approached the burning building, dismounted, and went running into the home. The place had been ransacked. There were several bloodied bodies scattered about that had been violently killed. I went into a bedroom and found a young woman, stabbed and bleeding profusely, but still alive. Although I was in no position to take on a rescue mission, I had little choice in the matter. I could either take her with me or leave her to die. She appeared lifeless as I carried her out of the wreckage and placed her on my horse. I rode for miles as I took her to my home hidden deep in the backwoods.

I lived alone in a small remote shack that was many miles from any other homestead or town. I nursed her back to life and she gradually recovered. The primary issue that immediately came to bear was related to our cultural divide. She was a white girl and I was a native. We didn't speak the same language, and she was very frightened of me because of the association to the brutal attack that had killed her family. The death of her loved ones and the destruction of her home had been delivered by a band of natives. In her eyes, I was one of the people that killed her family. It took time and a great deal of patience before she developed any trust in me. Through the years, we learned to communicate and eventually had children. We each lived out a good portion of our lives in this isolated and remote wilderness.

It was intriguing to have such a vivid and incredible vision, and even more amazing to witness my girlfriend's emotional response. She was sobbing as I shared this live motion picture with her that felt to be so real and relevant for both of us. It was an earth shattering revelation. This vision turned out to be the initial segment of a trilogy that ultimately revealed a greater storyline.

Another woman, who would end up becoming my second wife in this lifetime, had recently entered my world. I had met her through the community college program. We were spending a great deal of time together and one day I had a striking picture flash in my mind's eye. It was she, in buckskins, sitting on a horse with a disturbingly dreadful look on her face. The view was close up, and I was unable to see beyond her upper body. The picture continued to show up in my mind at random again and again until it became bothersome for me. I had told her about it, and neither of us could make any sense of it. What did it mean? Why did it keep appearing? One day when the picture returned, I became angry. I shouted, "*Okay… What???!! Show me the rest of it!!*" Suddenly the screen widened, as though the camera in my mind's eye was zooming out, and I could see the bigger picture. She was sitting on a horse in her buckskins, dragging a contraption made of two poles that were attached to the rear end of the horse. A body was lying lengthwise on the poles. Spontaneously, my point of view floated over the body, and as I looked down I was able to see the face up close. I was awestruck to see that it was my own! I was equally stunned to realize that I was as dead as a doornail. The repeating vision of the dreadful look on her face was of her deep grieving as she carried her father to his grave. It was shocking as the story continued to reveal more of what had happened. Once again, the vision was like watching a movie where I could feel the emotions and intuit what was occurring at a deeper level behind the scenes.

This was my daughter, and I had loved her dearly. The young woman that I found in the burning cabin in the previous vision was the mother of this daughter. This second regressive vision was an additional segment of the same life! As the story unfolded, I became aware of an embarrassing event that preceded my death. As a native, my cultural background held views around sexuality that were foreign to the white world. It was customary for young girls within the tribe to be introduced to sex, typically by way of being taught by an uncle. Given our isolation from the tribe, I had taken on the role of the uncle in introducing my daughter to the *how to's* of sex. When her non-tribal mother caught us in the act, she freaked out. She left in a rage on horseback, rode for miles to the nearest white man's village, and told the story. The men in the village followed her trail back to the cabin and killed me. My daughter had escaped and returned later to find my body. Wow! The astonishing parallels were beginning to make sense. The karmic ties were woven like steel thread through the heart of these relations. The depth of this mystical experience left me obsessed with connecting the dots for years to come.

The third vision unexpectedly emerged through a relationship with a female friend and business associate. We were sitting together in a park, having lunch one day, when the final scene came to light. Once again, it was spontaneous and I was able to convey to her what I was seeing as it unfolded. The scenario in my mind's eye was of two young boys playing in the woods. She and I were young friends except that in this incarnation she was a *he*. We were out in the wilderness hunting and playing with our bows. This was not at all unusual behavior, but what occurred created a life changing event for both of us.

My young warrior friend just happened to leap out of the brush as I was releasing an arrow. To my utter shock, it pierced his chest and quickly killed him. I was young and absolutely bewildered by the harsh and abrupt consequences of such an innocent accident. I was so upset, as well as frightened of facing the tribe, that I tied my buddy's limp body to a bundle of large sticks and floated him out into the river. I was aware that the current of the stream would carry him directly to the village where his body was certain to be discovered. I also realized I was unwilling to face what I expected in the way of punishment. I was filled with shame and an overwhelming sense of guilt. Perhaps I actually knew what kind of torture I would be put through as a consequence of this unfathomable violation. I'm not sure, but my expectations were severe because I instantly made the decision to leave the village and never return. This third vision was actually part one in the trilogy and tied the whole life story together.

After the accidental death, I had left the village and ventured off into the far reaches of the land to establish my own isolated place of residence. I lived alone for years and eventually found the young woman in the burning cabin. I took her home, revived her and in due time we had a child. I would ultimately end up being violently murdered for my apparent transgressions. It was a shameful life, and I felt deep sadness as I considered the impact it had carried for me at a soul level. I could feel the parallel dynamics in the relevant relationships, as well as in my overall life. The woman who'd been my daughter was currently my wife and seventeen years younger than me. This relationship turned out to be very much like raising a daughter. It seemed that I owed her something for abandoning her through my early death in the last go around. We also seemed destined to be lovers that did not have family relations to consider. My mission became one of helping her through the stage of development where she'd been abandoned in the previous life. I very much helped her to mature into an adult, and when the mission was complete I could feel at a soul level that it was done. Apparently, she did too as she soon moved on to greener pastures.

The other obvious connection through this review was with the sexual abuse in my childhood. What comes around, goes around. Whether you call it *karma* or *you reap what you sow*, it's all the same thing. My karmic actions apparently warranted me learning what it was like to be on the receiving end of such a violation of innocence. I was now able to understand the costly repercussions. My experience with child sexuality had been similar, in that I was very young and the relations were basically incestuous. Once again, my experiential learning had far surpassed the conceptual understanding that came through my book studies. Together, they gave me a deep awareness of lives beyond this one.

I later went on to be trained extensively in past life regression therapy and was able to learn a great deal through my work with others. The patterns in the regressions were always relevant to the life experience of each person's current living situation. The struggles and hardship screamed loudly for the attention that was much needed. Each memory pulled a string of events into view, and the vision of what each incarnation had been centered around became obvious. Many challenges were presented repeatedly through many lives. It lined up accurately and made good sense that we did not get to bypass our lessons. This universe had set the stage for every individual, as well as larger collectives, to encounter the appropriate situations required to bring lessons of the highest priority. You may fail miserably or die trying, but that lesson would present itself until the mission was accomplished. These eternal souls held no barriers to finding the time or place to make that final leap to the next level of growth. It reminded me of the video games, where you're required to touch all the right points and collect each necessary token to advance to the next floor.

Each life was experienced from a limited point of reference. Being a man or a woman, rich or poor, one race or another, shifted this single position of perspective. Every angle was one-sided, and yet living through many varying degrees of experience was bound to deliver a grander view of life in this human condition. Wholeness could ultimately be revealed through this eclectic array of viewpoints delivered through these multifaceted perspectives. The soul seemed destined to find a unified sense of wholeness and balance. The evolution of consciousness on every scale appeared to be inevitable.

Many years later, after the turn of the millennium, I enrolled in another hypnotherapy course. Our teacher was well educated, as he'd been a professor of Jungian Psychology at the University of Washington. Once again, I volunteered for a class presentation and experienced another powerful lifetime that had left an undeniable imprint on my soul. Reading and studying were informative and helpful for gaining knowledge of the general patterns and processes involved in being repeatedly reborn, however the personal regression took it to an entirely new depth of experiential understanding. This particular session was transformational and extremely educational in the most intimate way.

This simple life appeared to have taken place in the icy flows of the Arctic region. The culture appeared to be Eskimo-like, and my story revolved around caring for the village sled dogs. The scene opened with me playing in the snow with several young puppies. I absolutely loved these pups and spent a great deal of time caring for them as they grew into fully mature sled dogs. This may very well have been my job as a family or tribal member. The event that unfolded as a central theme in this regression was when I caught another tribesman beating the dogs for something they'd done which upset him. I witnessed his violent reaction, stepped in, grabbed hold of him, and stopped him from hurting the dogs.

The objectionable issue that arose was due to the fact that the aggressor, who I'd abruptly stopped in his tracks, was the chief of the clan. My position in the tribe did not allow or warrant me treating him in that way. It was expected that I should submit regardless of any personal feelings. I didn't see it that way. My love and responsibility for the dogs outweighed my desire to remain in good standing within the tribe. The posse of men who were assigned to correct my erroneous ways confronted me and placed me in front of a tribal council. I was unwilling to admit to a transgression and refused to conform to the demands of the council. I would not apologize, nor would I concede to the dogs being treated in that way. The method for forcing me to submit involved tying me to a short pole and bending my back against it until I passed out. The pain was unbearable and was supposed to be the driving force to change my mind, but I wouldn't give in. I went unconscious at that point and later returned to consciousness inside a container of some sort. The receptacle was made from seal skins fastened on top of a sled. I tore my way out of the enclosure to find myself in the middle of a vast expanse of ice and snow. I had been dragged to this remote location by my own dogs and family, and left to die. I was in excruciating pain as I staggered across the barren field of ice, knowing that I was gradually freezing to death. There were no landmarks for as far as I could see, and I could feel my body growing numb. I walked a long way before I felt myself stumble and fall into a frozen state as I took my last few breaths. It was extremely traumatic on an emotional level. The physical pain was not the core element that carried over. The underlying buried emotion was the severe hurt of being treated with such disregard by my own people. The thoughts and feelings that welled up in me, as I concluded I would soon die, were of revenge. I realized in that moment of the regression, that I had believed I would return and have my chance to get even. I was making vows of revenge as I faded out of that realm and on to greener pastures. I considered the tribal culture must have included reincarnation in its belief system, according to my closing thought stream.

What I experienced during the vivid regression enlightened me to a way of perceiving that could only come through firsthand participation. The character in that life, Iku (ee-koo), was ultra-attuned to the environment through his senses. This session left a permanent impression on my awareness and had impacted other students in a dynamic way as well. The presentation was videotaped, and I was able to observe it again later from an outside perspective. I was also inspired to write a poem:

Iku's Revenge

A mighty yet soft wind has blessed this soul.
There was a divine and earthly source of wisdom
behind that ancient wall of pain.
Iku (ee-koo) was an amazing man.
His Heart/Mind was singular.
There was no division.
He stood deeply grounded
in a state of unity consciousness

that we so desperately seek in this modern age.
He had a heartfelt sense of the environment
he lived and breathed in.
He could feel the energy of the sun
on the mountain...
like a gentle kiss to his soul.
He could taste the smoke of a distant fire...
through a gentle breeze.
His sense of smell was directly linked
to an inner vision
that was as accurate as the eagle's eye...
and as reliable as the seasons of change.
He could feel the heartbeat of the grazing elk
that would be his family's meal three days away.
His heart was pure and his love as constant
as the earth beneath his feet,
yet flowing like the mighty river
as the winter's ice becomes
the blossoming flowers of spring.
His respect for life
and his deep love for the forces behind it
are unfathomable to the modern mind.
There are feelings
and sensory awareness experiences
that cannot be touched by the intellect.
His knowledge was truly embodied.
Iku's sense of unity
with the living world around him
was never a concept.
It was an experiential reality.
He felt his way
through every moment of every day.
The love that arose in his body
in that final hour was unstoppable.
Like the rising sun and the ocean tide,

it was bound to find a way.
Iku did not die that day
in that frozen stiff, beaten and broken body.
He emerged from the cocoon in full glory...
with brightly colored wings
of yellow, violet, blue, and magenta.
The hatred and resentment
for what should have never been,
laid frozen in time.
He did not conform to the ways of his people
or bow to anything less than love.
His heart knew the difference.
It was the fire that burned at the core of his being
and had delivered him into this realm.
It guided his every move from within.
Like the great sea turtle that came and went
with perfect and divine timing...
his motion was without question.
Iku stood the test of time.
He was an advanced soul in a primitive day.
His wisdom and blessings of awareness are alive
His love still whispers sweet messages of peace
in the tall grassy meadows.
His vision flies high on the wings of a golden eagle.
And an ancient song can still be heard...
like a solo drum beat...
when the red headed woodpecker returns home.
Iku was as powerful as the forces of Nature.
They were one.
This constant and ever flowing invincible force
of love and wisdom... is Iku's revenge.
I took it to heart... when he said,
"Forgive... My Friend."

The interesting piece of this work was that the chief of the tribe who was central to the entire tribal conflict and ultimately put me to death, appeared to be my brother in my current life. I could feel the same dynamics at play in this lifetime and understand even more why there would be such underlying discord between us. I had a feeling this conflictive exchange had been bouncing back and forth for thousands of years. It didn't appear to be coming to a close soon. Our love for each other was strong, but the hidden dimensions of rivalry were far too obvious to deny.

My research in the arena of reincarnation gave me new insights into the unconventional episodes of madness that made no sense from a point of view in this current life. I couldn't help but wonder how much of the spill over from an unconscious pool of confusion was coming through trauma experienced in other lives. The traditional medical world did not consider these *New Age* perspectives as rational. My *alternative* views only validated my insanity for those who needed more evidence. Keep in mind the absurdity in labeling this multiple life perspective as *New Age*, when this view has been recognized in countless cultures for thousands of years.

Chapter 37

⮂ the body mind ⮀

Everything comes to us that belongs to us if we create the capacity to receive it.

—Rabindranath Tagore

What I could see so clearly, was regardless of the source of these sporadic waves of craziness, I had the same mission before me. Whether the initial upset had come through this lifetime or another didn't make any difference. Either way, I had to find the means to heal these emotional wounds before I would ever be set free. They were obviously buried within my consciousness which was somehow connected to my physical body. The relationship between body and mind was looking more like many shades of gray than black and white. I had made incredible progress through my Jungian-based inner work, as well as the Trager bodywork I'd stumbled upon on my way to the hypnotherapy training. I soon found myself intrigued by another style of bodywork that grabbed my attention fully as I passionately pursued it.

I enrolled in a school for neuro-muscular integration, which was a fancy name for a ten session style of bodywork that, like *Rolfing*, dealt with the fascia or connective tissue. There appeared to be a string of spinoffs including Hellerwork and Feldenkrais, each bringing a subtle twist to this basic modality. It seemed they each had something unique to offer.

The common premise was similar to the bodywork I'd participated in previously, in that the connective tissue was considered the layer in the body where the emotional memory is stored. These teachings focused on the Body-Mind and particularly a highly defined and strategic interaction with these connective tissues, which acted like a hard drive for the emotional memory. Once again, the repressed emotional pain could be accessed and released through specific physical manipulations. It was deeply fascinating and proved to be extremely effective. It was not unlike cleaning up and defragmenting the hard drive of a computer. Files were realigned as some were deleted and others restored. The system was upgraded by way of this much needed maintenance, leaving the emotional and physical body able to function more smoothly and efficiently.

I was invited to be the model for one of the teachers on the day that we studied the area below the knees. This part of the anatomy correlates with the early stages of childhood. The left side of the body connects to the right hemisphere of the brain which relates to feminine or mother based issues. The right side of the body connects to the left hemisphere and relates to the masculine or father based issues. The entire body is mapped out and every aspect of this intricate body-mind relates in some way to a person's mental-emotional being.

My experience of having my lower legs worked on was magical and surreal. After the completion of the session, when I first stood up and put my weight on my feet, I sobbed like a child. Tears were running down my face and I had no idea why. There was an enormous volume of emotional energy being released. It was bewildering to be in front of the entire class and unable to control the tears or the outpouring of emotion.

I went for a quiet stroll in a nearby pasture and felt like I had new legs. It was as if my spirit had not occupied this territory below my knees until now. I'd been completely unconscious of what was being released. No memories or recognizable thought streams were attached to the emotions that were gushing out. It was absolutely astonishing to feel my presence within my lower legs and simultaneously realize that I had not been aware of fully living in this portion of my body prior to this session. There had been an obstacle within my emotional body that blocked my awareness of occupying this region. As the blockage was released, this sense of connection naturally returned. I could suddenly see how a person would readily accept their ongoing physical sense of wellbeing, or state of mind, without question. Whatever we begin to experience as young children becomes familiar and accepted as normal. How could someone know otherwise? People in general didn't have the ability to realize what they were *NOT* experiencing in relation to wholeness. Leading up to this therapeutic event, I had no idea that I was missing out on anything in this region. This epiphany lit up my awareness of the treasures that lay beyond my current understanding. *"We just can't know... what we don't know."*

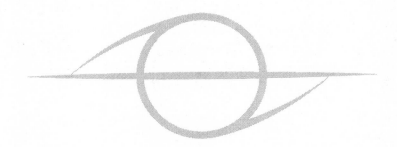

Chapter 38

✑ demonic possession ❧

There is something good in all seeming failures. You are not to see that now. Time will reveal it. Be patient.

—Swami Sivananda

Another point of awareness that came to light through this most recent venture was the degree to which my spirit was integrated and occupying my body. It was a mind-altering affair to realize that I'd been recognizably disengaged from this portion of my body, before fully inhabiting the lower floor of my personal temple. I reflected upon my mysterious experiences of being totally detached from my physical being, while somebody else had danced in this body I called mine.

I believed I was embodying this anatomical spacesuit for the purpose of interacting in this particular dimension of reality. It was like a material portal through which I could, in human form, experience this three dimensional realm on planet Earth. Taking care of this high-tech suit and maintaining its proper functioning was essential, however, I had also come to realize that I was not the only one that could occupy this precious earthly cloak.

The tremendous threat I was facing appeared to be twofold. My fragmented psyche was certainly a factor, without a doubt, but who were these other beings that vied for my body time? I enjoyed the many theories relating to the physical form and the mental emotional mapping that delved into the inner workings of this human condition, but there seemed to be another influence that I couldn't put my finger on. Where had the strange voices come from? What... or who was randomly taking over the helm without my permission? Were they angels, demons, ghosts, or extraterrestrials? They were simply entities of an unknown origin for all I knew. I was just a hundred percent certain that I wasn't the only player in this game.

My soul had certainly cracked wide open the day I fell into that divine field of light. I suddenly seemed to have access to another dimension of reality. I also felt vulnerable and accessible to the energy or entities in that foreign realm. It was one that I had absolutely no awareness of before *the fall*. Like my lower legs, I had no knowledge what-so-ever that there was space available within my consciousness, waiting to be occupied. I was entering another form of unfamiliar territory, wondering how I could ever comprehend what I was up against.

On many occasions, I had felt possessed by something that I couldn't identify or define. There were moments when it felt like flipping a light switch, and in an instant I could feel an entity enter my being. There were other times when it wasn't so black and white. When it was too late to fight, I would come to the realization, *"Hey… this isn't me!"* It was as if the driver's seat was wide open and available to whoever wanted to jump in, as I was thrown aside to the passenger's seat. I was taken on joy ride after joy ride, which didn't tend to end with any joy, at least for me. In fact, the typical outcome included intense pain, deep confusion, and another trip to the loony bin. This was a mystery I needed to solve as a matter of life and death.

One of the most obvious encounters in my experience of being possessed ended up bringing great and desperately needed clarity. It happened back in the mid '90s, when I'd found my way into the Mormon Church. They had come to my rescue during a time of great need and fed me when I was struggling to feed myself. This was at the peak low of hitting bottom, and I was in rough shape. I was anxiously seeking a clean and sober lifestyle and coming up short on places to socialize with healthy people. I took great comfort in the company of this community of Latter Day Saints. They were a Godsend when I had no sense of direction and no one to turn to. I felt genuinely loved and cared for in this church family. I was known to stir the discussion groups up a bit, which seemed to be genuinely appreciated. My questions and quest for knowledge were sincere, and my fellow seekers seemed approving of my push for understanding. I also enjoyed the interactions immensely and accepted an offer to be baptized, which opened the door for my ordination into the priesthood. As a priest, I was able to baptize my wife and children, which I most delightfully did. The Bishop had also come to our home to perform the formal ceremony for this second marriage and needless to say, my young wife didn't show up in buckskins this time around.

The Mormons were truly a lifesaver through this difficult phase of my misconstrued journey. The standard protocol for the Church was that every adult member was assigned a job, and I was soon invited to coach the men's basketball team. As a grateful recipient of such heartfelt generosity, I was more than willing to do my part. It was a fun and exciting way to serve, and I was pleased to have been appointed to this particular calling. The value for me having this healthy involvement in my life was priceless. As I was mentored and prepared for the position, a certain young man had been pointed out as a troublemaker. Apparently, he'd been involved with drugs, promiscuous relations, and was known for his violent and rebellious attitude. My superiors had recommended that he not be allowed on the team due to the difficulties that came with his involvement. I was decidedly and passionately opposed to this view. It seemed to me that this was the kind of kid that needed to be a part of what the church team offered, perhaps more than anyone. Pushing him away or shutting the door made absolutely no sense to me. I expressed my feelings very clearly, and I was impressed when they actually listened. They gave me the okay to allow him to play.

He was about eighteen when he came to join the team, and he brought a young buddy who seemed equally troublesome. It appeared that they were going to be a pair to contend with. I sat them down one day and told them straight out what the deal was, *"If you guys want to play... it will be by my rules."*

We talked a little bit, and they were both willing to agree, at least enough to get a foot in the door. We held a couple of practices, and the advisors had been correct. These guys were a serious handful. They had good skills, but were rowdy as hell and very difficult to control. Our first game unveiled the true potential for conflict that I'd been so prudently warned about. My number one troubled kid was really stirring it up with the other team. Not only was he pushing and being physically aggressive, but talking trash and insulting the other guys to the point of a fight breaking out. I pulled him out just before halftime. During the break I confronted him. I roared, *"This is not going down like this! If we're gonna have a conflict, it's not gonna be with the other team... it's gonna be internal!"* I still remember my words because they struck me later. When I said it, I meant we would fight it out on our own team between the coach and players. It actually developed into more of an internal affair than I had imagined possible.

I was anything but gentle with my approach. I was livid and yelling fiercely in his face. He grabbed me by my shirt, and we wrestled to the ground. He surprised me when he got the better position and pinned me down. In that very moment, I noticed something foreign entering my being. The possession was instantaneous and distinctly recognizable. I could sense

242

an immediate shift within my feeling body. Somebody pulled him off, and we got up from the court floor just in time for the second half to begin. Interestingly, I promptly decided to put myself into the position that I'd just taken him out of. What I and the rest of the team then witnessed was beyond bizarre. I was behaving exactly the way he had been! I was aggressive, malicious, pushing, and ready to start a fight. It was absolutely nuts as the bewildered referee stopped the game. That was it... utterly unbelievable! I chased the kid out to his car, belligerently screaming obscenities at the top of my lungs, as he tried to escape my violent pursuit. The rest of the guys looked at me as though I had lost my mind. I guess I actually had… one more time. I also went home knowing that I wasn't alone in my body.

I did my usual routine of breathing, relaxing, and letting it go but I couldn't shake it. The feeling was blatant and the exchange that had taken place was beyond obvious. On the third day, I called the Bishop and told him the story. He didn't seem terribly surprised and immediately offered to come to my home. I was grateful for the support and gladly accepted his offer. He brought an Elder with him and together they laid their hands on my head as they spoke in prayer. There was no doubt as to the effectiveness of their mission, as I felt the entity leave immediately. I could feel it moving right out through my skin like a cold sweat. I happily exclaimed, *"It's gone!"* The exit of this alien entity was as instantaneous as its arrival. This experience gave me a very clear sense of the process of being possessed. It was a wonderful learning opportunity that would serve me well into the future. As for the young man who was spontaneously exorcised, his life changed dramatically for the good as he went on to become an Elder, serving the church on a two year mission. It was a profound turn around that was obvious to his family and the church community.

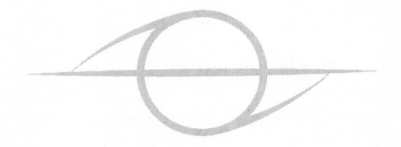

Chapter 39

✌ new labels ✌

No matter what people tell you, words and ideas can change the world.

—Robin Williams

Through my constant quest for a broader perspective, as well as deeper understanding, I stumbled upon a couple more labels. They seemed appropriate for the conditions that appeared to be at the forefront of my struggles. My spiritual or feeling body was extremely open and receptive, to put it mildly. I came across the word *Empath*, as in empathy or empathic, through my extracurricular studies. The description seemed to fit me to a tee. I was suddenly working with another label to live up to; however, *Empath* felt like one I could gladly deal with.

It seemed that I was sensitive on a level that the average person would never wish for. It was burdensome to feel so vulnerable. I did some research and found an interesting list of the varying degrees of empathy. The scale was primarily related to sensitivity, with one exception. The highest degree, level ten, included being able to affect the feeling body of the one being perceived. In other words, beyond being receptive and aware of another person on a feeling level, a ten had the ability to influence through that cord of connection. Imagine being able to recognize the anxiety in a loved one, and have the ability to soothe their angst by way of empathic intervention. It seems the highly developed empath could reverse the communication flow and influence this other person. Wow! This sounded like an open road to stepping into healing at an empathic level, and I recognized the incredible potential here. I was thrilled to realize this apparent curse suddenly held the potential for delivering tremendous blessing.

A second label soon emerged that was equally unfamiliar to me, Clairsentient. I was acquainted with the terms clairvoyant and clairaudient, but clairsentient had somehow escaped me. My hypnotherapy studies had taken me into the world of neuro-linguistic programming, or NLP, which relates to how we each process information through our five senses; the various modes of perception include visual, auditory, taste, smell, and kinesthetic. People in general tend to be more attuned or stronger in one of these particular modes. Some folks are primarily visual while others are more auditory oriented, etc. The clairvoyant is psychic through the visual mode, whereas the clairaudient processes through hearing. The clairsentient perceives psychically through the feeling body, or kinesthetically, which appeared to be a perfect fit for me.

I could feel things to the point of receiving information that shouldn't be available. My ability to perceive kinesthetically was classically at a highly psychic level. It was as if I could read minds through my feeling body. It wasn't so much the conscious thinking mind as it was the emotional substance. I could often read what a person was feeling beyond their own conscious awareness. It was as if I had a direct line into the subconscious minds of those around me, individuals as well as groups, whether I liked it or not.

Understanding this was an enormous step toward my being able to handle it, with at least a clue as to what I was dealing with. I readily took on these two new labels, like stamps on my forehead, reminding me of who I was when I looked into the mirror. It helped me to classify myself in a new way, with positive and definable terms. They seemed much more appropriate, precise, and fitting than *mentally ill...* which was purely negative, ugly, and a heavy burden to bear. I was so terribly tired of beating that dead horse.

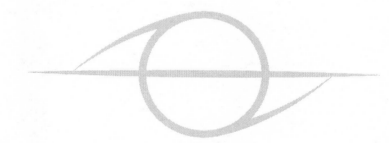

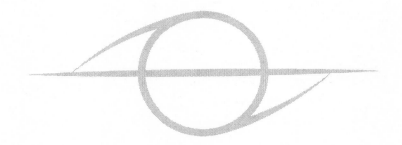

Chapter 40

❧ wireless transceivers ❧

Presumably there are energies, to which each human is sensitive, that we cannot yet detect by means of our instruments. Built into our brains and our bodies are very sensitive tuneable receivers for energies that we do not yet know about in our science but that each one of us can detect under the proper circumstances and the proper state of mind. We can tune our nervous systems and bodies to receive these energies. We can also tune our brains and bodies to transmit these energies.

—John C. Lilly

My sensitivity was certainly an issue to contend with. There was a thin veil between the madness that overwhelmed my mind and the chaos emanating from the world around me. It was difficult to see my insanity as strictly my own. So much of my feeling experience came through interacting with others. It seemed that we shared a great deal by way of thoughts and feelings, whether they were openly expressed or not.

I had learned to consider my mind in a contradictory manner to that which I was taught growing up. The idea of a person's mind being separate and strictly contained within the brain didn't seem accurate. The idea was, *"You have your brain, which contains your mind, and it's over there. I have my brain, which contains my mind, and it's over here... and the two are completely disconnected and separate."* The more I looked at this notion, the more it appeared to be utterly ridiculous. Early on, I had no computer or Internet to create such a clear association between these distinctly separate perspectives. The development of this technology would prove to be an awesome model for my understanding. It also appeared to be the actualization or physical manifestation of our minds being wirelessly networked.

The pre-internet image I held, from experiencing the process of sharing thoughts and feelings with others, was that we were more like radios. That is, we were transmitting and receiving within a sea of consciousness. Sure, I had a brain that was separate from my friends, but it wasn't necessarily the originator of the thought stream flowing through it, any more than a radio was the creator of the songs that played on the air. It was merely the tool, like a crystal, that could be used to dial in a particular frequency or channel. Depending on the chosen frequency, which is all too often by default, the source, quality, and stream of thought is determined. Some receivers are stronger than others. So it is with transmitters. We are not created equal in this department any more than with any other characteristics that vary within humanity. We each have our own equipment to tend to, according to its innate nature. My personal apparatus just happened to carry high intensity on both ends, which created a tremendous challenge to deal with. I could also see that getting a grip on this system was a doorway to incredible potential. Like Tesla, I was hopeful and determined.

I was beginning to see the dualistic nature of this situation more clearly. Much like my desktop computer that was hooked up to the Internet, I had an internal home based system to maintain. This gave me access to a separate online network of websites, created and maintained through other systems. The websites I accessed would appear to be playing through my system, as they were showing up on my monitor. In fact, they would be playing through my system, even though they were generated from another source.

In the same way, I have my own body/mind transceiver to take responsibility for, and it too is wirelessly connected to the entire collective consciousness of humanity. As I access the thought streams of the groups of people and individuals around me, like websites, they will show up in my own consciousness, appearing to be generated from within me. What a beautiful model, to use as a tool, for understanding the manner in which our minds are interconnected.

I also recognized how easily one could make self-judgments according to what showed up on the inner monitor. *"I can't believe I just had that thought!"* Then the appropriate judgment follows, *"If I'm having these kinds of thoughts... this must mean something about me! I must be... (fill in the judgment)."* This circular thinking could pull an individual into a downward spiral, which actually began in response to a random, non-personal thought stream, floating through a collective network in consciousness.

It seems that most people do not realize these thoughts flowing through our minds are not necessarily our own. To notice an ugly, disgusting, or hateful thought passing through and falsely surmise, *"This thought is coming from my own mind,"* is standard for the average person. It's easy to see how judging one's self for what's showing up on the screen can easily spiral into unfavorable directions, with such negative judgments drawing upon and attracting even darker sites. This process quite naturally generates a self-fulfilling prophecy, as the naïve witness is pulled into the depths of his own judgment, unaware that the original ugly source was remote. Like the Internet, just because it's on the screen doesn't mean it's yours. We have the same power of choice as to which windows we want to open and which ones we choose to close. *"It's not yours until you claim it!"*

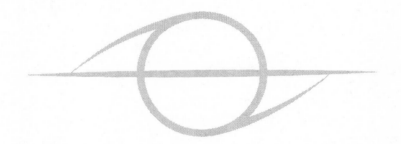

Chapter 41

๛ opening the seven seals ๛

You have resources yet to be unleashed. Make bold, courageous choices. Live as though you have the power to change the world – because you do.

—Carolyn Myss

The complexity of the human condition through the eyes of Western Civilization was becoming quite apparent. The Eastern perspective of the human system, however, appeared quite unique, particularly through the teachings of the *Chakras*. These Chakras were presented as power centers in the spirit or consciousness of the individual. There are seven strategically positioned within the body and an eighth just above the head. Those within the body, manifest in physical form as the endocrine system, and some theories consider there are actually twelve that extend out into the solar system, the galaxy, and perhaps beyond. This view was very intriguing to me.

Anatomy of the Spirit by Carolyn Myss provided excellent explanations as to the correlations between Chakras, specific spiritual imbalances, and the manifestation of disease, disorder, and other issues in the body. Her perspective made it apparent that the personal responsibility for one's health was deeply rooted. The basic premise being that the physical manifestations of disease and disorder originated at a spiritual level within the individual being. This was extremely educational and fascinating territory to explore.

I began to see these Chakras as vortices or portals to other dimensions. I felt as though I could go into my internal elevator and step off onto any chosen floor. Each level was access to another dimension of reality.

Now this may sound like science fiction but if you think of the five senses as accessing different dimensions, you may get a better feel for what I am attempting to point out. The visual realm is a different dimension of reality than the domain of sound or smell. You need certain organs to recognize each one exists. Without a nose you would be oblivious to the dimension of fragrance and find it imponderable. In this same manner, each vortex or Chakra is accessing a unique dimension of reality, all within the same universe.

Gary Zukav speaks quite clearly of the difference between the five sensory state of mind and a multidimensional awareness in his book *Seat of the Soul*. We are actually multi-dimensional beings that have collectively lost our conscious awareness of these individuated levels of existence.

In reawakening to our true nature, it is natural to find the way to a healthy balance. As we tune our awareness into these inner power gateways, the heart Chakra is at the center point where the higher and the lower Chakras converge. The heart center being central to the system also appears to be the favorable command post for the Kingdom within. It seems the lower Chakras are more related to our primal or animal nature, while the upper Chakras are more associated with our spiritual, etheric, or divine nature. The heart also proves to be the ideal instrument with which to rule this inner kingdom with, of course, Love on the throne.

I have noticed a tendency through a variety of spiritual paths toward activating and opening the upper Chakras while closing off or avoiding the lower ones. Once again, this seems out of balance and possibly detrimental. This physical incarnation is designed with purpose, and wholeness is essential to the full blossoming of the being.

Through observing one of the great Masters, Ramana Maharshi, it was apparent that he was in poor physical health for a good part of his life. His story of reaching this highly enlightened state of mind appeared to come by way of ignoring the lower Chakras, as well as the physical body. Although his self-realized state of awareness was profound, it does not appear to be a healthy or holistic approach. It seems that he was out of touch with, or in denial of, his incarnation as a human being.

Now, don't get me wrong. I believe we are divine beings, maybe even fallen angels, but it seems to me that we're in human form for a reason. It appears that we have been sent on this mission to develop the whole being, animal nature and all. To deny the lower Chakras as one reaches for the ecstatic states of divine consciousness appears to be another well-disguised avoidance strategy in my eyes. The result, as far as I can see, would be missing the primary point of this divinely assigned human incarnation.

My personal mission and sacred vow became one of opening the seven Chakras within the body. I envisioned being able to access all of them simultaneously, while striving for a balance of wholeness in this multi-dimensional existence. Integration and a sense of unity were becoming the prominent theme for this sacred mission, regardless of the mode of perception. Whether the point of view was from a social, psychological, or cellular level, the message seemed to be consistent. *"United we stand... divided we fall."*

Part 6

The Duality of Light

*"Caution has its place, no doubt,
but we cannot refuse our support to
a serious venture which challenges
the whole of the personality. If we
oppose it, we are trying to suppress
what is best in man... his daring
and his aspirations. And should we
succeed, we should only have stood in
the way of that invaluable experience
which might have given a meaning
to life. What would have happened if
Paul had allowed himself to be talked
out of his journey to Damascus?"*

—Carl Jung

Chapter 42

✺ bringers of the dawn ✺

Picture yourself in a boat on a river, with tangerine trees and marmalade skies. Somebody calls you, you answer quite slowly, a girl with kaleidoscope eyes.
— Beatles, Lucy in the Sky with Diamonds

I was at a peak high in my Sacre Voeu experience and somehow it seemed to align with a crescendo in time itself. We had just passed through the Y2K illusion of transition and enthusiastically realized we'd survived the predicted devastation without a hitch. It was at the tail end of December in 2000 that I attended the *Prophets Conference* in Palm Springs, which would blow my mind into an expanded orbit. I don't recall how I'd been informed about this event, or why I felt so driven to be there, but I certainly was. I truly had no idea what I was in for as I embarked upon this solo expedition.

The weekend lineup was absolutely outrageous, starring Gregg Braden, Jean Houston, Ph.D., John Mack, M.D., Steven Greer, M.D., Hank Wesselman, Ph.D., Drunvalo Melchizedek, Robert Anton Wilson, James Twyman, Doreen Virtue, Ph.D., Ilona Selke, and Neil Freer. In the first two hours I'd been exposed, through Neil's talk, to Zachariah Sitchin's theory of humanity's current status as a *hybrid* species. It all made perfect sense, as my suspended questions about the *missing link* in the theories I'd been taught in school, were satisfactorily answered. Homo erectus had been genetically infiltrated and the leap to Homo sapiens was extreme, due to an extra-terrestrial humanoid influence. The Anunnaki were among our forefathers, and they were not from this planet. *"Wow! No wonder humanity seemed so hell bent on trashing this earthly abode on the way to finding the next one!"* According to Freer, it was in our DNA. If you have no idea what I am talking about check out Sitchin's book *The 12th Planet*. It is spectacularly fascinating!

My mind was operating in a highly receptive state, and the expansion was overwhelming. It was a bit like seeing how big you can blow up a balloon before it pops. I took in more complex theoretical input during this weekend conference than I may have encountered through the totality of the preceding years of my entire life. It was certainly delivered in a more condensed fashion. My wheels were turning in overdrive. Consider this...

If you zoom out and take a peek at this earthly biosphere we call home, there is an amazing harmony between all life forms. The balance within nature is absolutely incredible. That is... with one exception. Humanity looks more like a disease or a virus that single-handedly disrupts that balance and harmony on every level. How could this be? Why would one species be so out of sync with such a finely tuned and balanced ecological system? The answer is apparent through the clear vision of this abstract looking glass. Our ancestral influence was not one hundred percent earth based. *"Whoa! And you thought telling your mother about the Czechoslovakian boyfriend would upset the apple cart."*

Steven Greer blew another window out of my self-made mental vault when he revealed his understanding of our government's current involvement with extra-terrestrials, as he passionately shared his mission to achieve total disclosure. His straightforward talk on our ongoing secretive close encounters of the fifth kind was instantly believable, and as an advisor to President Clinton on this matter I couldn't help but consider his credibility.

Doreen Virtue spoke of Angels, and Gregg Braden lectured on zero point energy. Drunvalo introduced us to *Sacred Geometry* which included a detailed orientation to *The Flower of Life*. Between Anton, Ilona, and Wesselman, I was left floating through visions of a holographic universe with angels, shaman and extra-terrestrial aliens drifting alongside me, as James Twyman fused it all together in a self-created score of mesmerizing music. The entire affair was literally mind blowing. The pinnacle for me was the introduction to John Mack's new book *Passport to the Cosmos*, which followed his National Best-Seller *Abduction*, and delivered great acclaim to this Pulitzer Prize winning author.

As a Harvard Professor of Psychiatry, he had stunned the world with the results of his extensive research with a significant number of clients who had reported personal encounters with alien life forms. The primary gist of the concepts he struggled to convey related to our general notion around the nature of reality. It seemed that through his work he had come to recognize the actuality of the dimensions of reality, which we quite naturally discount as imaginary and non-existent. The very premise of his presentation was a serious challenge to wrap the mind around... regardless of one's beliefs.

By chance, he'd run into a client on the streets of Palm Springs and invited her to come on stage during his presentation to share her story. It was utterly astonishing as she explained how she and her husband had been taking a drive into the nearby hills to star gaze for a romantic evening. They had noticed a red light glowing in the sky and made note of it as it occurred. They enjoyed their time on the hillside and nonchalantly drove home. There was one small catch to the overall experience they had just shared. When they returned to their home, they soon realized there were six hours missing from this romantic adventure, which neither of them could understand nor explain. She went on to speak of how the strange event left her emotionally disturbed, and why she would ultimately seek out a hypnotherapist to help her unveil what had actually occurred during that missing block of time.

Beyond the story telling, it was her emotional expression that impacted me so deeply. The hypnosis session had successfully revealed what her conscious mind had shut out. She was in tears, and so was I, as she spoke of the divine presence of these beings that had drawn them both into a light in the night sky. She explained that the red light was not a spacecraft or ship, but rather a portal to another dimension with the stars as the landscape. It was obvious that it was difficult for her to speak about this bizarre experience in a way that was easy for the rest of us to comprehend. I'm not so sure that even she was able to fully grasp the significance of her extraordinary encounter.

The message she had carried forward, and did her best to convey, was that the beauty she'd experienced during the abduction was what she felt compelled to share here on the earth plane. This was basically her assignment and what the *extraterrestrials* had requested of her. She cried as she described her feelings toward these magnificent beings of light. She expressed a deep recognition and knowing of these *aliens* as her true family. They were large in stature and beautiful beyond description. The only aliens I'd previously heard about were the little gray guys with the big spooky eyes. Her brilliant depiction was far from that image. The details of these creatures painted a picture more angelic than creepy. It was a transformational experience to sit with this open and authentic young woman as she shared her highly compelling story.

Dr. Mack spoke of the organization he had founded called *PEER*, a Program for Extraordinary Experience Research. He discussed in great detail this group's devotion to helping folks who'd been through these types of encounters. During his presentation, he invited anyone who had experienced anything like this to come to their table between lectures and connect with them. By the time his talk was complete, I was in a new state of awareness around my close encounter with *The Light*. So much of what was being shared aligned with my personal experience. These stories could have been my own, minus a couple of details. The *Shamanic* connections were common. A heightened sensitivity to the environment, including other people, was not unusual. The sense of being in contact with voices or beings from another dimension was typical. The feeling of having a mission to accomplish that would better mankind or the planet was also a standard response to this otherworldly experience.

I actually found my way to the table and decided I would share my extraordinary history. I quickly and quietly changed my mind when I saw the enormous crowd gathering. *"Wow!! Seriously? Is it that common?"* I didn't feel desperate enough to wait in such a long line to connect with this unusual organization, but I could definitely appreciate what they were doing. I could have benefited tremendously with this kind of help twenty years earlier. At this stage of the game, I had pretty much come to terms with my issues, or so I believed. The next series of events have been left to age in the deep and dark shadows of my subconscious mind. Some things are better left unsaid.

During a break I had gone to the merchandising area where books and other relevant items were being marketed. I had a few books in my hand as I stepped up to the cashier. I started to reach for my wallet... and poof! I was gone. I had experienced this *checking out* mode enough for this to be less shocking than you might expect. It was so NOT surprising that I hardly made note of it. The only oddity for me was that when I returned to my body, the woman was handing me back my credit card as I was still searching for it. *"How did you get that?"* I asked her point blank. She didn't even acknowledge my question as she completed the transaction, handing me the receipt and a bag full of books. I muttered a few words in confusion and walked away. Now normally I would have blocked it out of my mind, as I had become so accustomed to doing. *"I mean... c'mon... what else can you do with such non-sensical happenings?"* After so many years it just gets auto-filed in the *wtf?* bin. However, when my entire weekend had been devoured by unbelievable, highly educated, and documentable information relating to exactly what I had just experienced, I didn't shove it under the carpet so quickly.

Later in the day, I ran into a Warrior Brother from one of my men's circles. He and his wife had also shown up for the conference, coincidentally. He asked me, *"Did you hear about the UFO in town?"* "Huh?" I mumbled. *"What else do you say to that, beyond Huh?"* He went on to tell me of the *red light* hovering over the city for a long enough period for crowds to gather in the streets, as they stood gazing at this well-defined anomaly. He and his wife had both witnessed the event firsthand. I knew him well enough to know that he wasn't playing games or lying. The bizarre appearance was so aligned with the focus of the conference that it seemed like no big deal. I didn't hear any talk of this affair from anybody on stage. It went almost unmentioned, and yet my *taken* experience was too connected with all of it for me to sidestep or ignore.

I came home knowing full well that my many years of experience with voices and missing pieces held more for me than I had been willing to open up to. I continued my work with an expanded vision of what this Universe is made of, recognizing the systems theory to include more than humanity. There was another world full of beings that exceeded our capacity for knowledge and understanding. Whether we called them *Angels* or *Extra-Terrestrials* made little difference as to the quality of their true nature.

YES... it was easy to discount everything that didn't fit into my box of preconceived notions about *The Nature of Reality*. YES... the option to ignore what I couldn't understand was available and understandably attractive to a lot of folks for many reasons. I mean... think about it. Considering any of this *crazy stuff* as valid or realistic, forces a person to be faced with an enormous amount of challenging mental work, that requires a great deal of effort to sort it all out. It could mean restructuring one's entire mental-emotional infrastructure, which had been formulated according to the non-existence of anything beyond what the eyes could see, the hands could touch, or the mind could grasp.

The truth of the matter is... this can be damn scary stuff to look at! Of course most folks will passionately resist contending with this forbidden area of life. Expectedly, the masses will be inclined to deny or oppose dealing with any of this as reality based. Why open a door into expansive new territory, when you've struggled so long to achieve comfort in this modest but familiar space... you've almost come to terms with?

Suddenly, there's a fork in the road. It's the red pill or the blue pill. One direction means entering a frightening territory where nothing you have imagined to be true holds water. The other direction allows you to hold onto your comfortable and familiar perspective, without having to adjust or alter any of your views on *reality*. Can you see why the line would be longer in the *reject all incoming data* department? Whether the choice is conscious or not, most folks will automatically turn away from such an overload. That is, if they feel they have an option. The other truth of the matter is... I wasn't one of them.

My entire existence was falling through the holes of what I perceived to be real. This wasn't just a fun topic to explore or an interesting science fiction perspective to entertain myself with. I was focused on basic survival and desperately searching for freedom in a world that appeared to have limited options for a guy like me. The truth of my life story was that I was a social reject. I was doing everything in my power to act normal and appear as though I fit in, so as to avoid being locked up, tied down, and drugged into a stupefied state. I had been pushed to the edge of what I could handle, and quite honestly, was doing my best to buy into the *he's just crazy* story. A big part of me didn't want to deal with extra-terrestrials, angels, or voices from the other side, any more than the average closed-minded cave man. How much easier it is to say, "Oh... *it's just some crazy thinking... that occurs through this psychotic mind as a result of a chemical imbalance.*" Trust me... that's much easier to deal with.

My inner work was effective as I unraveled this knotted ball of emotional yarn that had been so twisted through time. I knew the pain and confusion emotional wounding could create, and also how clear the heart and mind could become through this healing work. I also had to admit that I was experiencing more than the confusion that arises through emotional trauma. I was definitely experiencing something quite similar to what was being shared through the stories of those who'd been courageous enough to step forward and speak their truth. My scope of awareness and attention had been expanded a hundredfold, and my workload increased significantly. However, I could not deny the possibility of this new awareness being central to my ongoing disturbance and disruption. As much as I wanted an easy path, I could finally see that this truth might very well set me free. I also had no idea of the level of science involved in attempting to understand the nature of reality. *"How far down the rabbit hole do you want to go?"*

As for being considered *crazy*... well which one was worse? Thinking you are Jesus, The Messiah of the Coming Age... or believing you have been abducted by an alien life form of an extra-terrestrial nature? It's really kind of a toss-up. Most folks would put you in the same basket for either offense. I was familiar with, and actually becoming comfortable with being judged as *out of his mind*. Delving into the studies that surrounded the entire ancient alien phenomenon would be no more disturbing to my life than any of the rest of it. I knew the routine well. *"Just don't tell the people that are in a position to punish you for looking outside the box!"*

Chapter 43

❧ stairway to heaven ❧

There's a feeling I get when I look to the west and my spirit is crying for leaving. In my thoughts I have seen rings of smoke through the trees and the voices of those who standing looking.
— Led Zeppelin, Stairway to Heaven

Three months after my wide-eyed encounter with this new world of possibilities, I lost one of the few trustworthy people in my life that I could be open and honest with without negative repercussions. My little sister Cathy died in the middle of March of 2001. Her fragile body finally gave out after twenty-four years of dialysis and three failed kidney transplants. Of the four children in our family, Cathy and I were the closest of the bunch. It had just naturally occurred that way. I was five years older and she looked up to me. She laughed a lot and believed me to be a painted faced clown, created just for her. Funny thing is, I loved being her clown and felt she was the constant audience designed just for me. She would fall over laughing at the smallest gesture. I could make a silly face, mutter a sound, and watch her go into hysterics. It tickled me deeply, and I cherished her presence in my life.

When she steered her path toward following in my footsteps to become a cosmetologist, it set us on track to work closely together for many years into our adult life. We had spent more than a decade working side by side in the Seattle salon. My life had fallen into an abyss of hardship when the business partnership was severed and we parted paths. Even though much time had passed, in the aftermath of this heart

269

wrenching disruption, I realized I was still adjusting to her not being in my daily life.

I had recently been through my second divorce with the young gal who was involved in the Sacre Voeu phase of my transformational living adventure. I was already suffering with some serious post-partum depression before Cathy's passing, so this was definitely the straw that carried a heavy load.

One day, within a week of her crossing over, I woke up unusually early in the morning. I hopped out of bed and immediately began getting dressed to go for a run. I put on my stretchy pants and a sweatshirt, and was sitting on the front porch getting ready to slip my tennis shoes on. Now this may not sound like a big deal, but if you knew me and my habits, you would definitely realize this was extremely odd. I didn't wake up in the early morning for much. I might possibly be persuaded by a well-planned fishing adventure with an old high school buddy. That level of excitement might light me up before the crack of dawn, but it would be a rare occasion. I certainly wasn't in the habit of *going for a run*. In fact, I couldn't recall the last time I'd felt up for that kind of activity. The truth is I was in a desperately depressed state during that spell, and *normal* would mean slowly crawling out of that warm bed at about ten a.m.

So anyway, I was sitting on the porch, beginning to put my shoes on, and I suddenly realized, *"Something weird is going on here."* At about the time I was awakening to the realization of the oddity of this situation, I felt a presence. Not just any presence, but most obviously and specifically my sister Cathy's presence, that I knew so very well. I could feel her as though she was right there with me, and I said out loud, *"Is that you?"* I could hear her reply within my mind like a telepathic response, *"Yes... it is."* So I wasn't hearing a voice coming from outside of me, but it was strong and clear. Beyond hearing, I was feeling a powerful physical presence. I was puzzled by it, and I asked her, *"Where are you?"* She responded, *"I am right next to you, by your side."* I could feel her presence so strongly that I was confused as to why I wasn't able to see her. I kind of squinted my eyes and looked to my side where she should have been sitting on the doorstep with me. It seemed strange that I couldn't see anything, and I felt a sense of embarrassment that I was unable to see her physical body with my eyes. *"What are you doing here?"* I asked softly. She replied, *"Do you need me?"* I immediately responded, *"God yes... are you kidding? I'm having a hard time with my life right now. I just went through a divorce... and now you are gone... and..."* She interrupted me with a reaffirming voice, *"That is why I'm here."* The conversation continued, *"Well geez sis... that's great... but for God's sake don't get caught up in my earth bound mess. I mean... don't you need to go to the light or something?"* Now the following message was the climax of this entire exchange, at least for me. She told me with such a deeply caring tone that it brought tears to my eyes. She said, *"Jeff... don't worry... It's all under control."* Now I read these words and they don't look like much, but the way she spoke brought a deep and lasting peace to my heart. I was instantly calmed, and felt an uncanny level of confidence in the divine nature of the universe, including beyond death. I knew in the depths of my heart that she was more than *okay.* This potent message valiantly confirmed that she had entered a heavenly realm and was in good hands. My heart and mind would remain at ease from that point on, in regard to her transition, even when the overwhelming sadness for the loss was undeniable.

I continued to put my shoes on and went for a run around the one mile loop, as she stayed with me for the entire trek. We casually conversed for the duration of the jog, and it was reassuringly delightful. The content escaped me shortly after the event, but it did leave a lasting impression. She came to me several times later on, and her visitations played an incredibly significant role in what was about to unfold in my life.

In all honesty, I didn't actually feel the initial visitation was random. What I mean by that is that I had inadvertently set up a transmission line that made this spirit connection highly feasible. I had given her a specific crystal the night I visited her in the hospital. This turned out to be the final visit we shared in her physical body. My parents had warned me that she was not doing well and would most likely not be conscious or capable of interacting much. I was prepared for the worst and happily surprised to find her energetic response to my presence. It was actually shocking and even more so as I recall the event.

She was out of her bed and up on her feet shortly after I entered the room. She had a pole that was holding her I.V. to contend with as she stood there with me, but it was nothing out of the ordinary for her. Half of her life had been spent with tubes of blood going in and out of her broken body. She was bright eyed, smiling, and her attitude seemed as confident as ever. We chatted for a bit with small talk, like hairdressers do so well, and the nurse soon gave a warning that the visiting hours were coming to a close. I had carried this mystical gift with a very specific intention. I presented it to her and explained, "*Cathy...* *you can call on me with this,*" as I handed her the crystal. "*Think of it like a cell phone.*"

I could see her wheels turning as she pondered what I was proposing. She smiled like only she could and was very pleased to accept this sacred present, as we unknowingly said our final good-bye. I did not expect that this would be our last time to look into each other's eyes. She seemed to be in pretty good shape, and I'd seen her survive a zillion times before when she looked a lot worse. My intention was merely to give her something that would provide a physical connection to me and the reassuring comfort of knowing that I was with her in spirit. I am grateful for that final gift, although it didn't exactly play out like I was expecting.

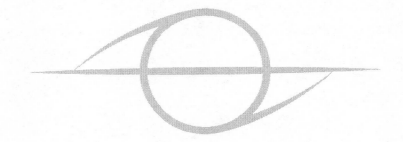

Chapter 44

✆ crystal visions ❧

Do you always trust your first initial feeling, special knowledge holds true, bears believing. I turned around and the water was closing all around like a glove, like the love that finally found me, then I knew in the crystalline knowledge of you. Drove me through the mountains, through the crystal like and clear water fountain, drove me like a magnet, to the sea...

— Fleetwood Mac, Crystal

The crystal I'd given her had a unique history. It was from a large collection or *family* of crystals that I'd been working with intimately for years. I told the story earlier of my first experience with the quartz crystal in the radio kit and don't actually recall how I became so enthralled with them later on, but I most certainly did.

One of the most outstanding occasions in relation to the crystals came through an unusual set of circumstances. I believe it was in the spring of '98, when my wife and I decided to take a joyride up into the Cascade Mountains. It was a lovely afternoon and we were anxious to get out of the house. We headed straight for the beauty of the high-altitude scenery. As we were driving out of town and approaching the foothills, we happened upon a little roadside Rock and Gem show. It was a little tent market that looked too cute to pass up.

We pulled in and took a stroll through the quaint little fairground atmosphere. There were a number of display tables, and we enjoyed browsing through the stones and the many trinkets and crafts these country folk had fashioned by hand. We stood in front of one particular stand with a display full of crystals, and I couldn't help but notice a bin near the cash register tagged with a hand written sign, *Special*. Inside were four crystals that were larger in size, significantly lower in price, and each had a red sticker attached. I questioned the attendant, and she said they just didn't fit in with the others, and that she was trying to clear her stock a bit. *"Wow... these are amazing crystals and the price is fantastic!"* I thought to myself. I quickly purchased the precious stones, and we were tickled with such a sweet find as we continued on our day trip.

I carried the crystals in my front pocket and soon discovered they were very attractive to the touch. I didn't really think much about it as I noticed myself wanting to hold them one by one, continuously. Within a couple of days, in some strange way, I found myself on a wild ride up into the San Juan Islands with the crystals as my guide.

These islands had already played, and would continue to play, a powerful role in my spiritual life. I had fallen in love with them back in '82, when I was on my honeymoon with my first wife, the mother of my children. We spent two weeks sailing a small boat through and around this magnificent and spectacular panorama. It was profoundly inspiring, and I made a vow to return to live in these islands one day, which I ended up fulfilling twenty years later. I had an intimate love affair going on with these beautiful little parcels of moat encircled earth.

With crystals in hand, I drove up to the ferry crossing and purchased a ticket to Orcas Island. I had no logical reason to go, nor had I prepared for this trip I felt so compelled to plunge into. As I sat in the waiting area for a couple of hours, I held the crystals in my hands. I was sitting outside at a picnic table that was situated to enjoy the view of the water. I sat peacefully taking

276

in the magnificent scenery, until something was so vigorously pulling my awareness into another realm, that I closed my eyes and embarked on an inward journey into the outer cosmos.

It was extremely vivid visually and as real as any other 3D experience I'd been familiar with. I felt that I was being taken on an expedition into a starry realm that held visions of value in some bizarre way. In other words, it was extraordinary and felt to be divinely purposeful.

I watched the light from a distant sun cast shadows on the moving bodies that traversed the heavens before my eyes, and it was thoroughly captivating. This cosmic display developed and wondrously transformed as I blissfully observed in silence. I found myself witnessing a star wars kind of scenario with enormous spaceships that were right out of a sci-fi movie. It was an absolutely incredible display, and there seemed to be an underlying theme to these interactions. At one point, I witnessed a dark craft coming toward the earth's atmosphere from the depths of space, and as it approached another starship emerged in the foreground. This magnificent and oversized spacecraft engaged the intruders, and obviously held the energy of the good guys. This was the beacon that was defending our earth colony, and capable of doing so beyond the shadow of a doubt. The gloomy spacecraft slowed as it approached and a telepathic communication of sorts ensued. The smaller and obviously less powerful shuttle seemed to recognize the danger in proceeding beyond the warning zone that was being declared, and backed off without any display of resistance. As it turned and began its descent into the dark abyss of space, I could clearly make out the evil face on the tail of the ship. The entire rear end of the craft was fashioned like the face of a gargoyle, and obviously designed to inflict fear. I felt a deep appreciation for the newly built and highly advanced technology of the defending battle ship that reigned over our planetary dwelling place. The streaming vision was extremely vivid and realistic. It didn't have the feeling of being a dream as I was fully conscious throughout the showing. It was a glorious display, and I felt honored to be able to witness this spectacular galactic event.

I did, eventually, take the ferry ride to Orcas, and met a few interesting characters along the way, but nothing astronomical occurred to my recollection. I anxiously searched for a room for the night and ran into dead-ends at every turn in the road. This overnight adventure didn't appear to be in the stars, so I headed home. The next day I was still feeling obsessed with the crystals, and although I didn't understand what the attraction was, it was profound. I probably looked like a child playing with marbles or toy soldiers in the dirt. I was just moving them around and feeling the energy that came through the various alignments. At one point, I was playing with them on top of the television cabinet and I brought a compass that I used for hiking and backpacking into the mix. I carefully and strategically laid the crystals in line with the four directions according to the compass. I had arranged them in several configurations, but when I placed them with the points facing outward and precisely in line with north, south, east and west... *KABOOM!* I mean literally, kaboom. I know how crazy this sounds and how hard it is to believe. Trust me... I don't typically tell folks this kind of thing, because it tends to make you look like a crazy man with serious mental health issues... but honest to God... this is what happened.

Chapter 45

৯ father sky's staff ৵

I ran into the fortune-teller who said beware of lightning that might strike. I haven't known peace and quiet for so long I can't remember what it's like. There's a lone soldier on the cross, smoke pouring out of a boxcar door... you didn't know it, you didn't think it could be done, in the final end he won the war, after losing every battle.
                        —Bob Dylan, Idiot Wind

The sky cracked open and rain came pouring down with a vengeance, along with thunder and lightning! I was alone when it transpired, and it completely freaked me out. I was frightened in the deepest way and muttered out loud, *"Oh My God... What have I done!?"* I was stunned and startled into a borderline panic as a voice came back and calmly stated, *"You pierced a veil."* This supernatural voice was arising from without and within simultaneously. I was astonished with the whole event and quickly gathered up the crystals, as I frantically scattered them about the house. I was frightened by the drastic response triggered by their close alignment.

When my wife came home, the first thing out of her mouth as she entered the door was, *"Did you see that freak storm?"* She had witnessed the violent outburst from a few miles away and heard it announced on the radio. My brother called me on the phone to tell me the same thing. Apparently, there was an emergency bulletin on the radio, mentioning this peculiar and unexpected lightning storm that seemed to arise from nowhere. It had certainly gained the attention of the local weather watchers. This was absolutely astonishing for me personally, because I had no doubt as to the causal factors. I told both my brother and my wife what I had done and neither of them seemed terribly thrown off by what I was proposing. They seemed equally dumfounded, but neither of them appeared caught in disbelief. There was nothing to be done and nowhere to go with this bizarre experience, especially as a mental health patient. We all just let it slide into the background of our awareness, along with the many other absurdities that remain unclassified.

The next day I created a new project for myself and it didn't feel optional. It also didn't appear to be coming from my conscious state of mind. I hand cut about a seven foot length of branch from a vine maple on my property. Instinctively and quickly, I took to carving out new homes for these wizardly crystals. Leaving them laying around left me feeling uneasy, and I was certain that I'd sleep better if they were secured, grounded, and properly aligned.

I used my buck knife to carve out a hole at the crotch of a smaller branch on the staff, buried a portion of the crystal tightly into the chiseled wood, and wrapped it securely with a leather shoestring. I carefully embedded all four crystals with the last one safely fastened in the fork at the top.

The strangest aspect of the project was witnessing my hands carving as though they were someone else's. It reminded me of *automatic writing* where the subconscious, or some other consciousness, takes over and a person strangely moves faster than normal. I guess this unusual behavior is often associated with channeling as well. I felt possessed and obsessed with carving and digging on this stick in rapid motion for the entire day. When I'd finished this mystical process, the crystals lined up like Chakras and the staff came to life.

Now I'm not talking about any movement of any sort. It wasn't like a walking-talking stick in a Pinocchio cartoon, or the brooms from Fantasia, for Christ's' sake. It just felt energized in an unusual and unique way. I noticed interesting effects whenever I carried it with me. Keep in mind, this wooden staff is seven and half feet tall.

I recall having it in the back of my truck one day as I was driving down the highway, and I swear the traffic aligned and moved harmoniously in sync. That's a rare occurrence in these parts, and certainly enough to get your attention. I ended up taking the staff into Sacre' Voeu and allowed many folks to encounter it, with only a select few permitted to touch it. The response was always fascinating.

The most phenomenal incident that I personally witnessed with this crystal staff was during an outdoor adventure with my kids. The three of us took a backpacking trip into the Enchanted Valley of the Olympic Mountains. My daughter was about 12, and my son 10. It was a very exciting journey, and I was tickled beyond measure to bring my children into such a wondrous and beautiful landscape. The impact of nature has always been enlightening for me, and I was thrilled to be sharing this depth of it with my two favorite beings on the planet.

The trail is about thirteen miles one-way, and we'd come about halfway in. The kids wanted to play in the water, and we weren't in a big hurry to reach the valley, so we decided to hang out at this campsite and spend the night. It was a gorgeous, sun-filled day, and the river was easy to access from here. We set up camp, built a fire, and fixed a little bite to eat.

Later in the day as dusk was drawing near, we were sitting on the riverbank, with me nestled between the two of them. I had the staff in my hand propped against the dirt in front of me. We were just sitting quietly, taking in the view and the majesty of this tranquil scene, when the most bizarre marvel occurred right before our eyes. Directly in front of us, about fifty feet away, a little sparkle of light began to flicker. It was strange and not easy to describe.

It reminded me of the *Wizard of Oz,* when the *Good Witch of the South* was about to appear. This little twinkle of light began and slowly expanded as it moved toward us. It was as if something beyond the veil was trying to appear, like a burst of effort to manifest from another dimension. It was eerie to say the least, and I felt a twinge of fear arise within our threesome. We were sitting closely together and energetically we were one. I couldn't tell from where the fear arose, but I felt it emerge and within seconds the twinkling light receded and disappeared. Even though it seemed like the prelude to something grander, it was a magnificent event.

The light appeared from beyond this world and was intimately reminiscent of the *pierced veil* extravaganza. I was extremely grateful to have my children witness this unusual phenomenon. For one, it was highly validating for me to have company, as I was so often inclined to question my own sanity. It was also enchanting to allow them the opportunity to experience something we could not define or fully comprehend. There is nothing like a mystical, otherworldly experience to open your mind to realms that you would otherwise deny. I am still appreciative and thankful for that bizarre little miracle.

Chapter 46

❧ mind enlightened network ❧

If you have built castles in the air, your work need not be lost; that is where they should be. Now put the foundations under them.

— *Henry David Thoreau, Walden*

As I came to recognize the value the quartz crystals held in the way of frequency modulation, I explored and experimented in every manner imaginable. I had purchased a thousand dollars' worth of high quality crystals from a wholesaler out of Arkansas when I first opened the store. I had procured a number of crystals from this distributor once before, and I appreciated having this new batch of stones from the same quarry. I've put great effort into seeing that they've been distributed and disbursed in an intentional fashion. I have offered them as gifts to family and friends, as well as other particular associations through the passing years. I have also carried them with me when I've traveled and carefully placed them in specific hands, and in strategic zones. Over a several year period I had crystals planted across the globe, from the volcanoes of Hawaii to South Korea, and as far away as a Himalayan peak on the border between India and Pakistan. The Himalayan crystal plant was definitely the coolest one ever, and by the grace of God it was captured on video.

My son has successfully fashioned his lifestyle around snowboarding and diligently forged his way into the professional status that brings him great encouragement to travel. He and a business partner/photographer went to India to shoot a documentary in the winter of 2013. As a favor, he took a particular crystal that I had chosen, strategically placed it in a stone cairn at the peak of a ridge, and video recorded this monumental event. What a deeply meaningful celebration for me to be able to actually watch him place a crystal in the snow-covered Himalayan Mountains. I was grateful and elated!

Perhaps it is easy to understand why I have tended toward keeping my *crazy* stuff to myself. So many folks are not only unable to comprehend this kind of thinking, but often lean into being antagonistic toward what they can't quite conceive of. Purely out of self-protection and ease, I've been quiet about my metaphysical explorations and experimental undertakings.

For me, I was setting up a network of relay stations around the world. I could personally connect with every single one of these crystals. They were packaged and stored as a family, and certainly originated from the same mound of dirt. They each had unique qualities and specific capabilities, but were connected at the very base of their creation, which creates a harmonic resonance.

I knew that they could be accessed and used in a wireless fashion. My intention for altering the collective consciousness of the planet could be channeled through these remote stations to impact humanity on a global scale. I didn't believe these stones were required to do the job, as it was clear that we were already connected through our collective consciousness without any crystals involved. It just seemed to be an effective way to amplify the impact and increase the intensity of the generative signal being broadcast.

"So... what if I'm completely out of my mind... as crazy as a loon?" This was the basic belief conveyed by so many that pushed to *fix* me. It seemed that even if I was stark raving mad, what's the big deal? I was *doing no harm* and unable to detect a downside or loss experienced by anyone involved. If this

crystal network was merely a bizarre way of entertaining my psychotic mind, then so be it. It wasn't hurting anyone and I was having a blast. The truth is… it made perfect sense to me.

I had only encountered one scary circumstance through my personal experimentations, and the cost was minor from what I could see. One day I was lying on my back on the couch, holding a certain crystal with a four-pointed window, in both hands on my chest. I suddenly was instantly sucked from the top of my head right down into the crystal. I had no intention of doing any more than holding and feeling into this crystal. It was perhaps the most bizarre event of my entire life, and that's really saying something. It was like a cartoon where a smoky body is drawn into a bottle like a Genie. I was alone, with no reference for time, so I was unsure if it was a two second or two hour journey. My guess was that it was quick. It seemed to have occurred in a flash. The weird part of it was that when I came back out, I had cold sores all over my lower lip. Never in my life had I developed cold sores instantaneously like that, and neither had I experienced having a handful of them appear all at once. This was one more crazy occurrence, never to be explained or considered beyond, *"Wow… that was weird!"*

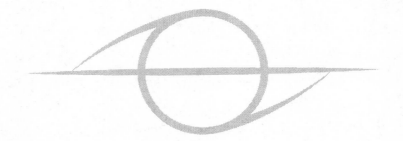

Chapter 47

❧ island time ❧

To be yourself in a world that is constantly trying to make you something else is the greatest accomplishment.

—Ralph Waldo Emerson

So, when I gave my sister a crystal and told her she could use it like a cell phone, you might now have a better understanding of where I was coming from. It seems to me that it worked better than I had anticipated. Her body had held fast to the crystal energy as she clinched it tightly before her departure. Her personal energy field was aligned with this crystal network and the frequency channel led her straight to me. Our connection was already tight and this additional contact created a quick access point from her spirit to mine. This is how I interpreted the metaphysical dynamics of this significant incident. Would she have visited me without the crystal? Most likely, but the visitation was strong and intense. Did this arrangement strengthen the connection? It appeared to play a heavy role, but who would ever know?

A short time after this event, we held a memorial service that would lead me to the next phase of my destiny. There was a strong turnout for this somber occasion, and many of her old school friends had shown up to pay their respects. One woman in particular caught my attention during the casual interactions after the service. She was a close friend of Cathy's from junior high school, and I hadn't seen her since they were young girls.

The uncanny attraction drew me into connecting with her beyond this singular affair. We connected via email for a while, and eventually got together in person. Early on, I became aware of the possibility of my attachment to her as being associated with subconsciously wanting to hold on to my little sister. We spoke openly of this underlying dynamic, and she was accepting as she expressed her understanding of the correlation. Even so, the attraction was strong enough to gradually pull us into intimate relations. Over the coming months, the relationship morphed into a girlfriend-boyfriend arrangement, in which we spoke intimately of the possibilities for the major change that we each dreamed of.

At what seemed to be a random point in time, as I was driving home from work, my sister suddenly does a drop-in visitation in the front seat of my car. What a shock to, out of the blue, suddenly have my sister come crashing in! She dives right into a serious discussion about me pursuing this relationship with her friend. Now this was not like a regular conversation where you analyze the words and define the message by way of verbal translation. It was more of an intuitive exchange through telepathy, which leaves an impression of obvious feelings around a certain subject matter. The question she was passionately presenting was about me moving forward with the plans that were developing with her friend. She seemed to have a deep knowing of the importance of this connection, and her question was basically, *"Would you be willing to do that?"* It felt like she was asking me a favor. What I remember clearly, is saying, *"Yes... I would be willing to do that,"* in direct response to her tender request. Was it for me... or her... or for reasons beyond either of us? I wasn't sure, but it felt right to move forward in the direction being highlighted in such a magnificent fashion. I was also banking on my trust in my sister as a spiritual ally.

The choice to step into, rather than away from, this stream of events would certainly prove to be critical to my life path. However, I had no way of realizing the magnitude of this choice from where I stood. It was a maneuver that required serious commitment, and it appeared daunting from my personal and limited point of view. Shortly after my drive-by spirit coaching session with my sister, my new girlfriend and I had conjured up an enormous plan of total transmutation. She was in a high level position with a major Seattle based corporation, so the leap she was proposing was radical to say the least. The basic vision we had fashioned included her quitting her job, me selling my business, both of us selling our homes, and the two of us moving up into the San Juan Islands. This surreal dream soon manifested in a magical and illustrious manner.

I was blown out of the water when I easily found both my business and my home being sold, without ever listing either of them. The gal that owned the coffee stand three doors down from the salon asked me if I was interested in selling. I responded immediately and the deal fell together nicely, as the sale proceeded without a hitch. My next-door neighbor, in a similar fashion, asked to buy my home. He wanted this adjoining property for his daughter to be able to live nearby, and purchased my property with no questions asked. They were both unbelievably smooth and effortless transactions.

When life offers up such mystical means of transition it becomes obvious that certain paths are meant to be followed, and this route was as clear as day. The girlfriend was also able to sell her home quite easily, and our dream was mysteriously materializing like a paper dragon. We moved up to Orcas and she purchased a large seven bedroom home that was currently operating as a bed and breakfast. It was a magnificent piece of property, and the idea of running a B&B was exciting for about a week and a half. I mean the actual reality of being bound to the home to answer phones and take care of guests was not quite as cool as the fantasy. Making beds and breakfast between guests became *not that fun* pretty quick. The excitement of the new love connection was dwindling rapidly, and our shaky foundation was shallower than either of us had considered. Our high romance relationship fizzled out in a matter of months, and I soon moved on. She was accustomed to running the show, so it wasn't out of the ordinary to see her go it alone. Her parents had followed her to the island, and she soon moved out of the B&B mansion to be closer to them.

As for me, I was very pleased to be out of the environment that I'd established in the prison town, and happy to be disconnected from my old situation. My mental health was teetering on the edge of the abyss during this big transition and sketchy through the breakup phase, but soon leveled out in a splendid manner. I rented a small apartment in town and found employment in the only barbershop on the island. It was a beautiful transition from the city life that I was so familiar with. I guess that is a bit misleading as it's all so relative when it comes to country and city living. I've never really lived in the big city. L.A... New York... I can't imagine. The closest I'd been to big city living was on the outskirts of Seattle, and that was for a short time during my early years. Since then I had continued to move North and West. I was now about as far northwest as I could possibly go within the continental United States. I was standing in the lookout tower on the peak of Mt. Constitution, gazing out over the inland waters to Canada, when I realized I could go no further in my current state.

I spent three years on the island and healed in magnificent ways. It was as if my soul was finally able to breathe in the beauty I was immersed in. A short time after moving into the apartment, I found a cottage for rent on the waterfront of a small bay facing the setting sun and spent the majority of my island excursion in that location. I hiked around the local trails and wasted many days exploring the state park. I ventured along the pathways to beach access that only the locals were privy to. I was secretly led to sacred sites and turned onto hidden vortexes tucked deeply in the backwoods. My mystical island love affair was blossoming. I often took my rowboat up into the mountain lake to fish and would find myself in awe of the stunning beauty. All alone in a landscape that could bring tears to your eyes, sitting in the middle of a paradise few would ever know, I would wholly realize how fortunate I was. The divine blessings were obvious and overflowing.

Chapter 48

❧ deliberate creation ❧

You have to grow from the inside out. None can teach you,
none can make you spiritual. There is no other teacher
but your own soul.

— Swami Vivekananda

I casually plugged into a circle of folks through the New Age gift shop in town and soon found my spiritual brothers and sisters in this quaint little community. I was intrigued by a local couple that promoted an *Avatar* program for *Deliberate Living*. I had studied many books about *creating your own reality* and was quite familiar with this basic premise. My first exposure to this perspective occurred at age fourteen, when I read *In Tune with the Infinite* by Ralph Waldo Trine, published in 1897. This popular modern-day metaphysical philosophy wasn't so "new" after all.

The Law of Attraction and *The Power of Intention* were common knowledge to the company I most often associated with. Dr. Wayne Dyer, Abraham/Hicks, and Dr. Chopra were among the many that had left a powerful impression on my evolutionary understanding. If I had my way, Deepak's *Seven Spiritual Laws of Success* would be unanimously accepted as the new standard International Bible. In my view, it's the most concise and clear teaching I have encountered, in the way of living a healthy spiritual life of responsibility and prosperity. I was well acquainted with the general notion that we are each manifesting the situations and opportunities that appear to show up randomly in our lives. I soaked in this pool of understanding that was glistening in the forefront of our most popular New Age teachings, but I'd never seen a hands-on course made available along these lines.

I signed up for the *Avatar* training and was so captivated by the approach that I continued on to the next three levels. The two beginning programs were presented on the island. The Master's course was held in South Korea, where I found myself as one of two Americans in a sea of non-English speaking Asian folks. With approximately two hundred participants, the majority were from Korea. Maybe twenty were from China, a handful from Japan, a few Canadians, and several from a variety of European countries. The course was taught in English, while a multitude of translators worked with the various groups of attendees. The work was transformational to say the least, and I ventured on to complete the final Wizard's course in Florida. Both of these upper level courses were approximately two week programs, and the training was intense. Upon completion in March of 2003, I was listed as one of 2500 Wizards from 33 countries who had achieved this level of training.

In the spring of 2015 I would attend a review of this *Avatar Wizard* course that held over 4000 students from 66 countries. These were only the students attending this particular event. There had obviously been ongoing growth and development in this international community, whole-heartedly devoted to creating an *Enlightened Planetary Civilization*. This was a powerful family to stand with, and I would honorably carry the teachings forward through the many twists and turns that still lay in the path ahead.

During the 2003 Wizard course I was fortunate enough to be in a position to connect with Harry Palmer, the founder and head honcho of the program. I carried a very special crystal with me, and in the back of my mind had considered it a nice gift for Harry, should I have the opportunity to meet with him personally. We coincidentally ran into each other in the lobby between teaching sessions, and following a brief dialogue he graciously accepted my offer. I was honored and confident this crystal was being received into good hands. The vibrational frequency of this wireless network was increasing and accelerating to levels I hadn't dreamed of a few years earlier.

I learned a valuable lesson in the mid '80s that stayed with me, like a close friend, through all of these years. A small book by Ken Keyes Jr., called *The Hundredth Monkey*, instilled the idea of consciousness being permeable and commonly influenced by a critical mass. The basic premise was related through a story where a group of scientists observed several islands off the coast of Japan that were occupied by monkeys. They flew over and dropped sweet potatoes onto the islands, and through observation discovered the patterns whereby the monkeys learned to wash the sand from the potatoes before eating them. The notion suggested, was that, as usual, the learning was by trial and error to begin with. The younger ones also watched and learned in a typical fashion for acquiring knowledge. However, at a certain point, all of the monkeys on all of the islands mysteriously and suddenly acquired this knowledge without the standard methods of learning. The *hundredth monkey* theory suggested that we are all connected through a common field of consciousness. The gist of the basic premise was that when a *critical mass* has been reached in a particular area of understanding, it permeates and saturates the consciousness of the whole of the species. The overriding message that I interpreted from Ken's book, and carried in my heart was, *"Reach for the stars, and rise to the heights of your greatest potential within consciousness... because you just might be the hundredth monkey to tip the scale!"*

Finding my way into a global community of people that were also reaching for the stars was inspirational and encouraging. My work was not in vain, nor was it in isolation. We were collectively forming an international team of torch carriers, and jerseys were totally optional. This was turning into some good fun.

You know, looking back, this whole Messiah trip was actually still running full steam ahead, although it was pretty much under the radar. I didn't acknowledge my drive to impact the collective consciousness of humanity with too many folks. I didn't speak of it with more than a few intimate friends, and like I said before, the medical community had completely stuffed the Messianic Syndrome files into the closet. I had been showered in shame about this conviction and quite deliberately pushed it aside, doing my best to disregard it completely. The truth of the matter is it didn't really mean much. The idea of a guy thinking he has some special mission to save the world isn't necessarily such a bad thing. As my life expanded into grander spheres of relations, I came to recognize this notion in motion, within the mainstream clouds of consciousness around the world. It wasn't actually that rare after all, and it didn't appear to be a disease or disorder to contend with. *"I mean... what's the harm in being passionate about doing your best to make something positive happen in the world? How could this altruistic attitude of having humanity's best interest at heart be considered a problem?"* Of course, it really wasn't.

Chapter 49

✎ the messiah's ego ✍

If you bring forth what is within you, what you bring forth will save you. If you do not bring forth what is within you, what you do not bring forth will destroy you.
—Jesus of Nazareth

The real issue hidden beneath this blatantly labeled disorder had more to do with the state of mind attached to it. In other words, it wasn't the idea of feeling compelled to save humanity and the planet that was problematic. It was the repercussions of a misconstrued ego that could create such havoc in an already highly dysfunctional society. It seemed that guys like Jim Jones, Koresh, and Manson had enacted plans that gave every good-hearted Messiah a questionable platform.

Now I am certainly not sitting in judgment about anybody that, quite honestly, I know nothing about. I've spent many hours soaking in the conspiracy theories that enshroud the murderous actions of unnamed evil-spirited souls throughout the history of mankind. I know that this game has been twisted in ways that none of us can ever fully comprehend. Every good person that has ever stepped forth to deliver a divinely inspired message has faced a dangerous threat from the world of darkness that reigns. From Jesus and Gandhi to Lincoln, Kennedy, and King, it was obvious that the Saints were murdered alongside the long list of others presented as subversive. *"It's not easy to recognize the good guys in a world that wants to shoot 'em all down."*

All I know, is that the status of having a *disorder* related to feeling I had a mission to serve humanity, was discolored in my eyes. The true territory in question was not easy to reveal, but it certainly wasn't the desire to serve. It was definitely the ego's state of maturity that determined how this questionable perspective would play out. It feels rather silly to point this out, given the development of the ego, or lack thereof, appears to be the make it or break it for every psychological profile that exists. The immature or distorted ego is at the helm of every threat we humans face with one another on this precious planet we share. If you are looking for the evil culprit behind man's self-inflicted suffering, you will find it lording over the command post of the *ego*.

So now that I've opened that door, what are we even talking about when we speak of the *EGO*? It's a bit like the word *GOD*. We throw it around as though we're all speaking the same language, and yet few will agree on the definition of either of these terms. We may as well be conversing in foreign languages; in fact it would be better if we were. At least in that scenario, the recognition of different understandings would be considered.

In all my years of searching for answers, and striving to understand the psychology of this modern mind, I have been presented with countless perspectives on the concept of *ego*. For me it is an area of great misperception and misunderstanding, equal to the overwhelming befuddlement encountered through the word *GOD*. This word *God* is really the epitome of comedy. Not the word itself, but rather the spectacle of people being so utterly confused by it. People commonly hate, fight, and go to war to kill each other, over the conflict that arises through their own misunderstanding of this concept. Obviously, there is nothing funny about conflict, hate, and war. However, the notion of fighting to the death, over something beyond human comprehension, is so absurd that laughter might be the most appropriate response a sane person could muster up; if you happen to know one.

298

Perhaps an overruling agreement that the human mind is incapable of comprehending *God* would make for a good beginning point. If we're unable to comprehend this notion, how do we find a way to be *Right*, while maintaining with certainty that everyone else is *Wrong*? I love that Jesus equated *God* to *Love*. It really throws a wrench in the conflict department, when you substitute the word *Love* into the statements made about *God*, that create so much conflict and suffering. People struggle to stand rooted in their hatred for one another when the conflict is merely about love. Crazy... huh? Consider the difference in these questions with a simple word substitution. *"Do you believe in God?"* versus *"Do you believe in Love?"* Different answers? Hmm...

So the definition I've developed for myself in the way of striving to get a grip on this concept we call *Ego*, goes something like this.

Be warned: This is unlikely to line up with any other approach you will run into. It's just my own attempt at wrapping my mind around this central theme that holds such a critical position in this puzzle-like matrix.

As embodied spirits, it seems we enter this world open-hearted and in need. We are functioning in a higher, more receptive spiritual capacity as we enter the physical body in the mother's womb. It's not far from the heavenly realm from which we descended, as we discover our basic needs are met in this warm and cozy little liquid environment, which seems to be self-sustaining.

Apparently, we don't come to realize ourselves as separate from the mother for quite some time after we are birthed. However, the physical disconnect that takes place when the umbilical cord is severed, pushes that soul into a constant state of need. The food is no longer on auto-feed, breathing is mandatory, and the warmth of nurturing must be deliberate through a conscious effort by the mother. The child is propelled to develop an aspect of mind capable of taking responsibility for this individuated being. The early development usually manifests through mustering up an audible cry to be fed or held.

The *spirit* of the child is now housed in a flesh and bone body that must be fed, protected, and kept at a proper temperature. This spirit child will now grow up in a physical body, and a conditional situation that depends upon the environment outside itself. The primary means of survival will come through personal interactions with the band of human life forms with whom this child will merge. Consider the complexity of this new realm. Imagine a free flying spirit that is drifting through a dream world where every need is met without effort, suddenly descending into a position of such dependency. Oh my goodness, what a shock to the soul that has unknowingly arrived! Soon that little mind begins to develop a sense of being separate and individuated.

The emerging ego is becoming compartmentalized as a fragmentation of the infinite mind from which it sprang. It is like a computer program or a phone app that begins to develop in this newly individuated being. This app is a required element for functioning in this three dimensional realm. It's like being in an online game that you can't play without the app.

The truth of this soul's existence is that it is one with the whole. An authentic or higher-self can function well in that field of awareness and no *ego app* is required. The deepest reality was being experienced pre-birth, however, that version of existence is no longer considered relevant in this world we choose to occupy for the duration of the incarnation. Here in this realm, we hang out in the domain of duality. Regardless of what is theoretically true, what appears to be so is that we are each separate beings in disconnected bodies. This is a brave new world we have suddenly entered.

The *ego* is the aspect of mind that develops, as a means of interfacing with this three dimensional realm, that presents one with the illusion of duality. *"Is it really just an illusion? Yes it is!... a very important one. You are here for a reason!"* The Ego is the much needed app for this Matrix, and readily takes the helm of the *I*. When a sentence begins with *I*... it is the voice of the ego that speaks. *"The Father and I are one."* *I* identifies *me* as a separate being, and this domain is under the jurisdiction of the ego. The ego app is operating if a person recognizes themselves as an individual. If it's not running, they are not capable of functioning as an individual. It's a required tool for this world.

This is what I was referring to earlier when I spoke of Ramana Maharshi. He was found lying in a cave, with bugs chewing on him, as he was starving to death. His survival was due to the intervention by loved ones that took him in. He was in an egoless state of ecstatic enlightenment. Eventually, his ego mind gradually regained functionality, and he was once again able to speak and take care of his basic personal needs.

I've also heard stories of Jesus experiencing times of not being mindful of eating or taking care of his personal needs. His ego, too, seemed to be falling away, as he wholeheartedly strived to fulfill his altruistic mission. Fortunately, he also had a support group that cared for him, when he wasn't exactly shining in the self-care department. This topic of self-care tends to blend well with the idea of loving support. There can be a fine line between dependency and a supportive alliance, which is certainly worthy of definition. It also seems extremely important to understand that the ego plays a critical role in this realm.

I often hear people say, *"You just need to get rid of your ego!"* They are speaking of something other than what I am referring to. What that is, I'm not sure. Without the *ego* I speak of, we are unable to function independently. There would be no reason or avenue for acting as a separate entity without the aspect of mind that operates according to this basic premise. Without the egoic mind, the true self would be lost in the oneness of unity consciousness and perceive nothing outside of it. The egoless state can look a lot like the state of awareness I shared through my fall into *the light*. That was a solid demonstration of a state of unity consciousness, as the ego-mind was sidelined. It was an awesome state to behold but not recommended for everyday functioning. If you really want to get a good sense of what I am attempting to outline here, go to YouTube and search for *Jill Bolte Taylor's stroke of insight*. She gives one of the most amazing presentations on brain/mind functioning I have ever witnessed. Seriously... if you haven't seen it, check it out. It is well worth the time.

My purpose in dissecting the concept of *ego* is to point out, that not only do we need this piece of mind, but that it is the primary focus for our personal development as human beings. The egoic mind is the component we are predisposed to develop. It is the aspect of self that is so often confused with the authentic, true, or higher Self. This is the conscious reasoning mind that does the *thinking* and is often referred to as the *false* or *lower* self. The Buddhists generally refer to this mental compartment as *The Monkey Mind*. This is also where mental/emotional health issues are processed and, therefore, where our inner work is required. It's the facet of mind we long to evolve. This is also the aspect that can and will achieve enlightenment. It is programmable and teachable. The ego does not have to remain in an immature or underdeveloped state. Nor must it remain entangled in narcissistic, sadistic, or masochistic levels of consciousness.

I hear so many teachings that speak as though the *ego* is a pre-programmed compartment of mind that is not capable of evolving. *"How ridiculous!"* What on earth would we be working toward if this were true? It is precisely the *self* that we are here to develop. The *TRUE* or *Authentic Self* doesn't need any development.

The funny thing about this whole *Messianic Complex* label that I felt so threatened by for the bulk of my life, was that it appeared to merely be another deep misunderstanding. This *EGOIC* mind, so foundational to man's basic functioning, in an immature state has a tendency to play God. The under developed ego, like a run-away robot, is inclined to take the helm as master of the vessel, posing as the Almighty.

This characteristic is no more ascribed to the implanted Messiahs than the general population of humanity. It's just a serious issue to contend with when they're coupled up. That is, when a person believing they have a Messianic role to play becomes partnered with an out of control ego that's running the show; it can be a frightening combination to contend with. Now we recognize a serious problem, and this appears to be the vision of ugliness that stands behind this mystically manufactured Messianic dilemma.

The obvious issue for me is that this out of control ego is consistently the true culprit, and it conspicuously dwells among the many. It need not be associated with a Messiah complex to create danger. Look at the countless profiles of the dangerous egocentric people throughout history, or even in the world we share now. Look at the ego-based minds that pose as Gods, willing to sacrifice the wellbeing of the majority for their own selfish gain. Why are we not targeting this obvious monster? Can you imagine the fortune that could be made selling drugs for that epidemic?

Think about it... *"Sir... we have determined that you have an Immature Ego Toxicity Disorder... and we're prescribing this new drug that generates the equivalent of two hours of meditation and prayer per day. Oh... and it's not recommended, or actually allowable for you to run for that political office with this condition."* Hey... I just might be on to something!

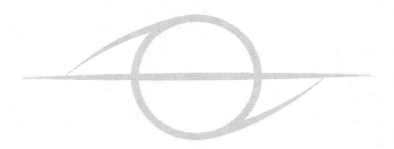

Chapter 50
᠀ archimedes pie ᠀

As far as the laws of mathematics refer to reality, they are not certain; and as far as they are certain, they do not refer to reality.

—Albert Einstein

It seems we have inconspicuously dialed into a highly suspicious aspect of mind on this introspective journey. This particular division appears to be paramount to humanity's suffering since the beginning of time. Interestingly enough, it ties directly into another previously mentioned area of concern identified as *Materialism*. This *ego mind* aka *false self* seems to be designed for the soul purpose of interacting with this material world. In fact, it seems to be the piece of mind that actually defines it! *"What?"*... *"YES!"*

This compartment of mind that serves as an app through which to interact, also serves as a filter through which we perceive. As it is indoctrinated and programmed for the purpose of behavioral functioning, it is also inadvertently being coded to see exactly what it has been told it will see. That is, programmed to believe and perceive precisely what the pre-programmed programmers before you were sold as *truth*. *"Can you wrap your mind around that?"*

The governing body that rules our educational process presents an environment that is pre-labeled and codified, so as to leave no room for error... or imagination. This multifaceted *science mind* proposes to be the master of understanding, and stands at the podium as the creator of all knowledge. We inadvertently and collectively bow to the God of science without a second thought. The child that dares to perceive in a way that's not scientifically and socially acceptable will pay the price, one way or another.

Non-science based cultures are nonchalantly pushed aside as *primitive,* and their knowledge stamped out as *invalid.* Pagan or earth based religions have been all but obliterated by this immoral disease of the *science mind.* The Shaman, Celts, and Wiccans have been trampled into the dirt, as the asphalt path to *civilized living* is strategically laid. We the common people, blindly and unknowingly, sit back, nurture, and bow to this Ivory Tower which lords over our souls.

I live in a territory where our *Native Americans* are still struggling to pick up the pieces left over from the total devastation that undermined their ancient and sacred knowledge. It appears that the *Aborigines of Australia* have faced a similar fate. We can see clearly, the obvious evil in this blatant violation, and yet the underlying dynamic goes undetected every day in our mainstream society. We cannot create a healthy society and allow this destructive force to continue. We need to revive the ancient cultures of wisdom before they are extinct. Our modern day witch burnings are carried out in sterile institutions, and crucifixions chemically induced behind closed doors. We cannot build a healthy social environment by locking the people up that don't fit into the mold of the status quos. We're running out of room, and one day the tides are going to turn. Let us find a way to move forward peacefully, as we ask ourselves, *"How on earth did we get here?"*

That is such an unfathomable question, and as I ponder it I realize the pointlessness in wandering down that endless corridor. Regardless of how we've arrived, the bottom line is, the current state of humanity's collective egoic mind has been formulated by our predecessors. Whether they were cave men, aliens, or a combination of the two seems of little consequence.

306

The predominant issue is this *ego* mind being indoctrinated by the social structure in which it emerges. That specific locale is inherently intertwined within the collective consciousness that continues to pave the way for each incoming soul.

Regardless of where the finger is pointed, in sorting out the cause, we are left with a serious obligation in this conflicted world we share. This socially centered ego mind is at the base of every incongruent movement which threatens our planet and our people, and is in dire need of persuasion and re-education. This is extremely unfortunate, and I am sorry to be the one to tell you, but this egoic virus has infected every single one of us. No man enters this domain unscathed. The collective consciousness of humanity, like a mud puddle, leaves its trace as you dive in. We are in this mess together, whether we are willing to admit it or not. Given this atrocity, the truly vital and pressing question remaining is, *"Where do we go from here?"*

The dogma of materialism has formed a powerful lock down when it comes to opening new channels of awareness. What I mean by dogma is the basic principles of science that have been created to support this covert Pythagorean mindset. The drive to deduce and break every musical note and slice of matter down to a numerical equation, has twisted the very nature of humanity. Spiritual beings have been reduced to numerically codified machines in the eyes of modern man.

The guiding principles that undermine our basic social structure hide beneath a materialistic based religion we are unwittingly soaking in. Our minds have been so completely and subliminally saturated in this materialistic persuasion that we fail to recognize its hold. The end result is a society that has forgotten what lies beyond the restricted visions of the science mind. The minds that incidentally venture beyond the boundaries of this artificial enclosure are either stamped out, or drugged down to conform to this limited way of perceiving. This man-made mindset pushes to control something that is far grander than it supposes. It unremittingly continues to fight a spiritual battle it is destined to lose. The truth and divine nature of reality is too glorious to be contained in this manner. If you want a peek through the smoke and mirrors of this science based material matrix, a good place to begin is *The Science Delusion* by Rupert Sheldrake. *Search YouTube for his banned TED Talk. (18 minutes)*

These basic principles have been used to anchor and tether the common mind to a chain of command that wholly denies that which science is unable or unwilling to prove. The default response for those experiencing *unusual phenomena* is simply, *"They are undoubtedly wrong… and if they persist, perhaps crazy."*

Scientific proof is hailed as the *final judgment*, the end all and be all of what is considered *real*. Experiences outside of this pre-determined *norm* are flagged as scientifically and socially unacceptable. Does this culturally promoted dynamic relate to the current condition of our overflowing mental institutions? The direct correlation is obvious in my eyes. *"I can't help but consider the similarities between **mental institutions** and **Indian reservations**, as the lifeblood of our spirits is silenced."* How many of us have been locked up, murdered, or persuaded to believe we were crazy, because our experience was outside of what mainstream science accepted as valid? From Crazy Horse to Galileo… this is not a pretty picture.

Chapter 51

❧ the bodhisattva's heart ❧

Love and compassion are necessities, not luxuries.
Without them humanity cannot survive.

—Dalai Lama

Interestingly enough, it is also in the realm of modern day science where we find our way out of this circuitous booby trap. Our futuristic quantum physicists are bringing us all back home with a deeper truth. It is now being shared openly, that those written-in-stone *laws of science*, with which we have been shaped and programmed, are insubstantial at a quantum level. It seems these formerly indisputable laws, which have been quietly and insidiously utilized as a means of keeping our minds in check... lest we stray from the herd... are no longer valid.

I still recall with deep gratitude, the day my friends and I took the ferry boat ride, and trekked across town to see the premier for *What the Bleep Do WE Know?* What an inspirational occasion, as we discovered that we really don't know much! Ramtha had finally made it to Hollywood, the world was no longer flat, and humanity's hope had suddenly been revitalized. The gateway to Quantum Physics was swung wide-open, and immeasurable scientific brilliance delivered to the common man on a silver platter.

Thanks to Dr. Emoto, millions have since witnessed the impact of *intention* on a drop of water. What a concrete visual for *The Power of Intention* in action, within the observable material world. That was over a decade ago, and since then the idea of our minds creating our own reality has become commonplace, in spite of the resistance from the insecure few who still find a way to feel threatened.

Opening the doors to higher pathways was easy on Orcas Island. I had left the city vibe far behind, and this sacred earth holds an intelligence of its own when you take the time to commune with her. My heart was blossoming like a lotus, and opportunities for expansion continued to show up. I found my way to the local Buddhist Community and through a brief introduction of several weeks was invited to take refuge with one of the Rinpoches. This Tibetan title literally means *precious one* and refers to a teacher that is recognized as a reincarnated Buddhist Master from a previous life. How freeing to be allowed to consider reincarnation for what it is without the undermining dogma that looks to obliterate it.

I was honored to have a Tibetan Llama who was willing to vouch for my spiritual well-being. I was even more honored when he gave me his name, 'Namka Dorje'. As a newcomer, I was taken aside and explained how this was a profoundly honoring event. I had a sense of this being a sacred gesture, and it warmed my heart to receive such a personal gift. This dedication carried even greater meaning as this *precious one* passed away a few short years later. I was still struggling with my sense of being okay in this world, and as I consistently searched for spiritual support, I continued to find it.

The island community was intimate, and a small local group had formed a *Deliberate Creation* circle shortly after my return from the Avatar Trainings. I was introduced to the circle by a female acquaintance I'd met through the barbershop. She was excited to connect me with this new bunch of like-minded friends, and it proved to be an undeniably good fit. We continued to meet once a week, and the group dynamics were favorable for making things happen.

310

Most of the people had been focused on Abraham's teachings, and my Wizard training was a complementary piece to add to the mix. The basic premise was congruent within the many approaches so popular at the time. Deepak shared his seven spiritual laws, and Abraham/Hicks carried *The Law of Attraction* like a torch. Dyer pushed *The Power of Intention,* and *The Secret* was lurking in the shadows. Our group pulled from every angle, and the synergistic power launched us each into a whirlwind of intentional creating. My primary desire was to discover and connect with a suitable partner. The deepest feeling within me said, *"first things first."* I had a lot on my plate in the way of creating change, but a sweetheart was at the top of my list.

My mental health was at a peak high, as I'd moved away from the pharmaceuticals in a major way. Just before I sold the home and the business, picked up camp, and moved out of town, I inadvertently discovered a doctor that realized how pointless the lithium prescription had been. What a breakthrough! As unfathomable as it is, it took over twenty years for a doctor to wake up to the reality of this destructive course of action, implanted in my life like train tracks. This brilliant man, I say with total respect and sincerity, officially took me off the lithium, and wrote a prescription for a drug I'd never heard of. I soon discovered that it had been around for decades. Interestingly, it had never been mentioned as an option. According to him it was fairly popular, but not so much within in my network of understanding. It was called Olanzapine and was typically used as an anti-psychotic for schizophrenia, as well as bipolar disorder. It was no angel for sure, as it came with its own standard set of side effects, but the enormous shift was due to the low dosage prescription that didn't require blood levels or close monitoring. I was no longer subjected to the long list of challenges that came with that unforgiving life sentence of lithium.

I felt my chain had been lengthened by a mile, and I had a new sense of freedom when I moved to the island. I found such peace and tranquility in my new surroundings, that I'd quietly tiptoed under the radar into a drug-free lifestyle. This was an enormous advancement for me. On those rare occasions when I was knocked off kilter, I was comforted to realize it wasn't such a big deal. I just had to take my medicine until it passed, and there was no medical hospitalization extravaganza to deal with or recuperate from. The most destructive and disturbing part of the medical system's intervention in my life had finally subsided. I was definitely making progress and my deliberate creation list no longer included *getting off lithium*. That mission had finally been accomplished.

I did, however, still feel the desire for a romantic partner. As my history shows clearly, I have been accustomed to having a girlfriend in my life. Was this just another form of addiction? That would probably be fair to claim, and difficult to deny as an accurate assessment. I was well aware of my dependency upon women in my life. I was born into one and raised by her as a stay at home mother. I grew up with two little sisters, and when I reached high school, the girls were everywhere. I then moved onto college and into beauty school, which was basically a warehouse full of flirty girls. As a hairdresser, *plentiful* would be an understatement when it came to romantic opportunities.

If I had a nickel for every woman that received a meaningful scalp massage as I shampooed her hair, I would be a rich man. My everyday relations with women in general were intimate and hands-on. I had undeniably become accustomed to having a woman by my side, and it wasn't a habit I was terribly concerned about breaking. I had more promising issues to contend with. Being *In Love* was an addiction I was willing to live with. Many sweethearts came and went through the years, and I loved every one of them. Still there were certain visions, and indisputable standards beyond romance, that I held as sacred.

I had decided long ago, when I came to recognize *self-actualization* as a need, that come hell or high water, I was going to attain this level of functioning. As a top priority, I would not allow this goal to be thwarted. In conjunction with this strategic target, I'd come to understand that a *self-actualized* relationship was also within the realm of possibility. I added this to the list of what I was determined to achieve in this lifetime. Since this particular goal was dependent upon another person, I was willing to forgive myself should I never find that certain soul mate. However, I was determined to at least die trying.

Interestingly, the pattern that developed included carpooling across the island once a week with my female friend. The trip was forty-five minutes each way, so we had more time for intimate conversation while driving than we actually spent at the meeting. Needless to say, we became close friends as we shared this devoted circle that delved into the heart of what we longed for in our lives. What began as a friendship ultimately developed into a romantic partnership, as she eventually moved into my cottage by the bay. My intimate list of what I truly desired in my life had been candidly displayed in our deliberate creation circle, and she was sold on the whole package. She was openly looking for a husband, and I certainly had a great deal of experience in that department. She was cute... I was charming... and we were beginning to look like a promising match. *"Third time's a charm... right?"*

Beyond this diminishing list of personal desires there was fire in my soul that had been secretly burning since the day it was ignited. Sure, I wanted a companion and a lover to warm my heart and my bed, but the truth is most of what I needed and longed for at a personal level had already been fulfilled. My children were blossoming in a most delightful way, and their health and happiness was more than enough to light me up. I had broken free of the tight grip of the city and all that it represented. I was basking in the sun of a new day dawning, surrounded by a natural beauty that radiated through the eyes of my comrades. I was contented beyond measure.

Even so, somewhere deep inside I was dying to share a greater value than I had thus far been able to. I was certain there were no drugs that could squelch this Messianic drive. It had survived through heaven and hell, and lived quietly in my heart and soul. The idea of this forced conversion was as ludicrous as suggesting gay people could be converted into non-gay people. Could somebody please tell me, *"What is wrong with this world?"*

I had been dancing with my *Inner Christ* in the form of a sacred symbol for over twenty years, and it was blossoming into more than I had fathomed it could ever be. This geometric image was a gift to me from the divine, and I held it as sacred and holy. It had been fashioned at my feet in the dirt of my inner realms, and emblazoned in the skies of my higher mind. This mystical image had developed a meaning that touched the very core of creation. It was a singular equation that encapsulated the vortex where time and eternity merge. It was the doorway through duality into the world of unity consciousness, and it was alive and breathing a fire inside of me that could not be denied. I was blissful on the surface, but churning in the depths of my being, knowing that I had a mission to fulfill. As beautiful as my life had become, internally I was up against a wall.

"How was I going to find a way to open the hearts of my fellow man to a notion I could barely wrap my mind around after twenty years of contemplation? How could I ever achieve such an astronomical accomplishment... as a mentally ill barber in a one horse town?" My anger was rising as I wrestled with this relentless yearning that haunted my dreams. Even the stillness was screaming loudly as my restless heart was driving my mind back into madness. This unstoppable Messianic drive was craving for a way to deliver the goods, and once again I had been tagged as the responsible party. *"Where could I possibly go from here?"*

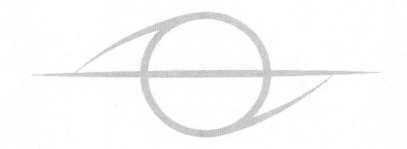

Part 7

The Silent Revolution

"Until one is committed, there is hesitancy, the chance to draw back — concerning all acts of initiative (and creation), there is one elementary truth that ignorance of which kills countless ideas and splendid plans: that the moment one definitely commits oneself, then Providence moves too. All sorts of things occur to help one that would never otherwise have occurred. A whole stream of events issues from the decision, raising in one's favor all manner of unforeseen incidents and meetings and material assistance, which no man could have dreamed would have come his way. Whatever you can do, or dream you can do, begin it. Boldness has genius, power, and magic in it. Begin it now."

—Goethe

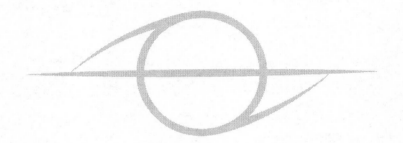

Chapter 52

❧ the wind of change ❧

Take me to the magic of the moment on a glory night,
Where the children of tomorrow dream away in the wind
of change...

—Scorpions, Wind of Change

My island adventure was coming to a close; I could feel it in the wind. It seemed that my soul had reached a crossroads, and it was obvious that I had a critical decision to make in the near future. A combination of events had collided with my own reasoning, and the push to move on was about to hit hard.

One day, I found myself meandering through the back roads of my rural neighborhood. As I was passing a local cemetery, I couldn't help but stop for a moment to take it all in. It was a beautiful day, the flowers were blooming, and a gentle breeze carried their fragrance softly before me. I stood dazed in a mesmerized state, captivated by the peace and tranquility that emanated from this mystical garden, solely dedicated to the other side. I caught my mind cherishing the idea of being laid to rest in such a magnificent setting, and blissfully dancing with the notion of a perfectly peaceful exit. It was a pleasurable occasion, but even so, it left me with a questionable impression.

A few days later, I was invited to go into town and meet with a woman who was offering psychic readings. I took great pleasure in sharing the insights that came through other peoples' inner guidance, and never felt prone to taking it too seriously. It was obvious that some folks were deeply in touch with the more subtle etheric realms and others... not so much. It was always interesting for me to sit with like-minded spiritual warriors, as they went through their own unique process of peering through the veil. I wasn't going with a pressing question in mind. It was more of a casual interest in checking out the local talent that drew me in.

I made the trek into town and found the bulk of her message easy to listen to. However, nothing in particular struck me as especially profound in the way of seeing deeply into my life. I was fairly unmoved, that is, until she highlighted a certain aspect of my future. She spoke confidently as she stated, *"You have so many things that you want to accomplish, and I want you to know that you need not worry about that any more. You will live a very long life. You'll have plenty of time to do everything you've dreamed of. You will live well beyond one hundred years."* Now this not only seized my attention, but lit a spark under me that burned like glowing coals. This was truly something that had bothered me. I was sorely concerned that my time would run out before I could accomplish the many goals I felt so devoted to. It wasn't that I considered her word as gold or expected this as an inevitable destiny. That wasn't the point at all. What hit me like a lightning bolt was the idea that this was a possibility I'd not realistically considered.

Most of my life was spent teetering on the edge of a precipice where death could grab me at moment's notice. I was surprised to have lived this long and didn't often consider longevity beyond the present day. In my blissful island wanderings, I'd slipped into a state of mind on the verge of melting into the sunset. I was in my late forties, and so tranquil and at ease that the thought of living another fifty years threw me for a serious loop. *"My God... I've been drifting into a mystically spellbound state... as though I am ready to join my sister... and yet I'm still a young man. At ninety years old, this state of mind is appropriate... but I'm half of that!"*

My dreams of being done with this earthly assignment were alluring. I could feel at peace with becoming another whisper in the trees. I was finding myself drawn toward the welcoming spirit realms that will eventually receive each and every one of us. It was just suddenly blatant and obvious that I was a bit ahead of schedule.

It seems funny now, but at the time it was very disturbing and deeply upsetting. Who would imagine a fellow being shook up by the proposition of having many productive years ahead? You'd think I'd have been dancing in the moonlight, joyously celebrating this wonderful news. As ironic as it is now, I recall the deep agitation I felt in considering my self-created vision of this potential crisis. My fear was of wandering around in a blissful state... ready to die... for fifty frigging years! The whole idea appeared as a nightmare to me. I could imagine a ghostly figure quietly, solemnly, blissfully roaming around in the forest, pointlessly hanging on for far too long.

The resulting surge of adrenaline fueled my heart to begin a serious evaluation of the situation at hand. My current state of affairs was not the result of a sudden event. I had gradually found my way into this tranquil paradise. My early days had been spent staggering on the edge of the busy city. I'd migrated north and west over the years, always toward the outskirts of town. The further I went, the more at ease my life became. The pace was slower in the rural areas, and a relaxed state of mind came quite naturally, far away from the hustle and bustle.

The problem I was facing was quite foreign. I'd never encountered or even imagined such a dilemma before. I was beginning to be so thoroughly comfortable with the tranquility that it was becoming troublesome to return to the intense commotion in the densely populated areas. Each time I would leave the island to visit the kids, or take care of business in town, it was increasingly challenging. The driving alone was a high stress shock to my nervous system. I had fully acclimated to the island pace that was literally thirty-five miles per hour, except for the twenty-five mile per hour limits in the park that I passed through every time I left my serene waterfront homestead. There were a few stop signs in town but mostly lazy, winding, two lane country roads stretched out through lush, pastoral landscapes.

After taking the hour and a half ferry ride to Anacortes I was gently launched into a stream of traffic that gradually transformed into a four lane highway, pushing well over sixty, with cars on either side. I felt like I was on a bumper car track, ready to be knocked out of bounds at any moment. It may sound odd, but in only three years, I'd made such an adjustment that the contrast was frightening. Every time I left the island, I would come back semi-traumatized, wondering how I could avoid the next demand for travel. I found myself staying at home for longer periods between departures and searching for reasons to not have to leave. What was haunting me in considering this new picture of living such a lengthy life was that my shrinking world was not developing into a long-term working model. My fear of being in the city, along with favoring this blissful quiet life, was reducing my livable area considerably. I was slowly and methodically becoming imprisoned by my own acceptance of this rapidly diminishing comfort zone. I could easily see the day coming where I would be so afraid to go anywhere that I'd become totally entrapped as a self-made recluse. That's the course I was on, like a magnetic pit that I was slowly being drawn into, and also the one that I feared. I did not consider the possible end result of agoraphobia as an acceptable option.

It reminded me of the analogy of the frog being put into steaming hot water and immediately jumping out. Whereas the same frog, put into lukewarm water that is gradually heating up, will stay in the pot until it boils. I could see the writing on the wall and realized beyond a doubt that I needed to face the music soon, if I ever expected to be capable of hanging out in the city again. With a good sense of the water slowly moving toward a rolling boil, it seemed the sooner I jumped out, the better. I was determined to make my move back to civilization.

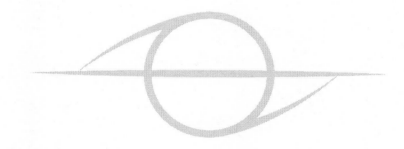

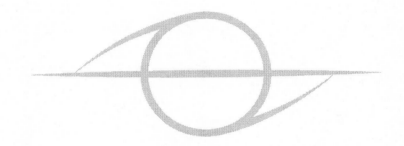

Chapter 53

❧ krido ishii ❧

Bird on the horizon, sitting on the fence. He's singing his song for me at his own expense, and I'm just like that bird... singing just for you. I hope that you can hear... Hear me singing through these tears.
—Bob Dylan, You're a Big Girl Now

Along with this charge to move on, I was feeling equally driven to launch my sacred symbol into the cosmos. Something had blossomed during my time away from the mainland, and this flowering was destined to emerge. My sense of its value had solidified, and I was certain that the motion behind this numinous image held a powerful purpose for mankind. I was well aware of the potential influence, and pleased with my own experience with this dynamism. At the time, I hadn't recognized the synchronicity between the symbol and myself being simultaneously ready for blast off.

The subtle vision of how to achieve my primary goal came to me like a softly lit daydream. There wasn't any magnificent Star Wars extravaganza or a fiery Shamanic vision of riding on the back of a Pegasus. It was so simple that I struggle to convey the transference of the message. I'd been chewing on a burning desire to put this symbol to use for quite some time, and what naturally came to me was the most direct and straightforward approach possible.

It was literally like being guided to swallow for the first time. There were no words involved in the message I was receiving, but if there had been they'd have said, *"Like this..."* with a big swallow to follow; like showing a three old how to blow her nose. You say, *"Like this... honey,"* as you demonstratively blow your nose, hoping she will eventually catch on to this complex and intricate maneuver. That's exactly what it felt like, except in this exchange I was the three year old.

What I gathered from the directive, was that I could easily carry this symbol, and all that it represented, into the collective consciousness of humanity by simply swallowing it into my own unconscious mind. As I pondered this notion I realized that I, along with everybody I knew, had become highly skilled at pushing stuff into the subconscious. This wasn't an original stunt by any stretch. The target in question was the Jungian *shadow* that we all so generously feed without a second thought. All that we had denied, ignored, and repressed was being swallowed into the unconscious realms of humanity's collective mind. The only thing different about this particular expression was that it was being consciously and deliberately pushed into the dark recesses with a definite intention and purpose. Now that was a new one! I'd never encountered such reasoning. If this collective unconscious shadow of humanity had any kind of an envelope to it, it was about to be infiltrated.

I went for a hike along the waterfront and sat quietly with the waves slapping the soft sand. I felt my heart and soul dancing in the revolution of the vortex this symbol so eloquently illustrated. I took in every aspect of the awareness I held in relation to this movement, enveloped it in my feeling body, and swallowed it down into the depths of my subconscious mind. I held it in as if it were a breath, and made sure it was sufficiently suppressed before coming up for air. I felt with certainty that it was being contained in the depths of my own psyche, at the very least. The rest was up to Mother Nature. Like blowing a wish through the down of a dandelion, my trust was in both the wind and the seedling. I let it go, *"So be it... It is done."*

Nothing astonishing happened in the starlit sky that night. That is, nothing more spectacular than what I witnessed every night as the stars conspired to sing me to sleep. No extraordinary animals wandered out of the forest to ensure an obvious omen. The bald eagles were plentiful and constantly in sight, so my vision had been permanently swayed. In the midst of another paradisiacal day, in a quiet blissful breeze, I knew that I'd just accomplished what my heart had longed to achieve since the beginning of time. I smiled gently as I graciously found my way home.

Ironically, there was a sadness of sorts that accompanied this deliberate launch. As much as it was a birth within the collective unconscious, it was a death of sorts for me on a personal level. I was fully aware of the law of detachment as it was so eloquently described in great detail by Deepak in his book of spiritual laws. I knew that planting this seed would mean letting it go. *"You don't pull on the shoots to see if the sprout is growing."* I wasn't sure if this would be easy, but I knew that my dedication to an effective strategy was strong. I was determined to do my best in following the plan. Planting this seed would mean discontinuing my constant tugging on this mental construct. It had matured and fully formed through the many years of mindful incubation and was thoroughly prepared to be set in motion. Like sending a child off to war, it was time to say goodbye.

I don't expect that many folks can grasp the unique awareness that was cultivated through this unusual relationship. It seems peculiar, even to me, as I purposefully consider it in this most intimate way. This symbol had literally come to life over the twenty year period we had shared. Like a foreign friend, I had given it a name, when it first came to me in the early '80s. Shortly thereafter the universe had responded in like, creating a two-part title.

I consciously and deliberately pulled two words together from my studies that expressed what the *being* of this symbolic motion meant to me. I found the Sanskrit word *Kri* through my Paramahansa Yogananda readings, which means *life force*. I was familiar with the Japanese word *Do, meaning The Way,* which was commonly used in association with the martial arts. Karate meaning *Empty Hand* and Karate-do meaning *The Way of the Empty Hand.* I combined these two words and called this symbol *Krido*, meaning *The Way of the Life Force.*

Shortly after my intentional gesture toward personalizing this deeply meaningful image, I felt the universe respond. Strangely enough it happened while I was on a short sabbatical... in jail. I'm embarrassed to share how I came to be incarcerated on this dismal occasion but, *"Hey... stuff happens."* I had somehow come into a relationship with a young woman who lived two counties away, and I honestly don't recall how we met. She was younger than I was by several years, and we never did get around to any kind of romantic connection, but I was certainly attracted to her. I had gone to visit her after hearing of an upsetting situation that landed her in the county courtroom. She was under age, and had been caught drinking and driving a friend's motorcycle on the street without a license. It was basically a teenage party, with a bunch of rowdy kids hanging out, playing loud music, and having a wild time. This was an activity I was quite familiar with. She just happened to be the one to get busted. I was in my early twenties, and being the responsible kind of guy I was, went over to support her through the process.

What then transpired was utterly ridiculous no matter how you look at it. Her sister and a few friends had shown up for this special occasion, and by the time it was her turn to receive sentencing for the crime, we were all sitting on pins and needles. The judge muttered through all the formal dribble of the proceedings and finally announced, *"I hereby sentence you to eleven days..."* and of course, me being the calm and collected young man I was back then, jumped to my feet in complete shock and yelled out loud, *"Oh Shit!"*

As you might imagine this behavior wasn't well received in the courtroom. I was as stunned and startled as everyone else in the joint, and quickly exited. To be perfectly honest, I actually ran out of the building as the judge ordered the bailiff, *"Seize that man!"* I didn't get far before the pursuing officer noticed me tucked in behind some brush on a nearby street corner. I wasn't trying to escape so much as in serious need of a moment to collect my thoughts. When I saw him driving in my direction, I came out of hiding and walked toward him. He seemed to recognize that I was embarrassed as I turned myself in and was actually quite gentle with me. He didn't bother to cuff me as he put me in the back seat, drove me back to the courthouse and presented me to the judge. The judge appeared on the verge of laughter as he informed me that my outburst had been very foolish, given his following statement. He said, *"If you could have waited thirty more seconds you would have heard that I was suspending ten of those eleven days. Your girlfriend is getting a grand total of one day in the juvenile detention center while I am sentencing you to two days in the county jail for contempt of court."* Slam goes the gavel.

So, like I was saying, this jail time had *embarrassing* poured all over it like syrup on pancakes. The one valuable thing to come from this asinine adventure arrived on the second day of confinement, when I heard a gentle voice speak clearly from within... *Ishii.* I was sitting at the table in my new little group home, when a voice spoke articulately and strongly

329

enough to rattle my cage. It was only one word and it instantly stunned me. I felt like jumping to my feet and shouting, *"Did you guys hear that!?"* But I knew better. I grabbed a Styrofoam cup and a pencil, and etched the name into the soft material. I quickly realized this was a response to my naming the symbol. It felt like an echo from the astral realms. I could just feel it somewhere inside and knew this was as significant as it was mysterious.

I put the two words together on the flimsy cup, *Krido Ishii*. It was immediately magical. Nobody else could ever understand the significance of this verbal repercussion, but for me it was a priceless gift from the divine. As with the symbol itself, I was bound to reach a deep understanding of the meaning of this title, through continuous contemplation of its relevance, to my ever-evolving awareness of the motion behind this symbolism.

I connected the dots slowly but surely as I struggled to gain a more complete understanding of this precious gem from beyond. Although the voice had not put spelling to the word *Ishii*, I somehow knew that it was written with three *I's*. I had seen the name *Ishi* once before, but it ended with one *I*. There was a familiar story about a Native American once touted as *the last wild Indian in North America.* He had reportedly wandered out of the wilderness in the early 1900's to be recognized as the last member of his all but extinct tribe. In the initial attempts to communicate, he was asked what his name was. When he responded, *"Ishi,"* they quickly assumed this to be his personal name and continued to call him by it. They eventually discovered this word meant *the people* in his native tongue, and that it actually wasn't his personal name. He was simply trying to let them know that he was one of the *Ishi*.

I took this meaning to heart, and used it within my sovereign quest for understanding. *The Way of the Life Force (Krido)* had been expanded to include *The People of the Way of the Life Force (Krido Ishii)*. It was beginning to make perfect sense, as to why the Universe was responding to me with a name. *The way of the Life Force* was meant to be coupled with *The People*. This was a powerful partnership being formed. The *Life force* was not capable of carrying this work forward without the *People of the Way* participating. The synchronistic harmony and alignment between the Divine, Nature, and Humanity was a prerequisite for the success of this Silent Revolution. This perspective aligned with everything I could understand about *free will* and the powers at play behind the scenes.

This self-perpetuating spiritual battle had been churning for the last couple hundred thousand years as a result of the *Lucifer Rebellion*. The entire crusade had culminated because of this *free will* imperative. According to *Urantia*, a two thousand page exposé on the history and hierarchy of the heavens, this war was inevitable. Even so, its completion required the *will of the people* to turn the final page on this seemingly never-ending chapter. It wasn't about God or the Angels forcing humanity into submission. Force would be pointless as the mandatory learning and evolution of understanding would have no reason to occur. The divinely inspired path being laid at our feet was meant to be followed by discovering and deliberately choosing *The Way*, rather than through its being forced, demanded, or inflicted upon the countless lost and lonely souls. Our true purpose, the whole point of our existence, is for this perfectly designed opportunity to naturally learn, grow, and evolve. This inherent motivation of the divine will is in extreme contrast to the notion of being herded like cattle into accord with an overpowering force of nature.

According to these channeled writings, Lucifer, as the highest Angel, broke away from Archangel Michael, and turned toward devising his own strategy of strong-arming humanity into submission. He wasn't buying the invisible God theory, nor did he have the patience required to allow for the evolution of Man's spiritual consciousness to develop according to his *free will*. As the *shining one,* he took a third of the Angels with him and they soon masterfully occupied and took dominion over the *free will* zone of Satania, where we find ourselves today; here on Planet Earth or *Urantia,* in the backwaters of a remote galaxy in the *free will* zone of a Universe within multi-universes.

This impending spiritual evolution of man's consciousness, like the rebellion, was equally inevitable, and the sole purpose for this ancient and archaic lineage of warfare. The hundreds of millennia that have since passed have allowed for great advancement and learning for all involved. Just as a young man will tear away from the family to individuate, mature, and develop; there also comes a time when it is appropriate for him to return. That time has come. The rebellion has all but exhausted itself, and the uprising of this current spiritual revolution is in order.

We are here to learn, grow, and develop individually, as well as collectively, so that we might find and choose, of our own accord, the path to harmonious relations. We were created in the image of the divine and given provisions to achieve this new way of proceeding beyond the fallout of the rebellion.

Krido Ishii is the invisible, all-inclusive banner which this new wave of light bearing souls gather beneath, and the axis that they dance around like a maypole. Like a black hole, it is a vortex, a portal, a gateway to the divine, which sits within a dimension of this reality we share. As an individual, I was grateful and humbled to be one of the accompanying souls in the distinct position to facilitate its birth. It just so happens that, for now, this would also mean letting go of something dear to my heart. Even though I recognized the glory in this maneuver, a heavy sadness seemed to overshadow any sense of accomplishment.

In the years of searching, I had gained an expansive understanding of this expression of *Ishii*. Through a martial arts program, I had come into contact with Japanese students who were extremely limited in their use of the English language. I considered this advantageous according to the manner in which I was seeking. I valued the opportunity to by-pass polished intellect and touch into this somewhat raw form of expression. In the locker room one day, I approached a couple of the young Japanese men and asked them about the meaning of this word *Ishii*. I had written it on a piece of paper and presented it along with the straightforward question, *"What does this word mean… Ishii?"* One student stuttered through his broken English, *"Oh… Ishii mean small stone, uhh… confidence… will."* The other young man chimed in, *Ishii have many meanings… mean many things."* I was totally thrilled to add a few more scattered pieces to my self-created puzzle, and busily pushed them from every angle that might bring greater connection and new understanding.

In time, I would come to recognize Ishii as *The People*, the small stone, relative to Krido, *The Way of the Life Force*, the large stone. Ishii represents the smaller or the personal will of the people, while Krido is *The Way* or the will of the Divine. These two forces were diametrically opposed and simultaneously conjoined in perfect harmony.

Many years later, I would encounter an older Japanese gentleman who would explain that this word *Ishii* means *Everything*. I couldn't help but see the correlation to the Taoist teachings of Lao Tzu. *Tao* meaning *The Way*, and *Ten Thousand Things* representing all of creation or *Everything*, the equivalent of *Ishii*. This living symbol displayed this relationship between God and Man in a resplendent fashion, and there was beauty here that washed my soul in starlight. This was a grand affair, and I was still almost alone in my celebration, as well as my sorrow.

I soon took a trip to the big city, and met with my son for lunch. I shared what I had done with the symbol, and he confirmed his understanding as tears ran down his cheeks. I was amazed that he was able to grasp the meaning of my efforts to this degree. I wasn't sure that it made a lot of sense to him until I witnessed the emotional acknowledgement of his own elevated awareness. I was moved beyond measure and elated to find my son able to share in this profound experience. My sense of being alone quickly faded into our loving connection as father and son. He was about 18 at the time, and his spiritual consciousness was beginning to sprout in a voracious manner. Our lives were moving toward a greater togetherness, and our dreams would one day merge.

Chapter 54

ᔾ love, money and civilization ᔿ

You never know what is enough unless you know what is more than enough.

—William Blake

Beyond these elevated visions of universal peace, my personal life was rocking like a ship at sea. My deliberate creation girlfriend and I decided to make a weekend trip over the border into Canada, with the initial intention of checking out a school for Acupuncture and Chinese Medicine. I had recently experienced some profound results through a series of acupuncture treatments with a local practitioner, and was feeling very drawn to this style of healing. The school in Canada was priced in a way that made this dream seem feasible. We made our way to Nelson B.C. and toured the private school, as we looked into the programs that seemed most fitting. The dream was expanding as we researched the possibilities, and considered what it would realistically take to relocate to Nelson for the duration of the three year course. In the midst of our fantasizing, we discovered that we could easily check *getting married* off our *to do* list while we were in town. I had already given her an engagement ring and somewhere in the back of our minds the clock was ticking.

We contacted a local gal through the newspaper to perform the marriage services. She quickly showed up with a couple of friends to act as witnesses as we were legally married in the hotel room. We were already on a new-lovers high, and behaving like drunken school children. Every day was filled with fun and the sweetness of young love, which was absolutely intoxicating, but somehow disconnected from the depth of yearning that had thus far carried me forward. Looking back, it was as if I had traded my relationship with *Krido Ishii* in for this innocent budding romance. It was delightful and exhilarating for the duration of our island adventure, but that phase was nearing its end.

One day, we took a double ferryboat ride and the subsequent drive to get to Port Townsend, which sits on the northeastern tip of the Olympic Peninsula. It's a quaint little seaside township that I'd become quite familiar with, as my brother had lived there for the last twenty years. Every now and again I would make the trip, fully prepared to enjoy the local marketplace. As I mentioned earlier, I was sure to visit my favorite metaphysical bookstore *Phoenix Rising*, as well as one other business that had become a regular stop along the way. It was the pub that was featured in the movie *Officer and a Gentleman*, starring Richard Gere. I just happened to love that movie as a young man, and it felt to me like hallowed ground. It was now called the Waterstreet Tavern and beyond the sentimental appeal of the historical décor, they had great food and a private brewery. It has since evaporated into the ethers, but it was an exceptionally cool place to hang out in those days.

I was beginning to see this general location as a nice way to step back into civilization without getting carried away. Port Townsend was definitely more populated than the island, and obviously more connected to the mainland. Even so, it seemed far enough away from any major metropolis to feel safely insulated from the associated madness. In the process of scouting around town we came across a particular advertisement for a *Bed and*

Breakfast that caught my sweetheart's eye. The story she then shared with me was mind boggling to say the least.

As a young girl, growing up in West Virginia, she had been captivated by a picture of an old Victorian home she'd discovered on the side of a cereal box. It somehow touched her deeply, and she cut out the picture and carried it with her over the years, even though she had no idea where it was located. The house that we were looking at in the B&B ad was the Ann Starrett Mansion, the exact same home that she held on that aging piece of paper. This young girl had somehow found her way to fulfilling this long kept secret dream, by revisiting this childhood fantasy as an adult in real life. Perhaps this deliberate creation theme truly was lighting the way. It was an amazing occurrence, and we readily made arrangements to return for a stay in this unique Victorian B&B.

Upon our return a few weeks later, we came bouncing in through the front door of this incredible mansion to quickly discover that this place had a longstanding reputation for being haunted. The enchanting spiral staircase had a story of its own as the last floating stairway of its kind. The walls were covered with newspaper clippings telling tales of the many ghosts that had been reported through the recent years in this historic residence. My new wife's initial response was one of being consumed with fear, but with a little coaxing she agreed to give it a go. This mysterious dream had survived too long to timidly turn away at the last minute.

For me, it turned out to be one of the most pleasant visits I had ever experienced. I could definitely feel the presence of entities in our sleeping quarters, but they seemed to have nothing but love for me. The Mrs. wasn't terribly impressed, but I felt like a petted cat, cozily sleeping under a sunbeam streaming in through the window. It was a remarkable experience and the story deepened as I felt my soul being magnetically drawn into Port Townsend.

I soon found myself looking into a home for rent a few blocks away, and discovered an intimate connection between the two historic residences. The Starrett Mansion was built in 1889, while the home we would soon move into was built in 1875, by Captain Morgan. These families had intermingled over a hundred years ago in this quaint little uptown neighborhood. There was a magical feeling of going back in time as we walked on the creaky, sloping, original wooden floors. The house squeaked and groaned as we moved about, and you could feel a summer breeze blowing through the single pane windows. It was in a delightful location in the uptown area, and Fort Warden State Park was in walking distance. The adventure was expanding in several ways as we geared up for the move away from Orcas and into this new, old living space.

Any sense of completion with my collective-level work was being abruptly overshadowed by the demands of this newly emerging personal direction. The entire planet seemed to be shifting beneath my feet. Along with the new marriage and our move to Port Townsend, my father had decided to disburse some of his excessive funds. I would love to tell you what a splendid experience it was to receive a bunch of money, but somehow it didn't work out like that. The truth is, as you've already heard, my family's relationship with money had never been regarded as healthy. It was actually the core element of the imbalance, within a family that suffered far too much.

The back story to this particular exchange began many years earlier, when my little sister was still alive. My father had come to my home when I was living in the trailer where the Mormons were feeding me, the same residence I lived in while attending the Community College through my disability program. He had come over to have me sign some papers that would appoint me a certain portion of the trust he had recently formed.

It was legally attached to a piece of property he owned in downtown Seattle. Originally, he'd run his business in this location, but it was now being rented to a third party. The newly formed trust was to be split equally between his four children. This transaction sounds wonderful from a distance, but the actual event was as ugly as could be. Well almost. It actually would have been worse had I not found that last ounce and a half of self-respect required to tell him, *"No thank you."* Truth be told, the actual conversation that transpired had a few self-propelled F-bombs involved. He was being a real ass to put it mildly, which wasn't at all unusual. It just didn't fit well with the idea of him supposedly doing me a favor. There was absolutely no sense of this business maneuver coming from a place of caring or compassion. It was more of a *spit in your face* insult, as I was being distastefully presented, and simultaneously implicated for, an undeserved hand out.

I have yet to understand the menial mentality behind these many heartless maneuvers. They've never ceased to amaze me, but this was most definitely a classic. The unspoken message behind the scene was, *"I'm not only going to treat you like shit, I am going to rub your nose in it at the same time... and if you want this money, you'll shut up and take the abuse."* Being driven by different principals and carrying an entirely separate value system, I wasn't desperate enough for the money to willingly allow this offensive approach. I basically told him, *"Why don't you take your money and shove it up your... uhh... where the sun don't shine... on your way out the door!"* as I escorted him to the exit. There wasn't any physical violence, but it certainly wasn't pretty. Keep in mind that while he's been putting his multiple million dollar deals together, his son is being fed by the Mormons and food stamps, going to school on government issued financial aid, and scraping by on an insufficient disability check.

I made it clear that this was one place on the planet I wasn't willing to be treated in such a disrespectful manner. My home was my castle, regardless of the dollar value attached, and a personal space I felt obliged to protect. Needless to say, my objection to his attitude toward me didn't go over well, as he resentfully proceeded to form the trust without my name involved. I certainly could have used the money, but not at the cost of my own dignity. Dignity was one of the few things I was attempting to hold onto in my fleeting world of ups and downs. I was actually quite content to remain unaffiliated with this sick and darkly twisted braid of love, hate, and money.

After a couple years went by and the situation shifted, particularly after my sister Cathy had passed away, I was quietly moved into the position on the trust that was left void through her departure. My father and I had calmed down a bit, and the grief of the loss seemed to bring us into more agreeable relations, at least temporarily. I no longer lived in his neck-of-the-woods when I was casually reinstated in the family trust, alongside my older brother and living sister.

Shortly after my appointment to the official documentation, this shadowy enterprise began to provide a monthly payout. It was about a thousand bucks a month that was suddenly flowing in on a regular basis. This happened long after my disability funds had come to an end, and shortly after beginning the solo phase of my adventure on Orcas. It turned out to be beneficial timing.

I was unquestionably appreciative and grateful for the abrupt financial boost. It was also unexpectedly easy to realize how a person could allow themselves to be mistreated or degraded in trade for the cash flow. I was progressively able to feel how this could readily happen, like slipping into a sleazy drug addiction, now that I was on the receiving end of this blatantly contentious trust fund. The monthly dividends kicked in during the final phase of my island living, and I was pleased to know I could survive with my simple lifestyle on that income alone, if it came right down to it. This awareness carried with it a pleasant feeling, a new sense of security, and a bit more.

Looking back, I see how a submerged level of agony and confusion was being stirred. This abusive father figure and his all-powerful money remained central to my mental-emotional imbalance. On one hand, this was the sliver in my thigh that motivated me to break through the intergenerational abuse patterns and rise up to be the loving father that my children longed for. This was undeniably the most beneficial consequence of this hurtful relationship that I had endured for as long as I could recall. Unfortunately, this painful dynamic had also created the torment that I associated with money, keeping me far from it. My frazzled psyche was torn in two by this situation that seemed to continuously undermine my tenacious pursuit of inner peace. There appeared to be no easy way to resolve the state of affairs that produced this constant upset.

Imagine somebody coming to you regularly, handing you a wad of money and simultaneously telling you *you're worthless*, as they give you a sharp slap across the face. You know when you see them approaching what you're in for. Now consider this happening from such an early stage in your childhood development that you accept it as natural. You love this person and have somehow come to believe they love you. However, for some odd reason you develop an aversion to the overall program. There's an attractive element and simultaneously something extremely repulsive. You get what you long for in the way of a father's attention, which comes in the form of a currency that society accepts in trade for almost anything. That's the attractive part. The downside is that this father's attention also comes as a hurtful persuasion of condemnation that cuts deep. There is always a put down, a cut, a slam of one sort or another that feeds a deep sense of inadequacy and leaves you wondering if you are worthy of love.

When I voice my disapproval for being treated disrespectfully, I am charged with being ungrateful. *"How dare you complain... after all I have done for you!"* An innocent and unknowing bystander could easily align with this perspective. *"What an ungrateful spoiled child!"* and they often did. Even my friends would question my dissatisfaction with my relationship with my father. *"Geez buddy... he just gave you a bunch of money... how can you complain?"* This was an additional layer to the mind-fuck game that seemed determined to pull me under one more time.

So here I sit, condemned by my family and peers for feeling abused and unsatisfied, because on paper I'm on the receiving end of a great act of generosity. Deep inside, I feel like a piece of shit for taking the money that symbolizes the abuse and all that undermines our entire society, but outwardly it's party time. *"Oh my God, what a mess!"* My emotional plate was suddenly overflowing. *"How can I find my way back to a Save the World perspective? That's a hell of a lot easier to deal with than this personal bullshit!"*

I knew I was capable of processing the pain from the past. I was very qualified to handle that inner job. I could forgive and let go of what had come before; however, this painful, abusive relationship remained before me. It wasn't merely in the past. It was a current and ongoing pattern that continued to undermine my efforts to maintain a healthy mind. Somewhere deep inside I struggled to let go of the hope that one day I would discover a loving and supportive father figure in my viewfinder. This unstoppable optimism kept me coming back for more. This burning desire for a loving father seemed insuppressible.

The money had somehow become a substitute for feeling cared for, or paid attention to, and it continued to twist my thoughts around love and money. Somewhere deep inside I resented money as if it were the demon that had taken my father from me. It had come to represent a living being that had selfishly received all of my father's love and attention, while leaving me fatherless. The truth of the experience was actually a step down from feeling fatherless. I'm quite certain that I could have more easily come to terms with not having a father. That story has an ending, which leaves space for resolving the emotions attached to the final outcome. My relentless agony was due to the fact that the relationship with my father was open-ended with an unfinished influence. He was the constant voice of disappointment and disapproval continuously pulling me down into the darkness of existence. His was the voice forever hell-bent on inflicting mental and emotional torment.

In the midst of the big move from the island, my father had mentioned critical developments in his business strategy that included selling the property that the trust represented. He explained that it would mean each of the three of us receiving the cash value of our share in a lump sum, rather than an ongoing dividend disbursement. He was basically selling it out from under us.

I pleaded and begged him not to do it as I openly expressed my concerns. I knew my state of mind was not in a good position to have a large sum of money at my disposal. The monthly check was perfect, as it provided a small steady stream of income, without the fear of loss that would come with a larger dose of money. As usual, my father's plan was based on his own agenda, and not designed nor intended to comply with anyone else's wishes or personal needs. It seems he was also born with a very special talent for making what could be presented as a gift; feel like a poke in the eye with a sharp stick.

My brother explained later that it was a tax-shelter move that saved him a bundle on a multi-million dollar sale of another commercial property. The motive, once again, seemed to be primarily self-serving. So as strange as it seems, even against my wishes, I was handed a check for a couple hundred thousand dollars soon after arriving in Port Townsend.

As you may have predicted, I was much happier, at least on the surface, to have the money in my hand than I had anticipated. Suddenly my friends were dying to know what kind of magic I had worked to inspire the Law of Attraction to respond in such an auspicious manner. Deliberate creation is an art form that covers a lot of territory, and even I was beginning to wonder what secret formula I had enacted to go from stark poverty to sitting on a pile of cash. *"Woo... hooo!! Money... Money... Money!"*

Everything changes with a little cash in hand. My new love affair was already bordering on a child-like persuasion, but now there were no limits. We were literally chewing bubble gum and flying kites in the sunshine of the open grassy fields at the state park. We bought a motorcycle with the last stash of cash we had right before the mother-load arrived. We spent the remainder of our savings knowing the fresh cash would inevitably arrive soon. Our thinking was already beginning to lean off-kilter. There was a definite rush involved, like taking a big snort of cocaine.

I bought her a brand spanking new car for Christmas, and put it on the front lawn with a huge red bow taped to the windshield. She quit working and we soon traveled more than I had ever experienced in my life. In the following months, we visited 28 states in the U.S. that I'd never stepped foot in before. We visited her deathly-ill father in South Carolina on one of our adventures, and then attended her sister's fancy wedding in Houston on a separate excursion. We had purposefully driven around in enormous sweeping circles on each of these occasions, which included crossing through the majority of the country. It was like the ultimate vacation package, with no apparent end in sight. Her track record for working had been consistent until now, and as a medical professional she'd made a decent living most of her adult life. After vacationing for a good portion of the year, I was beginning to wonder if she had any intention of working again. Our perspective had been abruptly and severely altered in relation to financial responsibility.

Chapter 55

ꙮ father and son ꙮ

I was once like you are now, and I know that it's not easy to be calm when you've found something going on. But take your time, think a lot, why think of everything you've got, for you will still be here tomorrow, but your dreams may not.

—Cat Stevens, Father and Son

I talked my son into coming over and staying with us for a while. We quickly dove into our shared dreams of video production. I bought some fancy computers and camera equipment as we plunged into this mutually empowered fantasy. My son was heavily involved in the snowboarding/skateboarding world, and videos were the central theme. This appeared to be an awesome project to reconnect us as father and son. Perhaps we could make up for the many times I had fallen short. I still held a great deal of guilt and shame for not being in my best form in his earlier years. My heart was still searching for an opportunity to fill in the gaps. They felt like big empty spaces linked to *being a high quality father for him.*

In the midst of it all, a part of me realized this excessive spending couldn't go on forever. At the same time, another part of me was saying, *"Don't buy into the scarcity thinking that creates poverty. You can always attract more money into your life. You can deliberately choose prosperity and abundance!"* It was like the angel on one shoulder and the devil on the other, and whoever was holding the checkbook seemed to be the one winning the argument.

It was a whirlwind of a ride for a couple years, and I am forever grateful for all that we experienced. One of the most incredible gifts that manifested through our efforts was when my son and I attended the video production course at the local community college. It was so much fun spending time with him and working together in such a creative and enjoyable fashion.

We both created several awesome video productions for family and friends, and shared them with everyone we knew. My grandmother on my mother's side had recently passed away at ninety-six years old, and I was able to compile the photos and songs required to put together a beautiful music video for the extended family as a tribute to her life. My son did something similar for his girlfriend's parents on their anniversary, as well as an exceptional production for his snowboarding buddies. We also did a very professional project for my wife's sister's wedding that was quite impressive. It was extremely exciting, fun, and emotionally rewarding to see the genuine response these loved ones had to the creative work we were producing.

Through this focused spurt of delving into commercial production, I had taken hold of a vision of my son's world that came in the form of a mental movie. It was a cross between his real life and a strange daydream of sorts. It was such a clear vision, that I took a screenwriting class, and ended up creating a full feature screenplay to put it to film. The completed work was impressive, and I was encouraged to send it off for a professional evaluation. The returning appraisal was remarkably positive, with little in the way of suggested changes. I was pleased to feel the heightened sense of self-worth that came through this unfamiliar accomplishment. The financial potential was obvious and exciting, but I soon discovered I was much less inspired to go through the process involved in actually selling the screenplay.

Looking back, I can see that the carrot attached to selling the feature was, once again, the almighty dollar bill. This pattern of consistently veering away from potential income is obvious to me now. A lifetime of divinely inspired aversion therapy had more than cured me of greed for money. The balanced perspective I truly longed for was still on my deliberate creation list. At the time, I considered this a department that didn't appeal to my passion, and allowed the project to naturally take a backseat to our ongoing video endeavors.

Even so, something incredibly magical seemed to develop from the formalization of this vision I held so clearly. It was as if through the writing of the screenplay I had cast a spell. The vision I had put to paper of my son's life unfolding as a professional snowboarder manifested right before our eyes. In the following years he moved into the mountain dream world that I'd described for the character representing him in the screenplay. The film also included the main character's initiation into manhood, which also came to pass in a similar fashion to what I had written. He and two close buddies attended a formal initiation into this sacred community of men that I was able to facilitate and participate in. This sacred event proved to have a profound impact on his personal development. The storyline for the character representing me also manifested in my personal world and even the *Krido Ishii symbol* found a place in the plot. The overall impact of the written screenplay, though it was not produced, was rather magnificent and even today it's something we both treasure deeply. In my father's eyes, this was all wasted time and money, but for me and my son, it was priceless.

That being said, an unromantic voice of reasoning was also chewing on me from within. Whether this was my father's voice in my head or just practical sense, it was strong. I could see the money going quickly, and knew for damn sure it would soon be gone if I didn't bring this spending spree to a halt. My son had stayed for the good part of a year before moving on, and it was undoubtedly an immeasurable blessing.

Chapter 56

～ meet me in the middle ～

I hope you never fear those mountains in the distance, never settle for the path of least resistance. Livin' might mean takin' chances but they're worth takin'. Lovin' might be a mistake but it's worth makin'. Don't let some hell bent heart leave you bitter. When you come close to sellin' out reconsider. Give the heavens above more than just a passing glance, and when you get the choice to sit it out or dance, I hope you dance.
— Lee Ann Womack, I Hope You Dance

Like clockwork, my daughter opened the door to deeper connections with her as well. We'd stayed in close association through the years and she and her husband would visit every so often. Like a storybook, they had been high school sweethearts, and married after several years of dating. A couple of years before my son's initiation, her husband had also followed my footsteps into the men's community through an initiatory ceremonial retreat. It was a profound shift in his life and interestingly, one he had actually asked for. He had come to me one day, describing the way he was feeling, which in my words was like having a boy's mind in a man's body. He felt there was something he needed, like the flipping of a switch, to move forward. I knew the feeling well, and considered this a strong indicator that he was ready. He was without a doubt ripe for this much needed transition, and it fell into place and worked out extremely well.

As a young couple, they had been pretty much on course for a standard, socially acceptable entry into adult living. After high school, she had gone on to graduate from Western

Washington University with a bachelor's degree in psychology, while he worked as a mechanic. They had since moved back from Bellingham, and were restarting their lives in an area north of Seattle where the majority of the family lived.

One day I was talking with my daughter on the phone, and she casually made a comment about us getting a place together. They were in an apartment in Mukilteo, which was precisely an island away from where I was living in Port Townsend. We had a ferry terminal that connected to the northern end of the island and they had one on the south end. We were separated by two stretches of water and a big island in the middle. She jokingly commented, *"We should just meet in the middle and get a place on Whidbey."*

She may have been casually expressing this cute little notion, but it was enough to get my wheels turning in overdrive. I carried a sense of need with my daughter that was much like the one I had just satisfied with my son. The time spent with him was deeply healing for both of us, and I longed to feel this heartfelt pain around my daughter-wound resolved as well. I decided to take her comment seriously, and we continued to discuss the subject until we finally made arrangements to meet in the middle. We each took a boat ride and met on the island for a father-daughter powwow.

I spoke with my wife and expressed how important it was for me to have this opportunity to live with my daughter. I had been torn from her life at an early age, and we both felt the pain of that major revision. I knew deep down, the healing required had a better chance if we could spend time in the same home. This foundational family element had been interrupted more than once.

At one point when I was in my trailer home, back in the neighborhood where the kids lived, she had come to stay

352

with me. As a young teenager, she was going through a classic rebellious stage with her mother. I was honored and thrilled when she offered to live with me, and wholeheartedly accepted her invitation. She moved into my home, but it quickly fizzled, and I blamed myself for the limited time she was able to stay. I don't recall the details, but I know my mental health was very poor through that juncture, and even she knew it wasn't a good situation for her. I wasn't stable enough to be in a position of responsibility, and her mother was quick to reel her back in, which she did without hesitation. This mishap only added to the hurt feelings, guilt, and shame of not being an adequate father to my daughter. In my eyes, I had failed once more, which only added fuel to my burning desire to resolve the agonizing pain.

As I considered the opportunity before me, I knew this attempt was going to be different. She was an adult now, and I was in a much better position to participate in the healthy relations that could bring the healing we so desperately needed. What I didn't talk to my wife about was the reasoning around my other driving motive to move forward. I was seriously struggling with the marriage and feeling quite powerless to do anything about it. It didn't seem conducive to my emotional health or my spiritual path, and my mental state had declined to the point of spending a great deal of time lost in feelings of hopelessness.

Regardless of my intellectual understanding of relationships and intimacy, we suffered day after day through emotional conflict and entanglement. I had initiated counseling and relationship retreats more than once, and the sense of an ongoing resistance between us was difficult to understand. The truth is my passionate charge to move into a new situation with my daughter was equally motivated by my desperate need to get out of the marriage I felt trapped in. My son's presence in our home had softened the situation to a large degree, but with him gone, it was increasingly difficult to cope with.

I was also well aware of the advantage to using the remaining money as a real estate down payment. This was the answer to my desperate search for a way to stop the continuous depletion of our savings. If I could invest the liquid cash in real estate, it would squelch the spending spree immediately. My confidence in deliberately creating abundance in the form of cash was rapidly dwindling, alongside my heavy sense of being stuck in a relationship that was less than satisfactory. I was tickled with this new direction and passionately jumped in with both feet.

My daughter and I met with a realtor on the island and began to get our toes wet as we ventured into the deeper waters of this monumental proposition. There was a great deal involved as we were moving into a joint purchase that required all four of us to qualify for this major transaction.

Interestingly enough, my vision for an ideal property had been formed while I was living on Orcas Island. At one point, we began casually looking at properties with the misty idea of settling down. I found myself generally disappointed with every parcel we explored, and one day my wife asked me directly, *"What do you really want in a piece of property?"* Now remember that our humble beginnings had been in a deliberate creation circle that was focused on attracting and creating your own reality, with no limitations. So when asked what I really wanted, I was easily coaxed into telling the truth of my desire without regard for what might be realistic. I readily described this property as a five-acre parcel with rolling pastures, ponds, old growth cedar trees, rich soil, and good sun exposure for gardening.

Her immediate response was, *"You'll never find that here!"* She was most likely accurate in her assessment, as there was significantly more rocky land than soft dirt on Orcas. It appeared that my vision was undeniably over ambitious for the market search we were tapped into. My instant reply would turn out to be equally valid and ultimately quite prophetic, *"Well… then we must be on the wrong island!"* I exclaimed.

As my daughter and I spent a few days riding around with the realtor in search of the ideal situation, it became obvious that we weren't encountering what either of us had envisioned. We looked at a half dozen homes without being impressed with the overall sense of what was being presented. One day the realtor pulled out a picture of a home on five acres that looked promising. The photo of the property was undeniably attractive, but it had one major flaw in my judgment. It had a triple-wide manufactured home rather than a stick-built structure. I had sworn to myself that I would never live in a trailer again, after my challenging time in the last one. It wasn't that it was an inadequate building as much as it was the mobile home had come to represent poverty and the hardship I had suffered through during that dismal spell. I had come to affiliate the manufactured home with a low point in my life, and I held a derogatory association toward being *white trailer trash.* Somewhere along the line, I became determined to avoid that correlation like the plague.

Given the limited choices for available real estate, we decided to take a closer look before shutting the door on this proposed property. We took a pleasant ride through the rural countryside, and enjoyed the beauty of the surrounding area as we approached the remote location. We drove up the long driveway, past the horses in the pasture, and as we encircled the home I was already head-over-heels in love. It was like love at first sight with a woman. By the time we had walked the property, and sat in the loft of the barn overlooking the valley, I was sold. I don't mean like, *"Yeah... it will do."* I mean more like, *"Oh my God... this is the divine manifestation of my ultimate vision for a piece of property!"* I was over-the-top in love, and my daughter was also genuinely impressed. It was everything we had dreamed of and more. There were at least a dozen large old growth cedar trees, two flowing ponds, rolling pastures that were cross-fenced and a really cool old-fashioned two-story barn. The dirt was dark and rich and the sun exposure was ideal. To top it off, the view of the valley from the loft of the barn was to die for.

I was literally ecstatic as I made my way home to tell the wife about the upcoming move. My daughter had also been given the go-ahead to make the decision based on her husband's trust. He had given her the *yes* without ever seeing the property or the home. We anxiously jumped into the negotiations with an offer that couldn't be refused. I was so thrilled that I wasn't able to pretend to be willing to lose this property. I had inadvertently stepped into the worst position possible for negotiating a good deal. I was so taken with the land that I no longer cared about the manufactured home, or the relative dollar value. I was more worried about the risk of somebody else discovering this land before we could complete the contract. I was in love with this property like I'd never experienced before.

We moved ahead at a quick and steady pace as we secured the purchase agreement and prepared for the major rearrangement. I must admit there were a few glitches in the hasty transaction. If I were to point the finger at anyone, it would be me. The biggest issue to arise came in the early winter when we discovered the roof, supposedly fixed, was leaking profusely.

356

It appeared questionable from the get go, and in my right mind, I would have surely been more thorough in my investigations. The timing was such that the home insurance inspectors had driven by shortly after we'd thrown a blue tarp over the leaky roof, hoping to put it off until winter passed. I soon received a notification stating that the insurance company would deny coverage if the roof wasn't fixed immediately, which would make our financing defunct. The bank could cancel the loan or call the note due if we didn't have the property legally insured. As the problem became urgent and insurmountable, we looked to the recent real estate agreements to find a path to reconciliation. The once confident realtor suddenly had no answers or recourse of action, and we were regrettably facing a substantial bill for the extensive repair. After a bit of whining and grumbling we found an outfit to replace the faulty roof, and everything fell back into place quite nicely, leaving us with a brand new housetop. That was the one major flaw in the deal, and it would have never happened had I not been so love-blind. Even so, we were thrilled to have forged our way into the dwelling on this magnificent property.

It was such an exciting time to finally have the opportunity to share a home with my daughter. I was so proud of her and her husband for having their act together enough at such a young age to qualify for the financing required. The entire extravaganza was the answer to a deep-seated and long-term prayer that I had been nurturing for years.

As expected, our time together was extremely meaningful and productive. There was something ethereal taking place that was immeasurable and less than obvious to the average onlooker. Just the close proximity between us impacted our relations in a way that was hidden beneath the surface and difficult to define. I could actually feel my heart healing.

My daughter is obviously a special character in my soul's ongoing development. There has always been a unique magic between us and I could more easily use colors than words to display how it shows up for me. Our paths were intertwined, and I took her declaration as gold the day she revealed the sentiment that she and her brother, once angels, had come to help me. She was an ally rooted deeply in the core of divinity, and we both knew it. One day, when we were living together in the previous trailer home, we shared a bizarre experience that we still talk about every now and again. It was an extraordinary incident, and we were the only ones to witness this event directly.

I had just left the kitchen and was walking into the hallway, as she exited her bedroom and entered the hall from the opposite end. As we passed in the middle we each instantaneously and simultaneously threw an arm block into each other. It may not sound like a big deal, but the feeling was utterly freakish. Neither of us meant to make the move or felt any precognition to the motion. Our arms moved at exactly the same time without either one of us instigating the reaction, and our wrists met squarely and precisely in the middle with equal force. There was perfection in the overall movement that was apparent to me. The nature of the transaction was irrefutably mysterious. She seemed equally mystified, as we were mutually stunned, amazed, and bewildered into a state of laughter. There wasn't anything unusual going on that either of us could imagine might have triggered this perfectly timed response from both of us. It felt to be life energy flowing through deeply ingrained habit channels from another lifetime. Perhaps she had been with me in the monastery incarnations where martial arts were a daily practice. It was divinely, mystically entertaining, and it sparked a deeper, enduring connection between us.

Chapter 57

✎ demons and darkness ✑

Whoever fights monsters should see to it that in the process he does not become a monster. And if you gaze long enough into an abyss, the abyss will gaze back into you.
—Friedrich Nietzsche

As beautiful as our father-daughter time together was, a heavy weight soon came to bear upon all of us. In the beginning, we were easily captivated by the appreciation and adventure in each unfolding moment. We painted walls, arranged furniture, and gradually nestled into our newly settled, comfortable, and cozy space. The superficial aspect of housekeeping and property management kept us fairly preoccupied for quite some time. As the months rolled by, there were undeniable issues destined to present themselves from a deeper, darker place.

Telltale signs began to emerge, indicating the likeliness of pre-existing entities posing a troublesome presence in our home. It soon became apparent that my son-in-law had a few gifts of his own to contend with. Like me, he was faced with a level of awareness that created disturbing challenges for him in the way of psychic apparitions. His neuro-linguistic receptivity, unlike mine, seemed to be more centered in the visual mode. He would report odd and interesting observations of images that slipped through the veil every now and again. His general attitude about his unique ability was one of humility, with perhaps a hint of reservation. He often seemed to be less than appreciative of his capability, as if given the choice he would rather not have to deal with it. I could relate to his perspective, and was also well aware of the beneficial side of the situation.

The story slowly revealed that the kids were encountering spirits or ghosts in the home that were bothersome. The hallway in particular had developed a dark presence that was bordering on unbearable for both of them. As interesting as this was, I was more attuned to, and concerned with, what was developing in the relations with my wife through this unanticipated family merging. I could feel a darkness arising in her that was also non-conducive to healthy family connections. The demons appeared to be pouring in through every crack and crevice as we continued to settle in.

I was acquainted with and confident in dealing with ghosts, spirits, or disincarnate entities. That was the least of my worries. What bothered me more was the issue of curbing the destructive patterns I could see coming to life in this recently revised family dynamic.

We quickly and directly confronted the darkness in the hallway. My son-in-law and I naturally fell into a trance-like moment where I was able to guide him through a process of delivering this lost soul to higher ground. I facilitated the transition verbally as he contacted and carried this entity into the light. The event was emotionally charged, and left a powerful impression on my young warrior son.

We had set the stage with some smudge and my handy concoction of Epsom salts and rubbing alcohol. This powerful combination, when set afire, created an all-consuming vacuum in the astral plane that opened windows where none previously existed. Many times, through the years, it proved to be a valuable tool for basic housecleaning. We held a few more rituals, and performed some much needed ceremonial duties, until we all agreed that our space was clear. We filled the void with sweet grass and sage, readily returning to our loving manner of intentionally saturating our home with good juju. The other issue, however, was not so easily set straight.

My children, including my son-in-law had been around me for many years. They were familiar with and accustomed to my uncommon manner of dealing with life. They had been vicariously trained to take responsibility for the inner-realm, so central to all relations. My son-in-law had received formal training through the men's community, and was well on his way to functioning as a mature adult in his early twenties. My wife, on the other hand, was not familiar with inner work or self-awareness in general. She was very intelligent and her intellectual understanding was sufficient, but her emotional development was a bit behind schedule. Her inner cauldron held a vicious brew that emanated outward like a broken microwave oven.

The core issue we continuously encountered was her innate resistance to uncovering the underlying issues that fueled this destructive shadow. She had repeatedly voiced an obvious resentment toward my relationship with my daughter, which pulled this subject matter into broad daylight. I had pushed for counseling and relationship workshops, time after time, which delved into this territory, and they were consistently helpful. As long as we had a teacher, mentor, or professional in the room, our communication was co-operative to a reasonable degree. We'd seem to be making progress in the short run, but it quickly dissipated when the external influence was removed. The solution was not coming by way of eradicating this father-daughter love connection. This wasn't an option on our table of negotiations. It was obviously something she must come to terms with from within.

When push came to shove, she quickly regressed into the old patterns of forcefully resisting any effort to uncover or deal with the source of the upset. It was extremely frustrating for both of us, and the negativity that was stirred in our home bounced around like a pinball. My daughter and her husband were feeling uncomfortable with the conflict that was emerging. I, in turn, felt great responsibility and pressure to correct it before irreparable damage was done.

The bottom line was that my wife struggled with feelings of resentment toward the love between my daughter and myself. Her father had abandoned her at an early age, and intimately witnessing this father-daughter love connection opened a deep wound. Although she could consciously see the obvious issue, the work to unravel it was much deeper, and this is where the strong resistance came up. It was a vicious cycle that only she held the key to.

Regardless of my understanding or the skills in facilitation that others could deliver, it was all hopeless without her willingness to participate. The intensity of the situation was escalating, and my heart was bleeding. All the while, I could see and feel the development in the relationship between my daughter and myself. We shared two years in the home together, and like the time spent with my son, it was priceless. The emotional wounds from years gone by were healing, and I could feel the deep strength between our hearts, even as my marriage was ripping a hole in my soul.

I also felt an increasing sensitivity to this new location we'd moved into. It seemed highly charged, as if we'd landed directly on a vortex deep within the earth. I soon discovered my home to be sitting on a major fault line that is listed as one of the most dangerous geological zones in the country. The potential for a devastating earthquake was uncanny. Somehow, it seemed that I was sensitive to the earth's energy in this unstable region. The property also had a strange history beyond the dark spirits we had personally encountered, that slowly came to light. According to the neighbors, this manufactured home was the third home to occupy this land, as the two previous stick-built homes had burned to the ground.

Our first Christmas season came as close to a repeat as I ever wanted to imagine. From a sound sleep on Christmas Eve, I was awakened to my daughter screaming, *"Holy shit!!!"* about three times. Startled by her shocking tone, I sprang out of bed and ran out into the living room to see the woodstove engulfed in flames, literally licking the ceiling. My son-in-law beat me by a breath and was chanting a frantic little tune of his own. They were in total shock as we anxiously quivered like jumping beans around the fire. Although it was comical afterwards, in that heated moment I realized how easily the mind can go goofy. I was fortunate to discover through the recent years, a strong tendency to be clear-minded in the most desperate of situations. This was one of them, and I readily reached beneath the stove and turned off the propane. That was step one. It looked like a freestanding woodstove, but it was actually propane fueled. Once the propane was turned off, the fire slowly began to recede. Between the four of us, we pulled our heads together and grabbed some baking soda, squelching the remaining flames to the best of our ability.

The mystery was easily solved, as we realized we'd gone to bed leaving a decorative candle holder with five large candles sitting on top of the unlit stove. As the temperature dropped that night, the thermostat triggered the ignition of the flame. The stove heated up until the candles melted, causing the wax to run down through the grate on top of the stove and catch fire. The liquid wax was burning, along with the propane, and the stove was completely enveloped in flames. There was no doubt that the home would have quickly burned to the ground had my daughter not awakened to the smoke alarm the rest of us slept through.

Somebody had called the fire department in the midst of the upset, and by the time they'd arrived, the fire was out. The home was full of smoke and we were out on the porch in our pajamas, as the full-sized fire truck came flying up the driveway. They quickly evaluated the situation and acknowledged that the fire was indeed extinguished. The crew graciously set up high-power fans and blew the smoke out of our home, making it possible to enter and breathe once more. The damage was surprisingly minimal, and we were tickled with the high quality candles that left no trace of black smoke on the white ceiling.

The immediate crisis had been diverted, but the idea of what had almost occurred continued to haunt us. We would ultimately encounter two more fires in this home, as we were called to go deeper with our entity removal. In all my fifty years of life, I had never experienced a fire in my home. Now, on the same property where two houses had previously burned to the ground, I am having one fire after another threaten my family and our home. For me, this was definitely noteworthy. It seemed the escalation of chaos and conflict was emanating from a deep source. I was troubled as well as relieved when the kids decided to move on to greener pastures. It was heartbreaking to see them leave, as well as a relief to know the unhealthy dynamics would soon come to a halt.

Somewhere deep down I knew that my daughter and I had achieved our goal. The healing had occurred through this two-year period of sharing a home, and the relational challenges had only strengthened our bond. I was also clear beyond the shadow of a doubt that this marriage was destined to be dissolved. My mission became one of seeing to it that it occurred as quickly and organically as possible. I had fulfilled my end of the bargain when it came to expended effort toward resolution. Our agreements had been clear and definite. This was a spiritual partnership. It was created to inspire and promote each of our personal paths to higher ground. It was designed to be a spiritually supportive connection, which was not based on the old school dynamics of dependency. The way it was playing out, it was becoming far more destructive than supportive for everyone involved. It was time to move forward, once again, toward the original vision of healthy relations.

I took great care to study our history and make note of where it had gone south. I ultimately realized that it was basically screwed up from the get-go. In reviewing our ecstatic beginnings, I had a clear recollection of her agreeing with everything I listed as important in life. My dreams... my goals... my ambitions seemed to align precisely with hers. She approved wholeheartedly of the pictures I painted with great detail. What I came to understand later was that she loved the ideas that I shared, and like a hitchhiker, was happy to go along for the ride as long as the vehicle was provided and manned. I was naïve, and apparently unguarded as I assumed we were the perfect match. I remember thinking and even saying, *"Wow... This is unbelievable... She wants everything in life that I want!"* I was thrilled as I openly stated, *"What a perfect match!"* What I came to understand is the huge difference between raising your hand in agreement with someone, and creating your own list of personal desires and goals in life. I mistook her approval of my passion and priorities in life as evidence of this being something we shared. I was completely wrong. The universe had graciously delivered one more very important and much needed lesson to my doorstep. I got it.

Something quite interesting had occurred early on that triggered a greater depth of investigation into this area of concern. As we entered into our joint venture, we suddenly began to have visitations from owls. They would flutter down in front of us in the middle of the day, as we walked the nearby wilderness trails. One early evening, an owl came swooping down and perched in the tree about ten feet from my front porch. He sat there looking me in the eye as I took his picture. They were appearing regularly in many locations, and my shamanic blood knew the underlying message must be important. I looked to my medicine cards and honed in on one particular meaning that seemed to shine brightly... *Deception.*

Wow, that's always a scary message to consider, but the messenger was relentless. I was feeling deceived and yet unsure as to how it was occurring, or to what extent. Things weren't lining up as we began to blend our life paths, but it wasn't easy to decipher exactly where the glitch was. What I ultimately realized over the next couple of years was that this deception was multifaceted. The core of the deceit was buried deep within her. This poor girl didn't have a clue about her true feelings or desires. Over a short period of time, I came to realize that she had highly restricted access to her deeper self, which was difficult for me to comprehend. There seemed to be an impenetrable wall between her conscious mind and her inner sense of being. Her deception was not as conscious as it may have appeared. I do not believe she had purposefully set out to lie, deceive, or take advantage of anybody. The issue was much deeper than that.

She sat in our circle and listened to my visions of how life could be, along with my passion for making these visions come to life, and found it attractive. She signed up and said, *"YES... let's do that together. I'm in!"* She had no idea that there was serious work involved in making it happen. She was not truly devoted to making the effort or expending the energy required for creating a healthy and joy-filled life with family and friends. She just appreciated the pretty picture I painted of the final outcome.

Her deceptive entrance into the partnership was innocent on a certain level. She was unaware of the depth of conviction I held, and was ignorant as to what it would take to create the reality I truly longed for. I had been immersed in my spiritual studies for decades, and for her it was like a cute cartoon image she had recently stumbled upon. I was drafting sophisticated blueprints of complex architecture, and she was playing with finger paints. She honestly didn't know any better. I could understand how the mishap occurred, and didn't hold her to blame on my way to resolving this indisputable dilemma.

After the kids had moved on, she came to a point of stating clearly that she wasn't willing to make the necessary effort to deal with her own stuff. I made my position clear and stood by our initial agreements to create the life we had dreamed of. *"If you're not willing to do your part, I am not willing to stay in this marriage. This is not what we agreed to or signed up for."* The beginning of the end was drawing near.

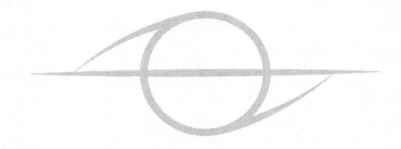

Chapter 58

◈ throwing in the towel ◈

I'm not crazy, I'm just a little unwell, I know right now you can't tell but stay awhile and maybe then you'll see a different side of me. I'm not crazy, I'm just a little impaired, I know right now you don't care but soon enough you're gonna think of me, and how I used to be. I've been talking in my sleep. Pretty soon they'll come to get me... Yeah, they're taking me away.

—Matchbox 20, Unwell

My state of mind was decidedly dwindling in this unsettling vibration of disharmony. The psychotropic medication that had been pushed to the back burner was suddenly at the forefront of my concern. I was heartbroken to find myself sliding back into a world of mental illness, and unable to deny the familiar issues arising for me. All of the typical symptoms were becoming prominent as my sleep patterns drifted into a troublesome zone. I was slipping into a dark abyss, and the demons were literally dragging me down, into an all too familiar hellish state once more.

One day, I was alone in the home while a host of demonic voices relentlessly nagged at my torn and weary soul. I was clearheaded and consciously aware of what was happening, but unable to break free. I wasn't frantic or out of control, which somehow made it worse. This tremendous suffering was taking place even though I was perfectly present and available to deal with it. All that I'd accomplished through my recovery was feeling like a complete failure.

The drugs weren't working any more, the side effects were blaring like a foghorn, and I was rapidly reaching a turning point that was bound to push me one way or the other. If ever I'd been at the end of my rope, this was it. I was deeply distressed to find myself in this dismal situation after decades of devotion and effort. I had come so far, and absorbed innumerable lessons along the way. I'd spent many years doing my shadow work, and been through countless programs and processes for healing my heart, mind, and soul. I had gained knowledge and ground along every path I'd traveled. My thirty year quest had included a variety of religions, as well as holistic medical approaches, hypnotherapy, past-life regression therapy, healing bodywork, Shamanic, Buddhist, and Native American practices. I knew this work inside and out. I had acquired and developed a truckload of skills, and was devoted with all my being to creating a healthy life. My extensive educational background had me sitting there... on the verge of feeling utterly incapable of coping with the torment of this overwhelmingly painful state of mind.

I was having a hard time accepting that I hadn't overcome the mental illness, and struggling to admit it to myself at this stage of the game. *"How can this be? Why hast thou forsaken me?"* I'm so deeply hurt, overwhelmed with sorrow and extreme anger. *"I can't fucking take this any more!"* I knew I'd made the choices that carried me into this situation, and had no one else to blame. I also knew I was capable of finding my way back to a peaceful existence far from here... but not today. I was thoroughly drained. Not the kind of worn out that you feel from sprinting a city block, but more like the complete exhaustion you experience after a lifetime of running marathons. I'd finally come to the point where I'd had enough. I was done. I had reached the point of no return.

I called my sister and confided in her in the midst of my crisis. Her last thirty years had been devoted to the medical field, and she knew my history well. Her interest in psychiatric nursing had mostly likely been inspired by her brother's disturbing struggles. She and I had been more at odds than aligned through the many years of battling with my mental health. Her views had consistently remained mainstream while I was busy exploring every alternative approach I could dig up. The sense of her devoted alignment with the opposing forces made for a difficult relationship. My lifelong quest was designed to not only overcome my health challenges, but to lead her to the truth. My personal goal was designed to demonstrate, through my own life path, that the solutions do exist, and that they're not owned by the multi-billion dollar pharmaceutical industry.

With all my heart I was devoted to this mission but on that day, all I could say was, *"I give up... I surrender. I just can't take this any more."* I told her in a way she could easily understand the nature of my mindset. I said, *"I see two choices. I either find a drug that can help me or I'm checking out."* I wasn't freaking out or playing any games. My attitude was not threatening or overly caught up in self-pity. I had truly reached the end of my rope, and was serious about my choice to not live with the suffering any longer. As for the tens of thousands of suicides that take place every year in this country alone... I get it. There comes a point where the perpetual pain is no longer tolerable. I had arrived at that very daunting, yet undeniable destination.

My sister was readily available to support me in my search for medical assistance. After all, she believed in this avenue and was relieved to see me surrender to what she perceived as the only answer. Between us, we found a clinic on the north end of the island that appeared to be geared for folks like me. I had nosed around on the Internet, and discovered a couple of drugs with promising possibilities. When the nurse practitioner sat us down and introduced a particular drug, I was already familiar with it. My response was one of agreement without hesitation.

This drug had been readily available for several years. It was new to me and from what I had read, sounded to be a hopeful advancement in the area of mental health. When the choice is between a new drug and death, it doesn't take much to persuade one into a state of acceptance. I was all in. Beyond my agreement, there was another serious challenge being presented. I had no health insurance, and this shit was over four hundred bucks per month!

I was in an extremely helpless state of mind. I was willing to give in to whatever I needed to. I didn't want to die, and I couldn't take the intense mental suffering any more. The path that would deliver any other option was the one I was desperately searching for. My sister was extremely encouraging and pushing for me to seek support from the family. She expressed a notion I hadn't considered, recognizing the value to our parents through this transaction. She thought they might actually feel good about being in a supportive position related to my healthcare. She stepped in and made negotiations with them, and they agreed to cover the cost of the medication according to her recommendation. I accepted the assistance without regard for any deeper feelings of confusion, guilt, or shame.

I despised the pharmaceutical industry with a passion. I hated the idea of my parents being able to dictate what could happen to my mind according to their monetary standings. I also knew full well this would be one more thing to hold over my head. I was disgusted to the core to be begging at the doors of the ones I had spent my lifetime running from... Doctors, Drugs, and Money.

Beyond my ego's battle with that version of reality, this appeared to be the only path out of this dark hole. I was in pain and desperate. I could worry about the superficial aspect of it all later. I was ruminating through my sorrow.

"Right now... I just need some serious pain relief in the depths of my being. I am surrendering to everything in my path that conspires to deliver me from this overwhelming suffering... even though it feels like I've just joined the other team."

What developed from here was absolutely magical. The new drug turned out to be beyond my wildest dreams in the way of relieving my misery. My mind quickly became clear, and I was utterly tickled to feel so content and hopeful. It had been a long time since I'd felt gratitude for a profound sense of inner peace. The depression and soul-nagging feeling was vanquished with one little pill and the side effects were barely noticeable. I could hardly believe it!

These pharmaceuticals had clearly evolved over the last thirty years. I was told up front, the length of the prescription would depend on the long-term damage to the kidneys. Although I knew this drug would be detrimental in the long run, it shouldn't be a serious concern for several years, and I was elated to feel better right now. I remember telling my kids that even if it shortened my life by ten years, it would be worth it. I was certain that I would rather feel good for a shorter life, than miserable for a longer one.

This particular drug was designed as an anti-seizure medication, and they had inadvertently discovered it to have a beneficial impact on other neurological issues, such as bipolar disorder. The second month of my prescription I was surprised to discover the time had run out on the pharmaceutical company's legal right to monopolize the pricing. The generic version was suddenly available, and unbelievably less expensive. This shift in cost made it affordable for me, which disentangled my folks from the shady affair. I was astounded to witness the price drop from over four hundred to less than twenty dollars per month, overnight. I was dumfounded by the timing and thanked God, and all of the angels responsible for this divine intervention. I was deeply and prayerfully grateful. It was an enormous emotional relief to feel capable of covering my own expense for the medication. I was utterly thrilled with the potent affect this overall maneuver had on my confidence, my mind, and my life.

With all of this positive motion, there was still one major shift required to complete my transformation, allowing me to live in peace. With a little help from my friends I was finally in a position to handle it. Divorce was something I was becoming quite experienced with, and this one would surely be my last. This exhausting marital game was unquestionably on the brink of being terminated for good, *"Three strikes and yer out!"*

Chapter 59

✎ a dose of humility ✎

There is something in humility which strangely exalts the heart.

—Saint Augustine

I was intensely appreciative of the turn of events that had just occurred. My most urgent prayers had been graciously answered, and I was suddenly functioning at a level that opened new doors. My mind was clear, stable, and at ease. The side effects were basically unnoticeable, and this was unheard of according to my lifelong comprehensive experience with drugs. I was literally on my knees in tears of gratitude. All at once I appreciated my sister, my parents, the doctors, and the pharmaceutical industry deeply. My entire view of the mental health field was turned upside down overnight, and it was startling to feel this intense, sincere, and deep appreciation for what appeared to be the enemy a short time ago.

I felt the universe had delivered a large dose of humility along with this generous answer to my prayers. I'd wasted a lifetime despising the medical and pharmaceutical industry that seemed to keep me locked in suffering like a caged rat. I'd spent decades dwelling on the pain and the shortcomings of this enormous body of highly devoted individuals, which had consistently held my hand through my many years of relentless nightmares. My father may have fallen short in the loving kindness department, but he gave what he had in the form of money, and it was time to appreciate the benefits it offered, rather than what it couldn't. Money wouldn't heal a wounded heart, but it could buy drugs and real estate, and suddenly I was thanking God for every bit of it.

I realized these drugs wouldn't exist without the steady development created through many years of trial and error. The ineffective ones were stepping stones leading to what was now available. I recognized the beauty in each phase that preceded those we were now benefiting from. The fact that I was alive to experience this new drug at all might very well be due to the systems default mode of locking me up during my inconsolable episodes of emotional confusion. My eyes had been opened.

It was like I'd been set high on a mountain, and suddenly able to look down upon a view that was foreign to me until now. It was as clear as day and completely obvious that there was no enemy behind the walls I had constructed for self-protection. The only enemy remaining was the ignorance that stood before me, and this was one that could be systematically defeated. I would dive deeper into my educational process, and ultimately solve this equation in a form that could be passed on to my fellow seekers. If I could find safe passage to an emotionally healthy state of mind, so could thousands of others that wrestle with the same demons.

From this place of stability, it was relatively effortless to make the choices needed to rearrange my world. The conversation about our marriage deepened over the coming months, and we were finally able to agree that this wasn't a relationship we would wish on anybody we cared for. We made a joint effort to disentangle our lives, and move forward gracefully without harboring resentments. We sat in the courthouse holding hands as we waited for our formal dissolution appointment. I still recall the stunned look on the judge's face when I answered his question about the reasoning for the divorce. I said, *"Your honor... we believe we might get along better if we aren't married."* He responded with a statement that verified the uniqueness of this perspective, and we were pleased to feel a sense of approval for our way of proceeding. We handled all of our legal paperwork and split the sheets peacefully as she moved into a place of her own. The property value had dropped significantly in 2008, which wiped out any equity that had been previously established through the large down payment. She was pleased to not have the mortgage hanging over her head, and I was happy to be able to continue to do what was necessary to hold onto the farm and my sanity. My attitude in general was going through a major metamorphosis as I abruptly found myself single, with a five-acre farm and a one-man barbershop. I was quite content with the idea of living alone, rather than being in a less than suitable relationship. I was also certain that I would continue my search for what I was looking for in a partner. I was now even more secure in my conviction to not settle for less than what I imagined could be. I still wanted to one day check *self-actualized relationship* off my bucket list before I died.

As for today, I was just damn happy to be disentangled from the relational net I'd been drowning in for far too long. I'd finally regained a solid sense of sanity, and it was a glorious occasion. On the outside, it was just another day in paradise, but on the inside I was spiritually lit up with an undiluted sense of joy. A new day was dawning, and I was grateful for this freshly rising sun. I'd thrown in the towel of surrender to what I perceived to be the enemy, and in a flash, was transformed into a stable-minded man with deeper compassion and greater understanding. My confidence was soaring and my determination was on fire. The life that I was ready to cash in, generously set me squarely back in the saddle again. Had I held one more silver dollar, perhaps they would have never caught this Midnight Rider. I thanked God for my empty hand and the wisdom to *know when to fold 'em*. My life was about to rock-n-roll...and I mean that in a good way.

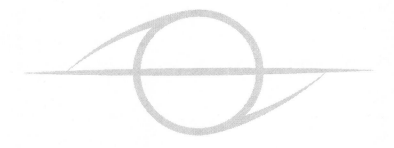

Part 8

Daybreak

"Darkness on the edge, Shadows where I stand
I search for the time on a watch with no hands
I want to see you clearly
Come closer than this
But all I remember Are the dreams in the mist

These dreams go on when I close my eyes
Every second of the night I live another life
These dreams that sleep when it's cold outside
Every moment I'm awake the further I'm away

Is it cloak n dagger
Could it be spring or fall
I walk without a cut
Through a stained glass wall
Weaker in my eyesight... the candle in my grip
And words that have no form...
are falling from my lips."

—Heart, These Dreams

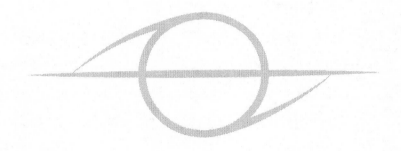

Chapter 60

✺ the other side of the fence ✺

I been double-crossed now for the very last time and now
I'm finally free. I kissed goodbye the howling beast on
the borderline which separated you from me. You'll never
know the hurt I suffered nor the pain I rise above, and
I'll never know the same about you your holiness or your
kind of love and it makes me feel so sorry.
— Bob Dylan, Idiot Wind

The phase of adjusting to the difficult marriage groomed me well for being happily independent. As the partnership slowly fell apart, I gradually became much more self-sufficient. What initially appeared to be a loss would ultimately prove to serve me well in this next stage of living. I had become comfortable with cooking, cleaning, and sleeping alone. For the first time in my life, I felt great appreciation for having my home to myself. It was an experience that seemed contrary to what I'd been accustomed to.

Most of my banked memories were wrapped up in longing for intimacy and connection. Suddenly, this state of aloneness felt like a newfound freedom, which afforded me the space to truly enjoy my life. In this spacious frame of mind, I was well aware of the benefits that had emerged through all of my relational struggles and challenges. Those lessons had been painful, but oh so worthwhile. My level of appreciation for the simple things in life had escalated in light of the distinct contrast with those complex days of suffering. Without darkness of night, how could we recognize the splendor of this precious daylight?

It was clear that my greatest challenges had delivered the most potent gifts. The sensitivities and levels of awareness that had previously left me feeling cursed were undoubtedly becoming the most powerful blessings in my life. I was discovering a level of genuine gratitude in my feeling body, that until now I had only read about. This grateful state of being seemed to translate directly into joy.

I spent my spare time caring for the land and the animals, while enjoying a peace of mind that flowed through the same valley where once danced daily conflict and resistance. This was a glorious phase of awakening to the joy of simple living. My relationship with nature and the astral realms developed and strengthened immensely, as my quieted mind was no longer creating interference. My desire for a simple and serene life was being fulfilled, and my dreams were all but complete. The starry visions that would soon unfold are somewhat surreal, even now as I live within them.

I had fully realized that I could enjoy my life as an independent individual. This much needed experience moved in me with great power. There was no doubt that the solo lifestyle was a viable option. Dependency would no longer drive my push for intimate relations. Nor would fear of intimacy keep me from striving to fulfill my lifelong desire for a healthy romantic love connection. I was still bound and determined to succeed in this department, if at all possible. Like they say, *"God willing and the creek don't rise."* The life changing difference for me was that my joy in living life was no longer dependent upon it. I moved forward with greater understanding and an even more refined sense of caution this time around.

Something enormous had shifted within the customs of pursuing romance in the recent years. Our newest digital technology was impacting the most intimate areas of social life, and I was preparing to test the waters. Living on an island that was largely devoted to retirement age folks, was hardly the place to find a lively dating pool. In fact, it was well known and quite obvious that the potential for dating in the local community was extremely limited. I was briefly hesitant before recognizing that Internet dating was the optimal method for having a chance of finding what I was looking for. It was obviously the most convenient and effective approach for interacting with a larger population of openly interested parties. I did a little shopping and readily signed on with one of the major players. I soon found myself entertained by the exchanges that took place, as I casually scanned the countless possibilities. It was easier than I had expected. There was no requirement to spend time traveling for in-person meetings, as I initially tiptoed into the pool by simply exchanging emails.

It's really quite revealing to converse directly with someone who is also admittedly pursuing a romantic relationship. It certainly takes guessing out of the game. It seemed that, typically, the level of attraction with each new connection was fairly obvious to both of us within a brief exchange. I appreciated not having to waste a lot of time sorting through the high volume of proposed candidates.

What I was searching for was grander than most of my acquaintances could fathom, let alone sign up for. I used my words to the best of my ability to convey exactly what that was. *"I am looking for an enlightened romantic relationship that is grounded in self-love and personal development. I want to form a spiritual partnership that equally supports both parties in blossoming to the fullest degree."* This was the primary goal I was solely interested in pursuing. I wanted to find that one-in-a-million partner who was just as driven as I toward creating a self-actualized relationship. I was devoted with my heart and soul to fulfilling this dream. For the first time in my life, I was also at ease with the possibility of this alignment not being in the stars.

I spent a few months communicating totally through email before I decided to get more deeply involved in the process. I was disappointed to find so many dead-ends as I met with several women in person. It wasn't happening the way that I'd hoped for. On one end of the spectrum were the women who chose to fudge on their age, or share a picture that was fifteen years old and fifty pounds lighter. One gal actually told me within the first ten minutes of getting together that she had lied about her age by ten years. *"Really... The first impression is one of deceitfulness? Wow... Thank you for making it so easy to steer in another direction!"* Those visits were annoying and a little disappointing, but short lived and easy to move past.

The scary one was when I invited a date to meet me on the island, and it took me two days to get her to leave. That encounter was disturbing from another point of view. She was somebody I could relate to, and I actually enjoyed her company. The connection was good, other than her certainty beyond the shadow of doubt that I was the one for her. Her overbearing attitude seemed to leave no room for how I felt about the entire affair. She was unable to hear my heart's hesitancy, and I was grateful and relieved to finally peel her off and move forward.

Each encounter was fine-tuning my scale of discernment. I was surprised to discover women looking strictly for a sexual encounter. I was blindly working under the old-fashioned notion that only men admittedly operated that way. Although, I recalled many younger years when this scenario would have

384

been a heyday, it was far from my focus at this stage of the game. Sexuality, although it is certainly an important aspect of romantic relations, was only a fragment of what I was looking for on this heart and soul driven mission. My quest was far more inclusive and expansive than physicality alone.

I went through ups and downs over a several month period, and at one point I had completely pulled my postings offline. Later on, as I was once more on the verge of giving up, I received a note from a woman who showed a pleasant interest in my listing. She seemed to be a genuine old soul and we began to chat a bit. I was moved by her pictures that indicated a deep love for her children, and quickly discovered that we shared a depth of perspective that we'd each longed for in a relationship. Our conversations were casual and friendly until the day she conveyed her feelings about the upcoming Father's Day celebration. She expressed deep sorrow over having lost her father and shared the hurt in her heart over his passing in the previous year. This was going to be her first Father's Day without him, and it was stirring up deep feelings of regret and sadness. I was inspired by her sincere and tender expression and in response wrote her a very intimate letter... from her father. Now some folks would call this message channeled, but in my eyes it was simply a matter of tapping into a father's heart and conveying a genuine love for his child. I had no difficulty in communicating appreciation for a daughter, knowing full well where that love resides. The whole motion was rather second nature.

This simple gesture became the fluttering of the butterfly's wings that creates a hurricane on the opposite side of the globe. She was moved deeply by my heartfelt expression and experienced a healing of sorts that left her astonished... and IN LOVE. She was instantly head over heels, lost in what looked like infatuation in my eyes. I knew that my words had touched her beyond measure, and I could understand the nature of her response. However, it wasn't significant enough for me to perceive it as the ultimate sign of things to come. I had reached out in a loving way and certainly intended for my message to carry an energy that could bring healing to these wounds I was so familiar with. I had not, however, intended to launch a full-scale romance through this simple act. She was beyond enticed and anxiously wanted to get together and meet in person. Interestingly enough, the timing was such that I was not fully available. A rather odd set of circumstances had unfolded that left me obligated to another previously planned encounter.

I had developed a dear friendship with a young man living on the island. We first met through the barbershop, and initially were drawn into each other's lives through our horses. At least, that was the excuse we used to connect on a more personal level. The friendship was very familiar, and he felt like family. I was old enough to be his dad, and I easily felt a genuine fatherly love for this brilliant, highly capable, young man. We had partnered up at the local gun club and took to shooting trap on a weekly basis. Our interactions were such that many of the men had assumed he was my son. We had gone fishing and hiking, and helped each other with a variety of projects, from putting a loft in his barn to chopping up a few truckloads of firewood. I readily held a genuine heartfelt appreciation for him, much like the love I feel for my own children. He was intimately involved in my life as I went through the divorce and had proven to be a powerful ally. His supportive friendship was strong and caring, and it meant a lot to me. When the time had come to consider dating, he had casually mentioned his mother as also being single. I was intrigued by the idea of being connected with him as a father figure, and looked into the feasibility of meeting his mother. *"Who knows... perhaps this family connection was in the stars."* I was running into a dead-end online anyway, so I decided to take a serious look into this intriguing possibility.

I quickly discovered that she and I were close in age. However, she was living on the other side of the country, and rarely made it out to the West Coast. We soon connected through Facebook and spoke on the phone a few times. She was immersed in her spiritual studies, as well as the healings arts, and our common interests seemed to indicate a positive match. My buddy and his wife had just recently delivered their first child, and it seemed like a great time to invite this new grandmother to the island for a visit. She could hold her newly born grandbaby in her arms, and we too could have a chance to meet face to face. It seemed like a perfect plan. I shared my idea with both her and my buddy and offered to help with airfare. She was delighted, and we set up the flight reservations to make it happen. Her arrival date was a couple of months away and this more recent Internet dating connection had unexpectedly emerged in the interim.

When this new online dating connection was suddenly on fire over the fatherly love letter, I was at a loss. I wasn't comfortable with beginning something that might complicate or interfere with the other invite I had just set in motion. *"Isn't that the way it goes?"* After several months have transpired with barely a glimpse of an opportunity for a serious connection, I'm suddenly juggling two potential relationships at the same time.

I quietly explained that I was not available for a couple of months, and shared with her the honest and complex reasoning. She was beside herself with disappointment, and yet boldly articulated her admiration for my integrity. She very much appreciated that I was not willing to entangle her in an open and unresolved situation. I suggested that we put our talks on hold until I'd met with the other woman, and completed that investigation. It was upsetting for her, and she expressed her strong knowing of this relationship as being divinely appointed. She swore that deep within her soul, she was certain that we were meant to be together. I had barely recovered from the last time a woman was so confident about her feelings and hesitant to take it too seriously.

As time went by, and I had engaged in a few more conversations with my friend's mother, I was getting the feeling there was less of a match here than I had imagined. Perhaps this was due to the obvious contrast with what was developing through the promising connection I had temporarily closed the door on. The pending emotional wave I was holding back was driven by a soul connection that touched me through a divine source. The silence between us was chewing on me from deep within. I found myself yearning for this budding romance that had been abruptly stifled, and I soon spoke up. I talked with my buddy's mother one day and after butting heads for a brief moment, let go of the sense of obligation to meet with her. It was already getting twisted into something unhealthy, and we hadn't even met in person yet. She was tickled to be seeing the baby, and I was equally pleased to have initiated the event. That seemed like enough for everyone involved. My young buddy wasn't terribly concerned about what developed between the two of us, and actually appeared a bit relieved to see it dissipate before it became fully entangled.

Two or three weeks had passed since the last interaction with my online relationship, as she humbly honored my request for a clean break. I quickly sent a message to this underground love connection *in waiting* and said, *"I would love to take you out to dinner if you are still available."* She still tells the story of running through the house when she received that letter, frightening the children as she screamed, *"My Universe just shifted!!"*

Chapter 61

❦ the heart of the matter ❧

Love is like a friendship caught on fire. In the beginning a flame, very pretty, often hot and fierce, but still only light and flickering. As love grows older, our hearts mature and our love becomes as coals, deep-burning and unquenchable.

—Bruce Lee

We spoke on the phone a few times, and one evening I suggested we have a glimpse of each other, before actually getting together face to face. She told me it wasn't a good time; that she was still in her apron after spending a few hours baking in the kitchen. She pleaded, *"My hair is a mess, and I don't have any makeup on."* I tenderly responded, *"If this is truly a deep spiritual connection... why should any of that matter?"* She softly agreed, and we each sat down with our laptops, Skyping our way into our first eye-to-eye contact.

I will never forget the moment we peered into one another's eyes, both slowly melting into tears. It was something I'd never experienced or even heard stories about. We sat quietly, tears flowing without words, gazing deeply into the windows of our souls. Our recognition of one another was intimate and intense, but not necessarily of this world. A minute or two passed before we began to speak. The early assessment, she was so certain of, had been accurate. This powerful connection was destined, and the foreshadowing of a spiritual partnership/romantic love affair that continues to blossom into more than I had imagined possible.

She came to the island for our first date and we had a blast. It was on the 3rd of July, which ironically is the day the island community holds the official 4th of July fireworks display. As she walked off the boat, and we strolled through the parking lot, we melted into an altered state. I had planned on taking her to a sacred sanctuary in a mystical forest nearby, however, the boat was late and our time was cut short for our dinner reservation. I explained that we wouldn't be able to fit the excursion in, as I soon found myself dizzily driving right into the park entrance. The wizardly vehicle suddenly had a mind of its own. It felt humorously peculiar to both of us as I said, *"I guess we're going to the sanctuary after all."* We laughed as we parked, and walked along the wilderness trail up the hill to the secluded building. I recall putting my hand on her back as a means of support while climbing the steep hill, and noticing my palm feeling magnetized to her body. It did not want to move away, and I quietly mentioned this curious feeling. As we approached the cabin-like structure, I heard a voice chanting from within the temple. I shared with her the oddity of the situation, given the sanctuary is typically a place of silence. There is a sign at the entryway that requests visitors remain silent once they enter. In the past several years I had not witnessed this rule being broken. We took off our shoes as we cautiously moved indoors.

In the center of this sacred space sat a man that appeared to be in Buddhist garb. He politely asked, as we approached, if we wanted instruction or merely to practice. It seemed as though he was expecting us, and we glanced at each other with a puzzled look, as we agreed to a practice session. We posed cross-legged on pillows, side-by-side, facing the teacher. After the sharp ring of a bell, we sat silently in meditation for what seemed to be an eternity. There was a timeless feeling of tranquility, and we were amazed by this initial dating experience that fell from the stars. To top it off, I'd carried my camera with me and asked the teacher to take a picture, which now sits upon the sacred altar in our home.

We did end up making it to dinner, and also watched the magnificent fireworks display from a friend's property overlooking the bay where the celebration is held. It was a fabulous event, and from that day forward, our lives gradually melted into one another. I soon discovered something through this love connection that I was previously unable to fully comprehend. The notion of compatibility had not held the meaning that I now see so clearly. This relationship has developed into one unlike any other I have ever experienced, in the way of ease and enjoyment. I had once again encountered an unknown in my life that instigated extreme transformation in so many ways. I tried to explain the feelings associated with this new understanding of compatibility to my buddy, *"It's like the three-legged race at the country fair, where two people each put a leg in a gunny sack... tie it tight... and hobble across the field together."*

I'd thus far only been tied to partners that made it all but impossible to move forward in a gracious manner. The past relationships had tended toward being more tortuous and awkward than enjoyable. I knew well what it felt like to struggle in a partnership, and of course it takes two to tango. However, suddenly with this companion, every shared movement flowed with ease and grace. There was a single-mindedness that made each motion smooth and effortless. The result was a sense of freedom, bringing a new level of joy which seemed synergistically magnified through our communion. I came to realize that this surge of joy stirred up more gratitude, which deepened the process and became cyclical; gratitude creating joy and vice versa. I knew what being stuck in a cycle felt like, but hadn't experienced it like this, in such a positive manner. This was a major breakthrough.

As happy as I was with this new experience and realization, it carried with it an awareness that flushed up an undercurrent of deep sorrow. Through this ripple of sadness, I looked back at the wasted years spent trying to create a similar dynamic in relationships that were incapable of functioning at this level. Suddenly, it was clear that this magical connection wasn't one you could just muster up between any two people. What I had unearthed was the alchemy of a distinct combination of two particular souls, which was extremely unique. I felt regret for all of the striving in past relations that held no possibility of becoming this. My pushing to reshape relations now looked as unfair as requesting a pansy to be an orchid.

I quickly realized that, once again I had been operating with limited knowledge, based on past experience. I readily let go of the regret and self-judgment for not knowing then, what I certainly know now. Another stream of emotional healing flowed through me, and I thanked God for the place in my heart that continued to believe. I deeply honored the warrior within, who held tight to this vision of a higher love.

We met in 2012, and are currently creating a story of our own. Perhaps one day that book will be written, but for now I'll keep it brief. This love connection has developed into far more than I had dreamed of. It dwells at the center of a richness in my heart and soul that will live forever. I am eternally grateful for the nature of life that allows such a dream to come true.

So... here I am... living the life of my dreams, with every piece of the puzzle falling gently into place, like *Snowfall on Cedars*. I am peacefully dwelling on my dream property. I have a simple life on a beautiful island in the Pacific Northwest with my barbershop three miles up the road. I have a dozen alpacas and a coop full of chickens, on a sweet little country farm. My children are doing very well, and my daughter has recently given me my first precious grandchild. My mental health is in top form, and I've discovered the love of my life, who is now living with me in our own little shared paradise. *"What more could a guy ask for?"* I couldn't imagine wanting more. Even so, overwhelmed with gratitude for immeasurable blessings, I continue to witness good fortune rushing into my already overflowing cup. *"When it rains... it pours!"*

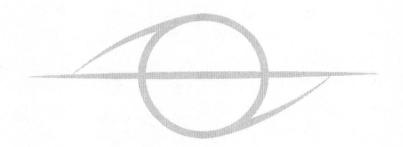

Chapter 62

❧ cellular blessings ❧

The way of fortune is like the Milky Way in the sky;
which is a number of small stars, not seen asunder, but
giving light together: so it is a number of little and scarce
discerned virtues, or rather faculties and customs, that
make men fortunate.

— Francis Bacon

One day I was sitting in the barber chair, reading a magazine, waiting for the next customer to arrive. I looked out the window as I noticed one of my regulars pulling into the parking lot. I watched him get out of his car and immediately noticed something different in the way he was moving. I know a fair amount about my clients, and over the years I've heard many intimate details of their personal lives. This man, in his early seventies, had a knee replacement that never quite healed properly. His back is out of whack, and he generally moves slowly, as if he's in pain. I can spot a guy by his motion from about a block away. This ingrained skill developed through many years of hands on attention to movement, as well as formal training in neuromuscular integration. When I noticed such a profound shift in his mobility, I found it peculiar, as well as noteworthy. By the time he'd walked across the parking lot, into my shop, and was approaching the chair… I energetically questioned him, *"What the hell did you do?"* I was expecting to hear about a medical procedure that resolved a structural issue of some sort. However, he proceeded to tell me of a liquid supplement he'd been using for a couple of months. He excitedly

395

jumped into a spiel about a new technology involving a *redox signaling* process in cellular biology. The concept was fascinating, but quite frankly I was sold before he'd shared any scientific information. What I'd witnessed with my own eyes was far more impressive than anything words could convey. I realized later how fortunate I was to have seen with my own eyes something that got my attention. I honestly don't think words alone would have inspired me to take a second look.

I got the feeling he was personally involved with this supplement, so I asked him up front, *"Is this a network marketed product?"* He said, *"Yes it is!"* and began to tell me about the business opportunity. I promptly told him, *"I'm not interested in the business... but I'm certainly gonna try the product."* So just out of curiosity I asked, *"How did you hear about this?"* He replied, *"My daughter told me about it."* I could sense his genuine enthusiasm and appreciation for what he was experiencing. *"Well it doesn't get any better than that... now does it?"* I muttered, as I grabbed my scissors and comb. He gave me a website to check out and our conversation readily turned toward fly-fishing.

That evening I went online and looked over the website. It was impressive. If this affected me the way it had my buddy there would certainly be a number of interested folks. The difference between buying the product as a customer and signing up to get a kick back for telling others was a 40 dollar onetime fee. It wasn't worth worrying about. If it took off... great. It could help cover the cost of the supplement. And if it didn't... no big deal. The risk was too low to be concerned. Christi and I were very anxious to experience the health benefits directly. *"Oh yeah...*

the mystery girl that I found via the Internet dating site... that has enhanced my life beyond measure... is named Christi. How do you spell it?"... I quizzed her. "Christ with an I," she replied, with a Mona Lisa smile.

So anyway, we ordered our first batch and soon began our 90 day trial. We quickly found ourselves noticing shifts in our health that would eventually escalate to an unbelievable level. In the beginning, we laughed it off and chalked it up to a placebo effect. We talked ourselves out of what we were experiencing because it seemed too good to be true. As time passed, it became obvious that this solution was altering our health in an astonishing way.

After almost forty years of cutting hair, my wrists had developed issues classified as *carpel tunnel,* according to the doctors. I was sleeping with a brace on my forearm and concerned about the pain while I was working. It was gradually getting worse, and the only solution I'd been offered was surgery. I'd heard too many scary stories, over the years, to stand in that line. I'd already decided I would find another avenue to generate income before I'd undergo the knife. Secretly, I was worried about making such a major shift, after a lifetime in one line of work. My back had stiffened to the point of making it difficult to bend over to pick up a comb from the floor. My shoulders were showing signs of wear and tear that made it painful to sleep on my side. It was easy to foresee this issue being next on the list of recommended surgeries.

Within a few months of taking the supplement, my wrists and shoulders had healed to the point that I was no longer in pain. Along with those specifics areas, my entire body had become far more agile. My clarity of mind and general sense of wellbeing had improved immensely. It appeared that my overall energy level had been noticeably strengthened. I was already beginning to wonder if my pharmaceutical remedy could finally be bypassed. It was amazing to experience and also exciting to consider the possibilities for helping others.

I told one of my buddies, *"I feel like doing somersaults!"* He thought that was pretty funny and made a comment about it leaving him with a comical visual. I was curious enough to experiment, and quickly discovered that I could actually do a somersault from a standing position, and roll right back onto my feet. The last time I'd pulled a move like that was as a wrestler in high school. I was soon doing somersaults, one after the other, with my two year old granddaughter on the living room floor.

Christi also experienced dramatic changes, and eventually discontinued a migraine medication she'd been taking for over twenty years. One day we were driving down the road where the scotch broom grows wild when she suddenly realized and screamed, *"I'm not having an allergic reaction!"* She shared stories of being admitted to the emergency room more than once, as the allergies triggered asthma attacks that made it difficult to breathe. It sounded like a frightening experience, and she was thrilled to be done with this long-term life-threatening issue. I remember the delight in her eyes the day she threw away her inhaler. Over the next couple of years, we experienced our bodies shifting into healthier patterns, as our overall health and general sense of wellbeing continued to improve dramatically.

We enthusiastically shared our experience with family and friends. Initially it was uncomfortable, bumping into the negative attitudes often associated with network marketing. However, in spite of the stereotyping, the results were pronounced enough to gain the attention of the people in our immediate circle. Our families would, one by one, step into each having an experience of their own in the way of astonishing health benefits.

A year later, I was looking at a network of over a hundred business associates, which had formed as a result of my initial efforts. I was not only thrilled to feel the health benefits firsthand, but also deeply moved to witness my loved ones, as well as acquaintances, being impacted in such a profound and direct manner.

Along with the personal health benefits and deep gratitude... was a paycheck. I'd suddenly found my way back to that $1000/month residual income I was so thrilled with a few years back. This time there were no strings attached, beyond my desire to share the wealth.

One of the most rewarding aspects of this endeavor developed through a connection with my sister, whose entire life had been immersed in the medical field. She and I had remained fairly distant for the majority of our adult lives. Our paths had been at opposite ends of the spectrum when it came to healthcare. Her first response when I approached her with this product was somewhat hurtful, to be perfectly honest. She appeared utterly close-minded as she laughed and exclaimed, *"Oh… Jeff thinks he's discovered the fountain of youth!"*

Throughout our history as brother and sister, she had looked through the eyes of mainstream medicine; while I was searching everywhere I could, outside of it. Her refusal to take a serious look at what I'd stumbled upon wasn't going to fly this time. This was too important to be sidelined due to opposing personal perspectives. The potential impact was far too great to let it slide by her gaze. I really got on her and pressured her to the point that she finally broke down and agreed to try it. I paid for the product and personally delivered it to her front door. Her husband was also quite negative about the network marketing idea, and between the two of them, I'm surprised I stood my ground. The eventual outcome was well worth it, as it ultimately became a dream come true.

She went on to experience amazing health benefits of her own. The outstanding story I remember vividly, was of the morning she awoke, stood up and yawned with her arms stretched over her head. Suddenly, she realized she hadn't been able to lift her arms above her head for years. This astonished her. Other profound shifts occurred that left her struggling to believe it… or deny it. At the same time, she was still immersed in doubt, and aggressively set out to discover the trickery used to accomplish this tomfoolery. It's funny now, but that's actually what she was thinking. Her overriding doubt and determination to understand how these impossible results occurred, actually led her right into the science that became the foundation for her own movement forward with the product.

Her husband went on to experience phenomenal changes as well. He shared a story of running around, throwing the Frisbee with the kids that literally brought tears to my eyes. This was an activity he couldn't have enjoyed a short while earlier. Their lives changed dramatically, and she ultimately redirected her already successful career. We eventually joined forces in establishing a Northwest Team to bring this product to the rest of the world.

My parents ended up having results that still blow my mind when I stop to think about it. A couple of months before I'd stumbled onto this stuff, my father had expressed his deep-seated feelings of resentment for growing old. He was about to turn 80, and his body was in rough shape. His hip was becoming increasingly bothersome, and he'd developed a serious limp due to excruciating pain in one knee. His blood pressure was high and the arthritis in his hands was painful enough to interfere with manual tasks. He was about a hundred pounds overweight, and unable to do much of what he wished he could. It was an unusual situation for him to express his feelings around his health issues, but I was glad he did. The timing was impeccable. His troubling concerns were about to be vanquished.

Within the first year of using the product, every one of these issues was resolved. His hip quit hurting right away and the knee surgery was no longer recommended after a few months. His blood pressure lowered to the point of astounding his doctors.

On top of all that, his hands didn't hurt any more. My sister recommended a dietary program that allowed him to lose over 80 pounds in the next several months. This was something he'd not been able to accomplish, although he had tried for the last twenty years. He'd actually gone to great lengths for more than a decade, including an expensive lap-band surgery that was completely ineffective. This new product had created an enormous shift in his ability to regain his health. It felt deeply rewarding to finally bring something into his life that he could appreciate.

My mother also achieved excellent results as she joined him on both the diet and the supplement. Less than a year later, these two would choose to spend their 60th anniversary on snowmobiles in Montana at a mountain resort. The entire family was amazed to see such a profound shift in their health... particularly at this age. It is still hard for me to believe, even though I witnessed it all. From a distance it appeared miraculous. My brother, children, and grandchildren would experience heartwarming results, as well as friend after friend, as the word continued to spread.

Chapter 63

⤳ micronutrient miracles ⤳

If people let the government decide what foods they eat and what medicines they take, their bodies will soon be in as sorry a state as are the souls of those who live under tyranny.

—Thomas Jefferson

Okay... so here we go. Apparently, the gateway to heaven's blessing was thrown wide open, because what follows is even sweeter than the icing on this already generously frosted cake. It just keeps coming...

I'd made a Facebook connection several years earlier with a young woman I'd encountered through a program called *Matrix Energetics*. Her father developed the course, and she was traveling the country, teaching alongside him when we met. As I was considering folks in advantageous positions for spreading the word, she came to mind. She was immersed in the healing arts and working with a large number of people across the globe. I contacted her via Facebook, and we had a brief exchange. I said, *"Hey... There's a product I want you to take a look at!"* She receptively replied, *"I'd be happy to... why don't you take a look at my product as well."*

We exchanged information, and quite honestly I was merely going through the motions to respectfully comply with her request. I was more focused on showing her what I had, than interested in her health products. Given my current state, I couldn't imagine anything else I would need. That is, until I caught a glimpse of what she was offering. I was shocked and amazed at the subject being delved into; *Micronutrients for MENTAL HEALTH*. This was new territory that had evaded my lifelong quest. I was about to be awakened to a higher level of understanding. (Go to YouTube and find *Julia Rucklidge,* on TEDx, entitled *The Surprisingly Dramatic Role of Nutrition in Mental Health -17mins.*)

The product my young friend was presenting had come out of Canada, and the story that accompanied it cut straight to my soul. Tony Stephan, the man responsible for developing this nutritional recipe, inadvertently found himself in the middle of a living nightmare. His wife had committed suicide shortly after her doctor prescribed drugs for a diagnosis of bipolar disorder. Her father had been down the same road fifteen years earlier. After losing their grandfather and more recently their mother, a few of Tony's children were also experiencing severe mental health issues. He was beside himself with upset over the hopeless attitude and lack of support through the medical field, as he pushed for more effective means of helping his family. The doctors essentially told him there was nothing he could do, and that his son would most likely commit suicide as well. He wasn't buying it, and he wasn't giving up.

This one man's refusal to accept the dead-end road that the medical world was offering, transformed into a priceless and immeasurable gift. His steadfast determination pushed him to prayerfully find answers that have permanently altered the world of mental health. He ultimately developed a nutritional recipe that would heal his children of their bipolar and schizophrenic

404

symptoms. It was so successful that he formed a non-profit organization to promote this mental health solution for the millions of others that suffer in the same way. As it grew into a serious movement, the Canadian government stepped in to shut them down. This escalated into a lawsuit that brought a wave of scientific attention to the product. It was soon to become the most researched nutritional health supplement on the planet. More than twenty private research labs, as well as fifteen universities, including Harvard, began to research the effects of this product. The results were astonishing and guess what? The Canadian government *LOST* the lawsuit! Along with the acceptance and legalization, it was mandated that the product be available to the public. This was over ten years ago! (The inside story is told through Tony's daughter's book *A Promise of Hope* by Autumn Stringam. *The Astonishing True Story of a Woman Afflicted with Bipolar Disorder and the Miraculous Treatment that CURED HER*).

My mind was suddenly spinning in circles. I wondered, *"Why was I unaware of this incredible breakthrough? Why had this amazing discovery not been announced to the millions of others struggling to find our way in this drug lord controlled world of mental healthcare?"* As incredibly excited and awestruck as I was to discover this amazing development, I was also deeply troubled on several levels. At a personal level, it pissed me off to have suffered through the many years this nutritional supplement could have been available to me. This micronutrient recipe was on the market long before I'd reached my final breaking point. Drugs were the only solution offered when I was in such desperate need of help. This flagrant error was enormous, and obviously based in the profit driven medical system that I was so deeply aware of. This was certainly not a new perspective, but extremely disturbing to feel the consequences hit so directly.

From another angle, Tony's heart wrenching story also highlighted the obvious lack of effort by my own parents. This man's accomplishments had created a vivid contrast between his children's dream come true and the ongoing nightmare I had painstakingly survived. I recalled an episode where a girlfriend had first come to hear of my mental health issues. She excitedly exclaimed, *"I can't wait to meet your parents!"* I was confused and questioned her as to connecting my mental health with meeting my parents. She naïvely stated, *"I want to read their books on the subject... so I can understand what it's all about."* I hadn't recognized the truth in this matter before her innocent assumption. The reality was... my parents didn't have a single book related to my issues.

Long before this event, I'd watched a movie called *Lorenzo's Oil* starring Nick Nolte. He played the father of a young man with an unusual disease. In this true story, both parents passionately devoted themselves to discovering a cure for their child, and ultimately succeeded. After seeing the movie, I had secretly fantasized of having parents that cared enough to dedicate their lives to discovering the solutions to my health issues. The reality was that mine hadn't lifted a finger, or even taken an interest in learning the basics. It cut to the quick, seeing these two extremes, side by side. I'd done my best to deal with the pain associated with the neglect, but it was being reactivated through this transformational event.

Tony Stephan entered the stage like a real-life superhero, proving that my wildest fantasies were totally realistic. He was a property manager at the time of his breakthrough discovery. He calls himself an *average Joe*, although his indomitable spirit proves otherwise. The driving force of his self-appointed mission was fueled by his love and compassion for his children. It was accompanied by his unwillingness to sit back and watch them needlessly suffer. He didn't have any advantage over my parents in the way of natural intelligence or ability. The distinction appeared to be in his value system. He was wholeheartedly striving for a way to stop the suffering of his children, while my father was busy bragging about his financial status. Tony's heart-centered priorities were the bottom-line difference and the cold hard truth made obvious the neglectful value system that had ruled my world. That deeply buried wound was once again being painfully poked and prodded.

On a larger scale, I was being reminded of the profit-based system that seemed hell-bent on using people as a means of generating billions of dollars, rather than helping them. I am certain that we would be completely appalled to know the dollar amount produced annually through pharmaceutical sales in the mental health industry. It is guaranteed to be horrendous. Google that one! It was evident that this profit-based healthcare system certainly wasn't looking out for our best interest. It appeared that anything operating outside of the money machine was not only being hidden behind an iron curtain, but actively pursued as a competitor to be stifled and shut down.

This product had been through the mill, including a government based lawsuit. It passed with flying colors, through intense scrutiny and screening of highly revered, and publicly recognized organizations and universities. This was no longer a debatable subject. *"So why on God's green earth had we not been notified?"* In a day when computer data systems are overflowing with capability and ease of access, it's obvious that the technical ability to inform people is not an issue. Every mental health patient list within the system is accessible with the click of a mouse.

So here we are, with a holistic approach to serious neurological disorders such as schizophrenia, bipolar disorder, autism, depression, anxiety, and ADHD. It has been proven highly effective beyond the shadow of a doubt in a superior court of law. In the meantime, our mental institutions, along with our prisons and drug recovery facilities, are literally overflowing into the streets. Even so, the governing body of our healthcare system finds no reason to inform people whose lives would be impacted beyond measure by such a breakthrough; not even those of us who have spent decades in severe suffering with these specific issues. *"Wow! That's a tough pill to swallow in a sitting position!"*

To be honest, I can't help but feel steaming anger when I consider the dynamics at play. I judge this to be an appropriate emotional response and one that is well founded. Rather than denying or burying it, my intention is to embrace it, as I consciously and deliberately use this anger to fuel my drive to follow in Tony's footsteps. I am standing up and choosing to be among the growing number of voices determined to get the word out. This *Silent Revolution* appears to be transforming into one that will not be so silent. I'm realizing I have something to say, and by God, I will do what it takes to share with others what I've struggled a lifetime to discover.

As grateful as I'd been for the drug that was helpful, it didn't compare to this drug-free alternative that should have been available to me ten years earlier. My five year period of relative safety from detrimental side effects had been exceeded. My kidneys were showing signs of deterioration that I could feel. My lungs were also being impacted, as I was continuing to become increasingly short of breath. The fact that I'd found this holistic approach to neurological health through nourishing the brain tissue, was another timely miracle. The truth is my time had run out on a drug that was knowingly doing major organ damage behind the scenes. I had admittedly been willing to live a shorter life in trade for what it offered, but this horrific sacrifice was unnecessary.

There was no doubt that the drug lords knew damn well these solutions could be achieved naturally, without risk to my internal organs. It was public knowledge to those in the industry. It was a major story in the Canadian media that was far from hidden. This micronutrient product had been highlighted on mainstream newscasts repeatedly. The secrecy associated with something so significant is inexcusable. It's obvious that the motives behind suppressing such a breakthrough are profit-driven. The system is geared in such a way that these mega-powered corporate entities have the ability to influence, regulate, and dictate what is publicly shared and promoted.

This is also how and why the network marketing industry is a major game changer. When John Lennon was singing about power to the people, he may have been missing a clear vision of how it might actually come to fruition. Within the monetary system, an approach has manifested that returns financial power to the people. The network marketing industry approached a two hundred billion dollar level last year, and continues to grow by leaps and bounds. The big money that keeps major corporations in power over the common person's choices in this world is losing its grip as more of us are being empowered at an individual level.

In this modality, each person is rewarded according to their ability to be effective. There is no inequality or unfair dominance of power to hold back the tides. Every player is allowed the same opportunity to prosper. The path to success comes by way of supporting others. This model only operates effectively in a win-win mode. Can you imagine corporate America running on these principles? If you don't understand this yet, please do the research to discover the truth about how this approach impacts humanity on a grand scale. Whether this is of personal interest or not, it's important to understand its value in a free society. (Go to YouTube and search *Tony Robbins On the power of Network Marketing*)

Chapter 64

༈ mindful uprising ༈

*All that is gold does not glitter, not all those who wander
are lost; the old that is strong does not wither, deep roots
are not reached by the frost.*

—J. R. R. Tolkien

I am elated to have finally established a healthy, drug-free lifestyle, after struggling for decades with mental illness. I have accomplished a goal that was not possible, according to the medical experts. I have made an enormous effort; searching far and wide for answers, discovering powerful solutions on my path of healing. Because of people like Tony Stephan, fighting tooth and nail to open unconventional doors, the way has been paved for the rest of us.

My medical diagnosis was generously delivered on a silver platter, almost forty years ago. Along with it came a long list of reasons, and an overwhelming body of evidence, as to why I could never recover or find a clean bill of health. The cards were heavily stacked against me. I heard this message, and like Tony rejected the restricted and limited perspective that promised to keep me disabled and dependent on drugs. I spent almost 40 years fighting a dead-end system, while blazing a path to a recovery, which was supposedly not possible. I have finally achieved this allegedly farfetched and unreachable goal. Thus far, I have yet to be approached with any proposals for trophies, ribbons, or medals. I have inadvertently discovered a department where heroic accomplishments are meaningless, when no corporate profit is affiliated with the achievement.

My good friend boldly exclaims, *"You really need to speak up about what you've accomplished! This is important and you need to share what you've learned with the world!"* I agree wholeheartedly, and as I look around, I realize there is no establishment designed to receive such a claim. Imagine going to the local medical clinic, hospital, or mental health institution to inform them of such a recovery. *"Maybe a few phone calls to the AMA or pharmaceutical companies could have a real impact... ya think?"*

It seems to me there are two obvious choices. One is to sit back and complain about the governmentally dictated healthcare system and profit driven pharmaceutical industry. The other is to rise up and make the effort required to educate and inform our shared community. This is exactly the nature of a powerful movement I see happening in the world today, and one I am wholeheartedly engaging in. If I'd sat around, expecting the current healthcare system to deliver the goods, I would have been found dead in the waiting room a long time ago.

Can you see the underlying premise here? Our society is being undermined by a healthcare system that not only dictates the definition of the disorders, but greatly profits through the tightly controlled prescriptive treatments. The choices are strictly defined and limited, regardless of the damage being done. There is an enormous payoff in keeping the masses believing they have restricted options and no chance of recovery. There is however, zero profit for the massive pharmaceutical industry when people discover they can become healthy without drugs.

There is an incredible lack of interest by the medical system, in people who have found a path to healing and recovery through alternative measures. Not only is there an obvious lack of interest, but an equally evident movement of resistance and retaliation. If our medical system is truly designed to promote health, this doesn't add up.

Try, for a moment, to step into the shoes of an individual who's overcome the impossible in an arena that impacts millions on a daily basis. Against all odds, they conquer an imponderable health challenge, and aspire to live a healthy and fulfilling life. Surprisingly, you look around and discover nobody seems to notice. I can't help but envision this same scenario in relation to the sports world. Imagine... the athletes have been told that a four minute mile is not possible. For years it's believed to be true. Then one day, somebody accomplishes the impossible and breaks the record. Soon after this limiting belief is proven false, many others follow suit. Now envision that individual breaking through that deeply ingrained belief, setting a new record, and nobody taking notice. *"Can you imagine!?"*

However, it doesn't happen like that in the sports arena. Our overall social values indicate more interest in accomplishments in the sports and entertainment industry than in the realm of mental health. That priority list changes rapidly when somebody goes ballistic with an assault rifle in an elementary school or a shopping mall. Suddenly, the importance of mental health shoots to the top of the charts. Unfortunately, it seems the reason for this abrupt shift is due to the fact that this tragic event has suddenly entered the entertainment department of social appreciation. Boy... do the media mongers love to capitalize on such tragedy! *"As sad as this is… as much as we want to ignore it… it is undeniably true."*

In the midst of my personal efforts to bring awareness to this holistic approach, I've run into many cautions and warnings about saying too much. *"Don't use the word cured!"* *"Don't talk about any specific medical issues… or make any claims about being healed."* When I heard this, I asked, *"If I've actually been healed… don't I have the right to tell the truth?"* More than once I was answered, *"No! The Law does not allow anyone besides the drug companies to claim the ability to heal."* **"Seriously? Wow… unbelievable!"**

There is still an uncanny fear in our society of being harassed by our own government. I see people walking on eggshells when it comes to speaking up about alternative health measures. We have doctors, using unconventional methods, showing better results with cancer patients than mainstream treatments, being shut down because they aren't following the government dictates. Shouldn't we be seeking out these methodologies rather than suppressing them? Effective treatments that don't use the mandated drugs are abruptly squashed. How can we collectively sit back and allow this to continue? The healthcare of *We the People* is being severely compromised, as it is siphoned through the filter of America's heartless money game.

In the year 2016, in America... Land of the Free... I'm told we don't have the right to speak the truth about healing with substances, beyond the drugs that are being shoveled down our throats. This boggles my mind.

Only recently have we created the technical ability to reach out and share our personal stories with the rest of the world. Our media is being decentralized through new technology that has rerouted our global, as well as interpersonal communications. The Internet has created social dynamics that are tipping the scales in favor of the common people. We're finding our way to honest and open disclosure of what's really happening in the world. We can now have a voice in our global community, despite the monetary-based corporate and governmental forces that would rather it were otherwise. We also have the opportunity to create a society, actively seeking beneficial health solutions, regardless of any connection to generating cash flow for mega-power corporations.

Thank God, and the awakened ones, for these amazing breakthroughs. There was a time, when the notion of being drug-free, sound of mind, having a healthy lifestyle, and an ideal spiritual partner, would have stretched my imagination to the point of ecstasy. I have envisioned this joyful drug-free stage as the epitome of life's fulfillment. Now that I'm here, I realize this is not the grand finale, but rather the entryway to fulfilling my true life purpose.

My lifelong quest to heal my mind has created a stringent path of self-monitoring, self-discovery, as well as self-discipline. I have developed a solid habit of inner observation through the years. Recently, I found myself sitting with the question, *"How can I be living the life of my dreams… and still not completely content?"* I asked myself, *"Wasn't that the goal?"* The inspired answer came quite readily, *"No… it was not the ultimate goal. It was a major stepping stone on the path to a far greater objective. You are but one of many. There is much work to do!"*

Through my studies, I came to recognize the nature of consciousness and the reality of how connected we truly are. As one of many, I know what it feels like to suffer. My heartfelt compassion for others runs deep. I also know what it feels like to be helped and supported. It's not within my nature to say, *"Okay… I got what I wanted… my mission is accomplished!"* We're all in the same boat whether we realize it or not. We breathe the same air and share the same social hardships. The issues I have faced on a personal level are only a reflection of the collective dynamics that create them. These disorders are systemic. My quest for sanity began in response to being born into, and living with circumstances that created severe mental health issues. As I look to my fellow aspirants, I see this is more common than not.

What I've discovered while unraveling this immense mystery is that I'm a minuscule element in this enormous spider web of humanity. The mental/emotional disorder and dis-ease that I've experienced are symptomatic of dysfunctional patterns that operate on a much grander scale. These are the pre-disposing factors to a mental health epidemic that is spiraling around the globe. From the individual in a small family to the social dynamics of humanity, and the governmentally dictated systems at large, every level is participating in and contributing to the underlying issues that create this shared suffering. *"You don't tend to stay clean... swimming in a dirty pond."* If we truly want for our children and grandchildren, the inner peace and sanity we desire for ourselves, we have a great deal of work to do.

I have crawled out of the muck and rinsed myself off. I now know the difference between a clear and a muddied mind. I also realize that many of my peers are still floating in the stench of a slimy swamp. We are all in this together. My long-range vision is set on participating in the cleanup of this collective pond, as well as instigating effective measures for ongoing maintenance.

I am reminded of a meaningful lesson that I found through a simple and concise story about, *Downstream Helping.* There is a contemporary fable that begins with a person walking beside a river, who sees someone drowning. He jumps in, pulls the victim out, and begins resuscitation. Soon another drowning person yells for help. The rescuer jumps back into the water, and pulls the second victim out in the same fashion. One after another, the drowning people come floating down the river, as the rescuer works tirelessly to revive each one. Soon, a large group of bystanders have gathered to watch the spectacle. Suddenly, the rescuer, even though the screams of yet another victim can be clearly heard, stands up and begins to walk upstream. One of the bystanders calls out, *"Hey where are you going? Can't you hear the cries of the latest victim?"* The rescuer replies, *"You handle it... I'm going upstream to find out how these people are ending up in the river, and why they don't know how to swim!"*

This *Downstream Helping* includes many levels of response to people in need, which do not address the underlying dysfunction, foundational to the suffering. We have the knowledge within our grasp to be much more effective than this. These diagnoses, labels, and primitive holding bins are a copout. They are the tools of an overtaxed system that is more designed according to cash flow than toward effective means of truly helping the individuals who suffer. We can easily do better. The decline in our mental health as a society has reached epidemic proportions. This isn't a random event that developed without cause. Nor is the understanding required to resolve the issues we face... rocket science. The solutions are readily available.

It is our basic value system that needs to be reconstructed, and this is a responsibility that each and every one of us holds. The transformation we long for begins at an individual level. We must not sit back and watch this unnecessary suffering. Our children need not face a lifetime of struggling to recuperate from this drug-ridden system that has taken so many down. Many of us have faced the eye of the storm and survived. The question is, *"Is this world ready to hear our stories?"*

I successfully accomplished what I set my sights on almost 40 years ago. Against all odds, I have stayed the course and attained a level of understanding and functionality that was once only a pipedream. I can see clearly the power in this deliberate path that has rolled out before me like a red carpet. What I was seeking, I found. I was able to discover the tools, as well as the understanding, required to establish the healthy habits of a functional mind. I encountered the means by which my emotional wounding could be flushed out and resolved in the depths of my psyche. I connected with the people and the products that could support my anatomical system in balancing the physiology that hindered this quest for wholeness.

"I stand before you a drug-free, healthy hearted, clear minded individual. I have developed a healthy romantic relationship with my spiritual partner, and we sit together at the center of our thriving and united family. We are setting in motion the means by which we might bring the healthy influence we seek, to the forefront of this world we share. Through these many years of striving, I have learned how to establish the path required, moving forward one step at a time. I am determined to utilize these highly effective practices, as I steer my intentions toward impacting humanity in a more comprehensive and personal fashion."

Early in my life, I put great emphasis on discovering a methodology for creating a depth of influence that would touch all of mankind. The *Krido Ishii* symbol transmits a potent dynamic to the base of the collective unconscious of humanity. I am pleased with this strategy and confident in the delivery. However, I've recently recognized an underlying motive for this uncanny approach. It was unwittingly based in the shame of stepping up as an individual who would be seen. My methodology was grounded in anonymity, as I secretly set out to impact the collective through this undercover mission.

From a position of faith and certainty, which comes by way of a healthy heart and mind, I see that I'm capable of more intimate methods of impacting people's lives. I am actively turning my attention toward working directly and cooperatively with individuals that share this vision for creating an emotionally healthy planet. Mankind is the single most toxic threat to this indivisible biosphere we share, and wisely the focal point for much needed change. We have a lot of work to do in rehabilitating the mental/emotional health of humanity and in so doing will transform our relations with this precious planet.

If we collectively correct our internal course and simultaneously direct our attention toward caring for the natural world we depend upon... we might very well stand a chance. *"I mean... what have we got to lose... besides everything?"*

Part 9

There is a Way

"Why does the mind habitually deny or resist the Now? Because it cannot function and remain in control without time, which is past and future, so it perceives the timeless Now as threatening. Time and mind are in fact inseparable.

Always say "yes" to the present moment. What could be more futile, more insane, than to create inner resistance to what already is? What could be more insane than to oppose life itself, which is now and always now? Surrender to what is. Say "yes" to life — and see how life suddenly starts working for you rather than against you."

— *Eckhart Tolle*

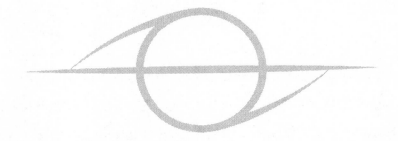

Chapter 65

❧ our true essence ❧

All God wants of man is a peaceful heart.
—Meister Eckhart

My initial awakening began in a flash of light. Through many years of seeking and searching I came to realize this phenomenal experience had revealed the truth of, not only my own true essence, but of the divine nature of all of humanity. I now see the core essence of man as but a reflection of this ocean of light we call *God*. The entire universe is an infinite emanation of this divine light of consciousness, which shines through all that is. We are spiritual beings who, like *the light*, are more than the form we gaze at in the mirror. The true self is inseparable from this pure essence of creation. Like the sun, it is forever shining behind the clouds of the ego mind that so easily masks its presence. This divine Self is constant and powerful. To experience this divine aspect of Self is to have discovered the Kingdom within. According to the teachings of Jesus, *"tis then that all else shall be added unto you."*

The solutions we seek are within us. The path to self-realization is not by way of becoming something more, but rather through unveiling and uncovering what already lies beneath the surface. We need not alter who we are on this quest for this luminous awareness, which brings true health and happiness.

The truth is... striving to be something other than authentic is exactly what leaves one feeling inadequate, and lost in a never-ending cycle of suffering.

The energy dedicated to the path of liberation is better spent on deconstructing the walls of illusion that have formed around each and every one of us. The ego mind that we use to navigate through each day is the aspect of self in which these destructive illusions reside. To lift oneself from the dismal suffering that comes through this clouded vision, one must tend to the emotional body, the egoic mind, and its shadow. Even the unconscious realms are accessible and available for alteration. We each have the capacity to reconfigure the beliefs, thoughts, and feelings that constrict our ability to experience the authentic, divine Self. As we do, we increase our aptitude for living healthy, productive, and enjoyable lives.

An emotionally healthy mind is one that naturally experiences feelings of joy and gratitude, while participating in healthy relations with each other and this planet we share. This is truly a realistic and auspicious goal that can be achieved by every earnest seeker.

Chapter 66

❧ our purpose ❧

Everyone has been made for some particular work, and the desire for that work has been put in every heart.

—Rumi

Humanity is here for a purpose, and each individual possesses the need to fully blossom. When this is understood, it becomes a primary goal in living. Every other need is structurally designed to lay the groundwork that makes this overarching mission possible. From empowerment to enlightenment, mankind is destined to progress along the spiritual path laid out before us.

Mental/emotional suffering is the result of being out of alignment with what truly matters in life. When our values are off-kilter, we feel the pain of the transgression. This is a natural, inherent, protective guidance response. It is the deeper mind steering one toward the values and priorities leading one to happy, healthy living. The greatest obstacles we face are often supported by the social norms, formed through a materialistic value system, which runs counter to a healthy model. As negative as that might sound, the beauty of it is, *WE* are the creators of this cultural stumbling block. As co-creators, we also have the ability and the power to change it. In so doing, we not only make room for healthy living now, but simultaneously pave the way for our children to dwell in a safer and more harmonious world in the future. Mental/emotional health and spiritual health go hand in hand; one begets the other. Striving for the highest rung in Maslow's ladder ensures the fulfillment of these greatly treasured prerequisites to healthy living. Realizing the importance of reaching one's potential is the key to creating a healthy life, as well as the loving community we long for.

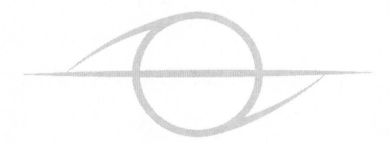

Chapter 67

❧ gateway to empowerment ☙

Victorious warriors win first and then go to war, while defeated warriors go to war first and then seek to win.

—Sun Tzu

Somewhere in the depths of my hungry mind, through the passing years, I discovered and created an exceptional methodology for self-empowerment. This symbol I've carried and studied since 1984 became the backbone to my quest for sanity. Through this vast and lengthy journey I inadvertently came to realize that sanity, in its purest form, is much like enlightenment. Once the initial threshold has been crossed, the soul is destined to reach this fully empowered state of development. Whether we call it self-realization, self-actualization, or enlightenment, makes no difference. The important aspect of understanding here is that this fully developed stage is a NEED rather than a luxury. Given this realization, the question becomes, *"How do we proceed toward fulfilling that need?"* Herein lies the purpose for my work, and the invitation I am offering you, the reader.

The path proposed is one of deconstructing that which masks the awareness of your true self, thereby eliminating interference with reaching your highest potential. The superficial aspect of self that is so often promoted in this fast-paced, shallow-minded, social structure is the tip of the iceberg. The chances are, you have no idea of the magnitude of your power as an individual. In line with that notion, how could we collectively realize the power we hold... united? Together, we look at this world we share, and grovel in the agony of the unjust and absurd manner in which our system drives us, like mice in a maze, searching for the next little piece of cheese. The root of the problem is that we have allowed ourselves to buy the program that defines that small chunk we scramble for. *Materialism* carries a heavy cost and we are on the verge of paying the ultimate price. Not only as burning coal fills our skies with toxic fumes and oceans of plastic threaten our planetary waters, but what about that piece of you that remains unnoticed?

This matrix of insanity is motivated by values that dishonor life as we know it. We are more than this physicality we embody. Your heart is a treasure house that gold can never attain. The true cheese we seek is the joy of living freely, in the healthy society we long for. It's not like it's not available; it's just that it's been withheld, hidden behind a monopoly board, and disguised as something you need to buy. To understand this basic premise, still leaves the question, *"How do we turn this ship around?"*

The mission before the true seeker is the path of dismantling the façade of reality that has been meticulously designed to keep us enslaved. It is not as difficult as it might seem, once the issue is revealed. You don't need to find Morpheus or ingest microchips for computer-generated martial arts performances. It is much simpler than that. However, it is easy to miss the fine line that leads down the narrow path ahead, and vitally important to remember, *"The Kingdom is within"*.

Chapter 68

♋ the real cheese ♋

God's love is too great to be confined to any one side of a conflict or to any one religion.

—Desmond Tutu

Imagine there is a diamond-like gem of light at the core of your being. Now consider that it exists on a feeling level. In other words, it's not something you can hold in your hand, but rather something that powers the heart of creation, and lights up a realm beyond the 3D world we see around us. It vibrates at a higher frequency than physicality, and the instrument you have been given to detect it is your heart. The only way to recognize and experience this light is through the feeling body. This single source delivers the fiery core of all that you have ever been convinced is worth striving for. Those things, goals, achievements, and accumulated tokens of greatness and power, are ultimately supposed to bring you wonderful feelings. It's a game we've been taught to play, whereby the source of joy within is supposedly accessed, when we meet the proposed criteria. We're programmed to create this self-fulfilling dynamic. Sometimes it even works. Not every superstar commits suicide or dies of a drug overdose. However, the truth is, you can bypass the game and go straight to the source, discovering a greater joy than you have ever known. Why?... because your attention is no longer being spent on the game. Your power of attention becomes focused on a single point, like a laser beam, and your pure intention is thereby magnified. The maze is sidestepped as the illusion of cheese is replaced with the real deal. It's a sure win.

Of course, it's easy for me to say, after forty years of groveling in the gutters. Obviously, it's been a rough road, and to claim this path is a piece of cake is like Lance Armstrong telling us how easy it is to win a bicycle race. Kind of silly, when I think about it like that. However, having a supportive and guiding hand can certainly make it much easier.

The primary purpose behind this approach is to tear down the walls of illusion that live in the darkest recesses of the mind; so as to enliven the heart and restore its capacity to feel. You don't need to prescribe to any particular religion, nor do you need to abandon one. This is not about religious dogma. It's about an effective path to living to your highest potential, cultivating a healthy lifestyle, and experiencing the depth of joy you were put on this green earth to know. If you find this notion attractive, come along and join the tribe. We have devoted our lives, heart and soul, to delivering the support that I have cried for in my darkest hours. Perhaps there is a way to achieve our dreams together. Check us out. We're just getting warmed up.

An Invitation

Where do we go from here?

Our vision is to help create a world in which intimacy, authenticity and emotional maturity are highly valued priorities.
If you are devoted to deepening your own sense of authenticity within your relationships in your social life, your work as well as your home life... while living as purposefully as you can imagine, then...

We genuinely welcome you to continue this journey with us and explore our other offerings. You can do so in the following ways.

- Visit our website at www.kridoishii.com. On the website you will find our interactive blog, video and audio presentations, as well as the online courses we offer.

- Join us on our Facebook Page:
  Beneath This Crown of Thorns

- Another way to get connected is by joining our Facebook Group: **Krido Ishii Foundation**, a non-profit organization created to bring this awareness to as many as possible, regardless of resources.

- And last but not least, feel free to email us at:
  info@kridoishii.com

This is a community effort. We are just beginning to organize. Be patient as we continue to expand and grow to fulfill the dream of a more empowered, authentic, connected humanity. Together, we are powerful beyond measure. Namaste.

Index

Made in the USA
Middletown, DE
17 July 2016